D1431973

ANNE BONNY: The Infamous Female Pirate
by Phillip Thomas Tucker

©2017 Phillip Thomas Tucker
ISBN 978-1-62731-045-1

Feral House
1240 W. Sims Way, Suite 124
Port Townsend, WA 98368
www.FeralHouse.com

Design by Sean Tejaratchi

ANNE BONNY

THE INFAMOUS FEMALE PIRATE

PHILLIP THOMAS TUCKER

FERAL HOUSE

TABLE OF CONTENTS

INTRODUCTION

TODAY, gender roles and definitions are changing and in flux across 21st-century America. But is this recent societal development that has made the headlines actually something new, as so many people believe today?

Fortunately, the most famous female pirate in history has provided us with the narrative of an extraordinary personal odyssey and an enduring example of one of the most improbable of lives at a time when almost all Western women were powerless in Western societies, on both sides of the Atlantic. Remarkably, Anne Bonny devised a novel means to gain personal freedom from the entrapment of a traditional restrictive gender role: a life as a pirate on the Caribbean. In this way, she gained a rare measure of respect and equality in a harsh patriarchal world, while mocking the ancient sailor's adage that a woman aboard ship was bad luck and an ill omen.

Rather than an aberration in the historical record, Anne Bonny's life can be viewed as an integral part of the overall human experience at sea from time immemorial. She first made her appearance aboard a pirate ship during the glory days of piracy in the Caribbean, which has evolved into one of the most romanticized and glamorized periods of history. However, the truth is that this so-called Golden Age of Piracy was anything but a romantic existence; it was an especially ugly business for everyone concerned. Most pirates of this much-celebrated period eventually met grisly ends in public executions by hanging—very nearly the fate of Anne Bonny.

Opposite: Statue of Anne Bonny [facing] and Mary Read by Erik Christianson.
Photo by Silvia Guijarro Parra.

Although Anne has become the best-known female pirate in Western history, relatively little is actually known about her life, like almost all pirates—some of the most elusive of all figures in history. After all, they were common criminals long before they were transformed into the romantic personages that have earned an honored place in popular history and memory. This work will be an attempt to fill in the considerable gaps in Anne Bonny's life, nearly three centuries later, without the multiple layers of mythology others have used to rescue the actual person for posterity.

Piracy has been an omnipresent part of life since the beginning of recorded history and continues to be today, in the 21st century. Its harsh reality, promising an early demise for the average pirate, is still being learned by modern-day pirates: On November 24, 2010, five Somali pirates, who had made the fundamental mistake in judgment of attacking a United States Navy vessel off the eastern coast of Africa, were tried and found guilty of piracy in an American court in Norfolk, Virginia: the first conviction of piracy on United States soil in nearly 200 years.

However, what was entirely overlooked by the national and international media was the fact that the conviction of the Somali pirates took place not far from where the most famous of all female pirates in history had lived most of her life: Virginia. Anne Bonny died in the Old Dominion's Tidewater region near the end of the American Revolution in 1783.

After turning her back on everything that she knew in South Carolina in the pursuit of a sense of personal freedom away from patriarchal society's restrictions for women on land, Anne found herself at center stage of an intense international rivalry—one that had long been played out violently by the European powers in the Caribbean. With the death of Queen Elizabeth I in late March 1603, the Elizabethan age of privateering ended, buccaneers ruled the Caribbean in the 17th century, and the lucrative "sweet trade" of piracy reached its highest point in the late 17th and the early 18th centuries. But the true zenith of piracy in the Caribbean was the period between 1714 and 1724, and this is when Anne Bonny arrived on the scene, disguised as a man, with Captain John "Calico Jack" Rackham's pirate crew. As fate would have it, though, by the time that Anne joined the crew of Captain Rackham in 1718, the dark art of piracy was already beginning to die.

Beyond the seemingly endless romantic legends and *Treasure Is-*

land–inspired pirate stereotypes—including the mistaken perception that these ruthless sea rovers were good-natured Robin Hoods—who were the real pirates who sailed the Caribbean's waters? And what were their personal stories that drove them to become pirates? How much of the actual truth can be separated from fiction, especially in regard to Anne Bonny?

After all, the pirates of Anne Bonny's day were the some of the most distorted and fictionalized personalities in the annals of history, ensuring that the real persons have remained elusive to this day. Because their lifestyles guaranteed hanging if caught, they naturally needed to keep their criminal activities secret. Therefore, many pirates served under aliases to disguise their true identities. Another reason that few stories about their lives exist today is because most were illiterate and did not leave letters, diaries, or memoirs, or other written accounts.

The life stories of female pirates were especially rarely recorded, meaning that the narratives of these unconventional women generally died with them. And because large numbers of pirates were hanged by the authorities, few pirates of either gender survived to tell their tales. In many ways, therefore, the average pirate of the Golden Age of Piracy has remained a mystery in the historical record to this day, and an excessive number of myths have filled in these gaps, including those in Anne Bonny's life.

We do know a few details, however. After her capture in 1720 as a capable crew member on Captain Rackham's sloop, just off the coast of Negril, Jamaica's westernmost point, Anne became widely known to the general public as "Bonn." Luckily for us but unfortunately for her, Anne then went to trial before the High Court of the Admiralty at St. Jago de la Vega, today's Spanish Town, Jamaica, and it was here that Anne's daring endeavors were revealed for the first time. This was a very unusual development, seeing as so few pirates, especially women, ever went to trial. The trial exposed the full details of the daily voyages—literally a hidden history of clandestine criminal activities—of the notorious "Calico Jack" Rackham crew during the summer and fall of 1720.

One early 18th-century author attempted to combine the scant available evidence provided by the trial with some personal information that he had acquired firsthand, in order to fashion the first biographical sketch of Anne Bonny. But the author employed a good deal of poetic license and sensationalism to embellish Anne's life—along with that of Mary Read, who served with Anne on Captain Rackham's sloop, the *William*—hoping to fill the public's insatiable appetite and guarantee high sales and profits. Therefore, Anne's life story reached a wide readership when this small book, written by a former sea captain under the alias of Captain Charles Johnson, was published in May 1724 in London, England. Reprinted many times, this popular work, which is still in print today, was titled *A General History of the Robberies and Murders of the Most Notorious Pyrates*. For the first time, the personal lives of the major pirate leaders, such as Captain Rackham and Captain Edward Teach (also known as Blackbeard), were detailed.

Johnson's publication caused an immediate stir in London. In regard to preserving these fascinating life stories, the timing of the book's debut was fortunate, as the relatively brief Golden Age of Piracy had come to an inglorious end only a few years prior. The colorful historical era distinguished by Anne's most unconventional way of life—that is, a democratic society on the high seas—was already an anachronism. Piracy had already been targeted for destruction by the most powerful nation in the Western world, even by the time that a young Anne first sailed the Caribbean.

When she was captured by the English, Anne was trapped by a host of changing circumstances and harsh new realities that were entirely unknown to her. The European upper-class elite, the opinion of the public, and the wealthy sugar cane planters, bankers, investors, stock market manipulators, and slave traders had all turned against the pirates with a righteous vengeance (conveniently ignoring their own hypocrisy and profit-seeking at any cost), because their highly lucrative commercial interests had to be protected to maximize soaring profits.

Therefore, the full might of the English government, society, and military turned their wrath upon these mostly lower-class raiders. As an equal member of the Captain Rackham crew, Anne was sentenced by the British court in late November 1720 to be hanged—not for murder or robbery, but for engaging in petty criminal activities that hardly threatened the extensive interests of the wealthy, aristocratic elite on both sides of the Atlantic.

Unfortunately, much of what Johnson wrote was invented. Knowing a good tale when he saw one, the opportunistic Englishman focused more on Anne's personal life than her pirate experiences. In truth, Johnson merely followed the conventional descriptions of a long-existing tradition of exaggerating the stereotypes of 18th-century female warriors and crossdressers—tantalizing stories that were immensely popular with the curious English public, especially men—to shape the sketches of Bonny and Mary Read into exactly what his curious male readers wanted to hear. Consequently, the enduring romantic fiction has to be separated from fact in order to discover the true Anne Bonny, which is the principal objective of this book.

To fill in the sizable gaps in Anne's life story, Captain Johnson, with keen instincts and marketing savvy, provided the most scandalous, titillating, and colorful possible sketch of Anne Bonny, thereby obscuring the real person she was. As intended, Johnson's ferocious version of Anne was a sensation. Consider that early 18th-century England was a patriarchal society, where women were severely repressed and kept in subservience, according to the dictates of tradition, custom, and culture. By telling the stories of bold and assertive female pirates, Johnson captured the curiosity of the reading public, and his publication was a bombshell to the extremely conservative sensibilities of Western society. Quite simply, he shocked readers of both genders by describing unorthodox behaviors in women—aggressiveness, boldness, and resourcefulness—that overturned long-held stereotypes and ridiculed the traditional order of a patriarchal society.

Of course, what was most outrageous to the public was that Anne Bonny not only dressed like a man, but also that she so openly flouted and boldly challenged the most demeaning stereotypes about women. Such behavior, including displaying courage in combat, raised seldom-asked questions about the time-honored concept of masculinity and its true meaning. Johnson provided examples that were unimaginable to readers: how a young woman wielded ingenuity, audacity, and personal bravery (a higher trait that was thought to be exclusively the domain of males) against well-armed men. Most shocking of all, she dared to break out of the severe limitations, barriers, and restrictions placed upon her sex by society's conventional values, by her own initiative, regardless of the cost—a true revolutionary woman.

Above: Map of Ireland, 1766.

According to the beliefs of the patriarchal world, women were not thought capable of excelling outside the traditional bounds of a lowly domestic existence. Thanks to the stereotypes about an alleged inherent inferiority and the overall powerlessness of the female sex, any women aboard ship on the open seas were almost always viewed as psychopaths, misfits, or prostitutes. Any rational and accurate characterization would pose a stiff challenge to existing gender identities and roles, because such masculinity in women directly challenged the masculinity of men. According to this paternal way of thinking, women could accomplish little work of real significance, especially in a man's world, on the field of strife where courage was required. Therefore, any such obvious historical examples of strong, dynamic women, particularly those in leadership roles, that so thoroughly contradicted existing gender stereotypes were called social deviants.

Instead of the bloodthirsty, excessively violent, if not pathological, female pirate of romantic legend, who was emphasized in Johnson's book, Anne Bonny was in some ways a normal sailor who performed her duties as any other crew member aboard Captain Rackham's ship. Contrary to the caricature that has been perpetuated to this day, she was not driven by psychopathic urges, madness, or a killer instinct that finally found release far from society in the Caribbean. Most of all, Anne possessed the identical basic human wants, needs, and desires as any young woman of her day. Although she was different and quite exceptional in many ways—a deliberate breaker of traditions and rules of a paternal society that posed severe limitations on her—this did not make her a psychopath.

While the brief biographical sketches of pirate captains in Johnson's 1724 book (the so-called bible of pirate historians) have been for the most part verified by corroborating evidence, the true facts of Anne's life have been far more elusive, in large part because she slipped back into obscurity after her escape from the hangman's noose in Jamaica. Having survived brushes with death on numerous occasions, Anne left her life of piracy behind and returned to her adopted homeland in the South, eventually setting down in the Tidewater region of Virginia. After not even two years spent raising hell as a swashbuckler, she transitioned smoothly into an ordinary world, her past hidden over the course of her long life by her new role as a mother and almost certainly a grandmother.

As part of the overall glorification of Caribbean piracy, which conceals nasty truths to present an idealized portrait of pirate life, generations of imaginative historians, myth-creators, novelists, and filmmakers have distorted the true contours of Anne Bonny's life beyond all recognition. In the process, they have twisted and obscured the real person.

A popular 2006 work titled *The Most Evil Pirates in History* included a chapter on Anne Bonny. But in truth, Anne Bonny didn't come close to qualifying as one of the "Most Evil Pirates in History." Contradicting the popular stereotype of the pathological Amazon, she displayed none of the psychosis, abnormality, or bloodlust of a deviant personality, while leading an average pirate's life—one that she loved for its freedom and opportunities, rather than its robberies and brutalities. No evidence has been found of Anne having killed or hurt anyone as a pirate, including when capturing ships.

Nevertheless, what Anne so boldly challenged was male-dominated concepts of honor, faithful service, devotion to comrades, and courage, especially in the face of danger where manhood was traditionally proved in combat and crisis situations. In truth, Anne's role as a feisty fighter who battled men in mortal combat was part of a distinguished tradition that had nothing to do with piracy: a martial legacy of women around the world that had been long suppressed by patriarchal society's denial of the admirable qualities of female warriors, including courage. Indeed, generations of male writers, scholars, and historians have long denigrated a distinguished tradition of female warriors that was truly global, including in Anne's native Ireland. As a young Irish woman sailing the Gulf Stream, Anne unknowingly drew upon a lengthy practice of female Celtic and Celtic-Gaelic pirates and warriors who had fought against foreign invaders, including the ancient Romans and Vikings.

Today, Anne Bonny has been cast either as a swashbuckling heroine who was even more fearsome than her male crew members, or most often a breathtaking blonde or red-haired beauty--a simplistic caricature of a modern Wonder Woman for popular consumption by males, especially by the vivid imaginations of Hollywood scriptwriters. Even more romantic myth about Anne Bonny's life was added with the rise of feminism in the 1970s. Anne was then portrayed as a bold, ultra-masculine lesbian, apparently fueled by too much testosterone and an uncontrollable aggression, to support the prevailing feminist and political agendas of the day: the transformation of the "bad" lesbian of the 18th century into the "good" lesbian of the 1970s.

Thankfully, America has become much more tolerant in the 21st century in regard to individual decisions and personal choices of mates, regardless of sex. Hence, some of the shock value of the mythical Anne Bonny has been negated by time. In contrast, more conservative writers and mostly male historians, with their own agendas to create even greater distortion, have too often portrayed Anne as a cheap prostitute and a "super whore," who was little more than a sex object. So, at different times in history, Anne's image has changed based upon the political mood and leanings, without much regard to the historical facts.

In the end, both men and women and their respective political agendas have been equally guilty of manipulating Anne Bonny's image to support their biases and prejudices and to fit their particular personal and political needs at the moment.

As early as 1724, Anne was portrayed by Captain Johnson as a pathological female maniac cursed with a homicidal temper and unstoppable rage, in order to enthrall his readers with his trademark sensational portrayal. All of these considerable distortions and exaggerations—beginning with Johnson in 1724, spanning throughout generations of male historians, and later by feminists in the 1970s, over more than 250 years—have muddled the truth about who Anne Bonny was. Indeed, her true persona lay neatly between two extremes: the radical feminist view of Anne as a supercharged, overly aggressive lesbian and the conservative male view of Anne as a promiscuous whore. Before she engaged in piracy, and like many adolescents, Anne early experienced her fair share of personal family problems and setbacks in life, in no small part due to the limited opportunities and the lowly place she occupied to in 18th-century English society. From the beginning, Anne's life was troubled, if not tragic, in fundamental ways, counting her illegitimate birth in Ireland, her mother's early death in South Carolina, and later estrangement from her father just before she left South Carolina to become a Caribbean pirate.

Not unlike so many modern women today, the personal and family problems that Anne faced were mostly not her fault, and she wrestled with the consequences of her own personal failures and mistakes--a kind commonly made by young people while growing up and adjusting to the world. After breaking with her authoritarian father and gaining her freedom, she sought to create a new life for herself in the Caribbean: hers was literally a case of running away from home. Anne's decisions can be seen partly as the result of her dysfunctional family background and illegitimacy, a situation that certainly caused Anne a degree of inner anguish at a time when birthplace, family background, and social status determined one's course in life.

In the end, Anne Bonny became a victim of the popular myth and stereotype of the fierce female pirate, devoid of all feminine instincts and feelings. For the most part, Anne's life aboard a pirate ship was neither glamorous nor a romantic adventure, as long emphasized by the myth-makers. For the average Caribbean pirate in 1720, life at sea was serious business that focused primarily on daily survival in difficult situations, especially when on the run from swift-sailing pursuers, especially the ships of the English Navy. There was no glamour to be found while riding the waves, seasick from the tossing ship, or from subsisting on a meager, awful diet of rations, feverish from tropical diseases, and discomfort in cramped, rocking quarters on a sailing ship far from land. Everyday sailors' duties and assignments were exceptionally demanding and arduous. Marked by far more monotony than excitement, life aboard a pirate ship could be an exceptionally short one if the vessel sank, or if captured by the authorities, who showed no mercy for pirates, according to official policy from the highest offices in the land.

It is now time to take a fresh look at the life of Anne Bonny to present a more accurate and corrective view, and fill a missing gap in the incredibly rich field of pirate and women's history, with this book aims to do. To discover the real Anne Bonny, it is time to move well beyond the enduring myths of the negative stereotypes of the sexually charged, ultra-masculine, crazed, and hopelessly neurotic woman pirate, who fulfilled society's imagined descriptions of what was considered the most perverse and despicable to males in 1724.

Contrary to the enduring mythology of a psychotic woman motivated by greed, bloodlust, or love (regarding her relationship with Captain Rackham), depending on the author's imagination and bias, Anne exhibited many qualities that were actually quite wholesome. In addition to being a mother and wife, Anne became a colonial Virginian and an American after her pirating days ended. She lived most of her life according to these definitions not found in Johnson's 1724 account. Anne Bonny was a proud citizen of a new republic, the United States of America, that had yet to declare its independence. Appropriately, this new nation had been forged from turbulent, revolutionary spirits comparable to her own, when she had sailed the with a youthful bravado and a naïve innocence about the world at large.

A complex, versatile woman with a varied background from both sides of the Atlantic, Anne was different from other colonial Americans for a variety of reasons. First and foremost, the importance of Anne's Irish background has been almost always ignored by historians, who have overlooked her formative early years when her character and personality were forged. What has been disregarded is that a vibrant Celtic-Gaelic culture and experience early shaped this young woman of nonconformist spirit to a significant degree. Quite simply, any accurate understanding of the true Anne Bonny is impossible without an analysis of her Irish background and its impact on her and her decisions: one key to understanding why she decided to become a pirate in the Caribbean. To this day, the contributions of Irish women have been long neglected in the historical record, and the story of Anne Bonny has suffered in consequence.

Anne was raised first in Kinsale, Ireland, and then in South Carolina, after her father migrated with her and her mother to one of America's busiest ports, Charles Town (now Charleston, South Carolina), to start a new life. She still carried a distinctive Irish brogue, traditional Celtic-Gaelic ways of thinking, Irish belief systems, and even a distinctive personal manner that was Irish. Anne was also a hybrid of two distinct environments, a product of both the Old World and the New World. Like her Irish roots, so her South Carolina's roots are equally important for any realistic understanding of her as a real person. During her eventful life and beside her pirating days, Anne possessed a wide-ranging degree of transcending personal experiences as an Irish woman, a planter's daughter, a mother, and a wife. She was an Irish woman, a South Carolinian, a Virginian, and an American, and she should be analyzed in all of these contexts.

Demonstrating a longing for autonomy and a fulfilling life far from society's rules and arbitrary dictates that had placed so many artificial limitations upon her, she sought to carve out a new identity and independent life for herself far from South Carolina, her abusive father, and confining patriarchal society. What also has been often overlooked was the fact that Anne and her comrades waged a very personal social and economic war against an exploitative system of powerful bankers, merchants, speculators, ship owners, investors, slave traders, lawyers, speculators, businessmen, and even King George himself. This system had long sucked the life and hopes out of the lowly common people (often little more than slaves, especially indentured servants), ensuring their repression, misery, and poverty for their entire lives. Therefore, Anne Bonny and her comrades, who consisted mostly of lower-class, common people of many nationalities and ethnic groups, fought against the wealthy elites, social and class injustices, abusive governments, and an elitist ruling aristocracy on both sides of the Atlantic, in a timeless struggle between the haves and the have-nots.

Her life was much like that of the main character in Thornton Wilder's 1930 novel, *The Woman of Andros*: Chrysis, in her personal trials during a lengthy search for the meaning of truth and a measure of peace in a hostile world, tells the story of everyone's fundamental struggle. In this sense, Anne Bonny embodied the universal spirit of all people who stood up to fight against what was the most unjust in their lives, representing the oldest of all plights, which still continues today among people around the world. Naturally, the spirit of Anne Bonny still exists to this day: an almost instinctual desire to strike back at what is unfair or just plain wrong. Her unforgettable story is pertinent for future generations as well, in regard to American society's rapidly changing values in the 21st century.

As an effect of America's evolution into a more equitable society in the 21st century, its military has become degendered—which was unimaginable in Anne's day—and thankfully, the concept of the supposed "weaker sex" and ordained subordinate roles for women in society no longer holds its customary place of prominence. Therefore, a new look is required to reevaluate Anne Bonny's life story from a fresh and more honest perspective, to present a more accurate and true portrait of this young woman of courage and character.

Clearly, Anne was ahead of her time, accepting some of the stiffest challenges of her day in order to win the right to forge her own way in life and live on her own terms. After more than three centuries, it is time for a new and more honest look at the astounding life of Anne Bonny beyond the well-worn stereotypes and romantic myths, to present the real person for the first time.

Phillip Thomas Tucker, Ph.D.
Washington, D. C.
July 17, 2016

THE SCANDAL
THAT SHOCKED
KINSALE, IRELAND
1698-1708

AS THROUGHOUT THE PAST, the 17th century, when Anne Bonny was born in the south of Ireland, was not a kind era for women across Europe. The very social foundation of European life and religion, which mandated complete subjugation of women to their husbands' will as part of God's divine plan, was partly based on the alleged inferiority of the female sex. Some authorities even maintained that women had no souls. According to the arbitrary dictates of patriarchal society, God had created "the fairer sex" for automatic obedience in a world dominated by males. Free-spirited, outspoken, and unconventional women were even put to death in England—the last in 1685—and in Salem, Massachusetts, during the witch trials of 1692–1693.

Anne Bonny was about to face a great many barriers, obstacles, and disadvantages, as Western society had designated to her a lifelong inferior and subservient role long before she was born. However, unsung women of spirit and determination occasionally rebelled against the submissive role as defined for them. Consequently, one English author lamented the reality for white women of Europe during this period:

Opposite: Photograph of the port of Kinsale, Ireland, where Anne Bonny was raised.

"Women, like our Negroes in our western plantations [in the West Indies], are born slaves, and live prisoners all their lives."[1] Born on the western fringe of Europe, Anne Bonny was one of those defiant women who rebelled against what she correctly viewed as a deeply entrenched system of oppression that denied her individuality, dignity, and worth as a person.[1]

However, the sheer physical beauty of Anne Bonny's homeland hid many ugly realities of daily life for women. Perhaps no place in Ireland was more picturesque than the south of Ireland, especially County Cork, Munster Province, in springtime, when this land of beauty was warmed by the Gulf Stream. Without providing details in his 1724 book *A General History of the Robberies and Murders of the Most Notorious Pyrates*, Captain Charles Johnson, who exhibited some of the traditional British prejudice toward the Irish, merely described how "Anne Bonny was born at a town near Cork, in the kingdom of Ireland . . ."[2]

But Johnson missed the mark by failing to pinpoint Anne's actual birthplace. Indeed, it was not in the south Ireland port of Cork, or Corcaigh in Gaelic. She was in fact born in the small fishing village of Kinsale, Ireland. Founded by Anglo-Normans and thought to have once been the home of ancient Irish kings, the coastal town of Kinsale was situated near the Old Head of Kinsale sixteen miles southwest of the larger port of Cork. After Cork, Kinsale was the most important port in the county.

Johnson was correct in describing Anne's mother as a house servant named Mary, or Peg, Brennan. The date of Anne's birth is still uncertain, because of the lack of records and documentation: Some modern historians have claimed that she was born as a love child on March 8, 1700, while other historians have placed Anne's birth year at 1698. At this time, the best available evidence says that 1698 was the year of Anne's birth, and that she was born Anne Ni Cormac.

Mary Brennan was an attractive young woman who served in the household of a married and respected lawyer of Kinsale, William Cormac, who was Anne's father. With reddish hair and greenish-brown eyes, like her mother, who occupied the lowest rung of Irish society, the illegitimate little girl was named Anne. This was hardly a promising beginning for an infant girl into a highly religious, traditional society—almost medieval in sexual matters—in which birth and social status were vitally important not only for future success, but also for survival.[3]

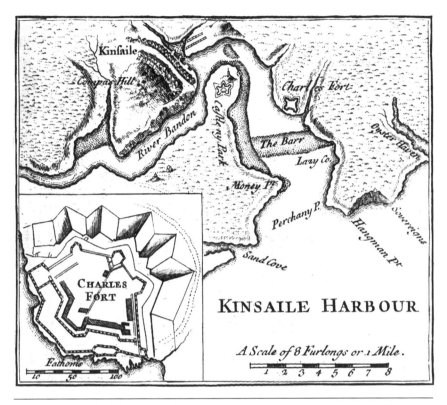

Above: Kinsale, Ireland, where Anne Bonny was born in the town opposite Charles Fort.

Anne's homeland was nestled in a picturesque region. An Englishman described how Kinsale was "defended by a strong fort called Charles's Fort; and on the opposite shore there are two villages called Cove and Scilly; the inhabitants of which are generally native Irish and live in low built houses, made of mud, on a beautiful eminence . . . facing the inlet of the harbour."[4] As a Catholic, Mary Brennan most likely had been raised in either one of these two "villages" that revealed nothing of prosperity or possibilities for upward mobility.[5] Built in the late 1670s, the star-shaped masonry bastion known as Charles's Fort guarded the river that approached Kinsale harbor from the south, while the bastion's sister fort, James's Fort, which had been constructed earlier than Charles's Fort, stood closer to the town of Kinsale.[6]

Although not recognized by historians who have focused excessively

on only her pirate activities in the Caribbean, Anne possessed a distinguished lineage and heritage on her father's side, the Cormac family. But
in her paternalistic world, such a background was negated by her gender.
Beginning in 227 A. D., Cormac mac Airt, the son of Art who was the King
of Tara, was "the most celebrated of all [Irish] pagan monarchs," during
the period before St. Patrick brought Christianity to the island. A wise,
far-sighted ruler, Cormac mac Airt first established not only a uniform
set of just laws to govern his Gaelic nation but also established schools
for teaching history, to enlighten his people with martial lore. He also in-
stilled military discipline to create a true warrior society. Clearly, he knew
that the key to his people's survival was to be well prepared for war, especially since a vulnerable Ireland long had been victimized by invasions.

During the third century, Cormac mac Airt (or Cormac Mac Art)
represented the sacred kingship of Tara, the ancient seat of power in Ireland. County Meath, from which he ruled, overlooked the fertile northern
part of the Central Plain: the famous Hill of Tara. Known as "the wise
warrior," Cormac "revered truth and prized peace," while enjoying a successful reign. Despite being more than a warrior-king of the traditional
mold, Cormac was also known for his wisdom as a sage judge and philoso-
pher. A general prosperity flourished among his Gaelic-speaking people,
who reaped the riches from the fertile soil. One ancient fortified point
atop the sacred Hill of Tara is still known today to the Irish people as
Cormac's House. And an O'Cormac branch of the Corca Laoighdhe family—almost certainly Anne's paternal line—had thrived in its southwest
County Cork home since the 16th century.[7]

Displaying the sophistication of the literary traditions of his reign
and with the assistance of some of Ireland's most renowned historians,
King Cormac was the author of the Saltair of Tara (or Cormac's Saltair),
which was a history of the Celtic people "from the world's beginning."[8]
Most significantly, this "noble work," which was widely considered to be
"the best summary of history" of Ireland, recorded "the succession of
their kings and monarchs, their battles, their contests, and their antiqui-
ties," which was known as the "Saltair of Temair [Tara]."[9]

The words of an ancient poem from Tara and the "Book of Bally-
mote" (1391) sang Cormac's praises and revealed the ancient paternal
lineage of Anne Bonny:

"Temair, choicest of hills,
For [possession of] which Erinn is now devastated,
The noble city of Cormac, son of Art,
Who was the son of great Conn of the hundred battles:
Cormac, the prudent and good,
Was a sage, a filé [poet], a prince;
Was a righteous judge of the Fené-men,
Was a good friend and companion.
Cormac gained fifty battles:
He compiled the Saltair of Temur."[10]

In addition, solid evidence has also revealed that the Cormac family of County Cork was also descended from Milesius, King of Spain, through the bloodline of his son, Heremon (Érimón). However, the most reliable documentation has indicated that Fiacha Baiceada, son of Cathire More, king of Ireland in 144 A. D., was in fact the Cormac's family's founder. The ancient name of Cormac meant "son of wrestler." However, some genealogical experts have suggested that the name of Cormac also signified an ancient "charioteer." An anglicized name that reflected the realities of the English conquest, Cormac was the Gaelic equivalent to the name Charles. Cormac also gave rise to the common surnames of MacCormack and McCormack.[11]

As though it were a portent of her future life as a pirate of the Caribbean, Anne's birth took place under a convoluted set of circumstances. The chain of events that led to Anne's birth began when William Cormac's wife became so ill that a physician advised her to "remove for change of air" at a distant location in the rural countryside. This fact indicated that the Cormac residence was probably located in the heart of Kinsale, near the busy waterfront. In such a bustling port, diseases brought from foreign lands were quickly spread when gangs of seamen came ashore to visit the town's brothels and crowded taverns, while mixing with the local population. Therefore, William Cormac's wife "chose" a healthier place that "was a few miles' distance from her dwelling, where her husband's mother lived [and] Here she sojourned some time, her husband staying at house, to follow his affairs."[12]

Although unintentional, this was an appropriate word employed by Johnson, because one of William's "affairs" included the pursuit of the pretty servant girl in the Cormac household while his wife was away. Mary Brennan remained behind to care for the house and "to attend the family" in Mrs. Cormac's absence: an ideal situation for a successful seduction. But Mrs. Cormac, perhaps anguished by mental torment (if she still loved her husband) from her growing suspicions and the obvious growing bond between her husband and the pretty maid, might also have intentionally left her home.

After all, William had too often showed Mary special, if not excessive, favor, including "several actions of kindness" noticed by his observant wife, who correctly sensed something deeper was in play. William's passion for his wife had either recently plummeted or never had burned very brightly to begin with if he had married for money and social status, which seemed to be the case. Mrs. Cormac's love, wealth, and high standing in society were insufficient to contain her husband's obsession. A natural rebel who had a penchant for breaking rules and defying convention despite being an attorney—which made him think that he was above the law in regard to societal norms and sexual indiscretions—William Cormac possessed an adventurous spirit, and his reckless, freewheeling ways were demonstrated both inside and outside of bed. Like an adolescent schoolboy, he was smitten with Mary's youth, appearance, and pleasant personality: she seemed to be the antithesis of his wife.[13]

But William Cormac had competition for her affections from a younger and equally ardent rival. To William's disgust, this equally infatuated suitor, younger than William and closer to Mary's age, was of dubious character. The young man, a tanner, hailed from a lower-middle-class background that was higher than Mary's own, but much lower than the attorney's.[14]

However, in order to fool Mrs. Cormac about what was going on in her own home behind her back, Mary utilized the relationship with the younger man as a clever screen to mask the clandestine affair with Cormac. Mrs. Cormac was not a jealous type, or she certainly would have never allowed the attractive young lady to stay in her own household, close to her husband's greedy grasp. Mary's low social status had initially seemed sufficient to bar any such possibility of a clandestine romantic relationship between a respected Kinsale attorney and a maid, to Mrs. Cormac's class-conscious, upper-crust mind and society.[15]

After recovering from her illness, Mrs. Cormac returned to her home from her mother-in-law's house unannounced one day. Because her husband had not visited her or and his mother during the four months that she was sick, nor even communicated with her, she had intentionally not informed him of her return in order to ascertain what was happening in her own household—and perhaps even in her own bed. He was doing nothing to cover his tracks, such as feigning concern for his wife's welfare. Clearly, Mr. Cormac's behavior was now out of control.

Evidence had been gradually piling up that the philandering attorney, who outsmarted himself, had engaged in sexual escapades with his pretty maid. But Mrs. Cormac's suspicions were proven when she arrived in the morning to discover that Mary's bed was undisturbed from the previous night. However, for final confirmation, because her reputation and standing in society were at stake, the lady of the house had one more trick up her sleeve. Mrs. Cormac dismissed Mary early one day and then, revealing a well-conceived cunning that rivaled her husband's own, she lay in the darkness of the maid's room that night, waiting for the visitor who was sure to come seeking sexual favors. As expected, her husband arrived in a heated passion, sneaking into the maid's small dark room. She recognized her husband's eager voice when he asked, "Mary, are you awake?" As he had so many times over the past four months, he took off his clothes and proceeded to make love to her. More than ever before, Mrs. Cormac now had reason to hate Mary Brennan.

She also made another discovery in Mary's room: Several silver household spoons that had gone missing, which were hidden under the covers of the maid's bed. These expensive silver spoons had been placed under the sheets by Mary's young suitor, the tanner, who had stolen them. He had taken them out of his pocket and stashed them when Mary had accused him of theft and threatened to go directly to the "constable" in Kinsale. Worried about Mary backing up her threat, the tanner, who took full advantage of existing opportunities at the Cormac house, had then professed his innocence in unconvincing fashion. When Mary had checked the kitchen drawer for the missing spoons, he then slipped into the bedroom to place the spoons under Mary's sheets. After she had conducted a futile search for the missing items, the young tanner quietly sneaked back to Kinsale to escape Mary's anger.

Eager for revenge against the uneducated maid, rather than her husband, who was guilty of not only betrayal but also infidelity, an enraged Mrs. Cormac called the authorities of Kinsale and had Mary thrown in jail on the trumped-up charge that she had stolen the spoons. But her lawyer-husband was too deeply in love with Mary Brennan by this time to allow the injustice to continue.

His wife's revenge fueled William's wrath sufficiently to ensure a permanent separation between them. Mrs. Cormac then officially charged her husband with adultery, an accusation that extended Mary's stay in the Kinsale jail. Some evidence has indicated that Cormac himself was briefly jailed for adultery, but this was unlikely, as he was a respected attorney with good legal connections, especially with the judge. However, Mrs. Cormac and her family possessed considerable clout, and the story could have been true.

Mrs. Cormac's wealth, as well as Mary's low social status and the swiftness with which she was incarcerated, might indicate that the Cormacs were Protestants and that Mary was a Catholic. Irish Catholics had long been regulated as second-class citizens by their British Protestant conquerors, who controlled a subjugated Ireland, and County Cork was mostly Catholic. The brutal ruthlessness of Oliver Cromwell, who slaughtered countless numbers of Catholic soldiers and civilians in southern Ireland under the belief that he was doing God's will, had won Ireland for England. So, in the eyes of the conservative and religious-based community of Kinsale, Cormac had committed a double indiscretion against the Church though adultery and also against his Protestant faith, because Mary was almost certainly an "untouchable" Catholic.[16]

All of this personal drama and inflamed passion in the Cormac household was set in the most serene of natural settings that seemingly scoffed at human folly and foibles. Ireland's abundant warm rains, combined with ocean winds from the Gulf Stream, transformed the land along its southern coast into a beautiful green idyll during the spring. Not even the ancient Romans had been able to conquer Ireland—they were stopped by the English. Hibernia was the Roman name of this stunning island, which had been coveted by all who had gazed upon it. Numerous ports existed at inlets and bays along the Ireland's southern coast. Kinsale's size was sufficient for conducting a thriving commerce, which supported William Cormac's law practice. Along with his legal profession, William was also prosperous because he had married well.[17]

John Robert Shaw, a British soldier, described the busy port where Anne was raised. He marveled at the "Cove of Kinsale [and] Kinsale, especially in the time of war, is a place of much business . . . The cove is a convenient and beautiful harbour, and lies about seven miles from the city of Cork."[18]

Meanwhile, the Cormac drama that was the talk of all Kinsale continued unabated. Mary Brennan, the unlucky pawn of the love triangle, languished in prison month after month until it was discovered that she was pregnant. The overall public sentiment of Kinsale and even the judge then softened toward the unfortunate Mary, as did Mrs. Cormac, whose desire for vengeance had subsided somewhat. The people of Kinsale knew that Mrs. Cormac had acted unjustly against this common woman with a good heart. In addition, this was a drama about class. Consequently, the townsfolk, mostly Catholic, stood behind their fellow commoner, in opposition to the Protestant, aristocratic Mrs. Cormac.

In the end, Mary was acquitted of all charges and released from jail. From the turbulence that had caused the greatest scandal in Kinsale's recent memory, Anne was born in 1698, a love child in the truest sense. Therefore, Anne never would be accepted by William Cormac's mother and class-conscious family, who had naturally sided with his wife and refused to acknowledge his new daughter.[19]

Around the same time that Anne was born, Mrs. Cormac, from whom William was estranged, gave birth to twins by another man, evidently out of personal revenge for her husband's infidelity. This development shocked William, who was somewhat of a ladies' man with a lofty ego based on his class, status, and privilege, and who had not realized that his wife had been sexually active outside of the marriage as well. Thereafter, William and his wife lived separately and had no sexual relations. William kept his distance from Mary too, due to community pressure, an attempt to salvage some personal honor, and perhaps also out of guilt. Because he was an attorney, he probably also tried to at least publicly

adhere to his marriage vows, which were legally binding: a necessary façade under the circumstances.

Any additional romantic involvement with the maid was bound to
destroy not only William's reputation, already bruised from the scandal,
but also his livelihood as an attorney. In such a conservative and reli-
gion-prioritized environment as Kinsale, a divorce was unthinkable, and
would be guaranteed to ruin his legal career. But William ultimately followed the dictates of his heart, as his daughter Anne would later do in
the course of her own life, and eventually rekindled his relationship with
Mary and his daughter, Anne. And this time, the bond between the three
became permanent.[20]

Consequently, Anne grew up in Kinsale, enjoying a relatively normal
life close to the seafaring world of the port town. Kinsale was a thriving
port, a fishing center, and a medieval tangle of cobblestone streets, with
a history going back to the Anglo-Normans, who had invaded and first
settled a community near lucrative fishing grounds on the warm Gulf
Stream. Here, in County Cork, Anne was raised with the sea in her blood.
She also experienced a distinctive sense of the tortured heritage of these
Celtic-Gaelic people.

Strategically situated on high ground, nearby Fort Charles overlooked the wide bay that led to the Irish Sea. The decisive battle of Kinsale in 1601 had been one of the most important clashes in Irish history,
as Anne eventually learned. Here, the heroic but futile last stand of the
fast-fading Celtic-Gaelic world stood against the might of Protestant
England, whose aggressive imperialism had early targeted Ireland for
subjugation. After the defeat of the Irish Catholic forces at Kinsale, Ireland's complete conquest was just a matter of time.

Catholic James II had ruled England until his Protestant subjects
forced him from the throne during the Glorious Revolution of 1688.
Along with the Protestant William of Orange, James II had fled to France
before coming to Kinsale—the first English monarch to set foot on Irish
soil—in mid-March 1689, bringing with him a sizable Jacobite army in
an audacious bid to conquer Ireland. Not long after James' landing, the
first Protestant resistance against the resurgent Irish Catholic tide was
crushed at nearby Bandon, County Cork, just northwest of Kinsale. After
the Jacobites swept north during this springtime of hope, James II and

the Jacobite rebels were decisively defeated along the River Boyne at the battle of the Boyne on June 14, 1690.[21]

Besides its rich history and Celtic-Gaelic traditions extending back for centuries, Kinsale was also blessed by nature, allowing it to become one of Ireland's premier harbors. The heart of the little town was nestled between the high ground (Compass Hill) and the rocky shoreline of the wide harbor that accommodated large, oceangoing vessels. Sailing north up the Bandon's broad waters, vessels were greeted by green hills, with the port town situated at the base of the high ground.

Above the waterfront, wharf area, commercial buildings, and fine homes that lined the harbor, the town's remainder was spread out along the gentle slopes of Compass Hill. From this commanding perch that overlooked the wide harbor and the Bandon River, Anne likely gained an early appreciation of nature. Likewise providing a source of inspiration, the blue waters of Kinsale harbor, the Bandon River, and the sea might well have called to her at an early age.

Although she was illegitimate, Anne enjoyed a relatively privileged upbringing compared to most Irish Catholics, because of her father's money and love: an almost certain recipe for a spoiled child. William wanted his daughter to live at his home with him, while his legal wife continued a separate life in another part of Kinsale. But he faced a dilemma, because he still received a yearly allowance from his wealthy wife, and she wanted to reconcile their differences as advocated by William's mother, who continued to attempt to reunite the couple. This allowance was too lucrative for the attorney to ignore. But most of all, William naturally felt love as well as a moral obligation toward his daughter. Therefore, William developed a novel strategy and began presenting Anne, dressed in male clothes, as a young boy to disguise her true identity. In this way, he could pretend that he was training the "boy" to be a lawyer's clerk to assist in his law practice, while keeping his daughter close by his side like a responsible father.[22]

For community approval, to avoid continued scandal, and to reap his wife's allowance, William needed to conceal the fact that the child living with him was his own daughter. His rich wife continued to pay an annual allowance to him, destined to last nearly five years, as part of their separation agreement, in part because William's mother had willed her estate to the couple and Mrs. Cormac's twins. Revealing that he followed his heart, William had stubbornly refused attempts to reconcile with this wife for the twins' sake, even after he learned that Mrs. Cormac was pregnant. The tragic deaths of the twins from disease then allowed William to focus his attentions exclusively on his daughter, who early overcame society's rules about so-called proper dress that differentiated the sexes.

In the Cormac home where she had been conceived, therefore, Anne was raised in traditional boy's clothing. Nevertheless, and more importantly, she benefitted from a loving father and mother, who either occasionally visited each other at William's home or at some discreet location. Anne also enjoyed a relatively elevated station in life by growing up in the Cormac household. William continued to represent the principal merchants, leading citizens, and ship captains, who sailed around the world in a variety of commercial enterprises. Although no documentation has been found, his law office was probably located along one of the narrow medieval streets near the harbor.

Thanks to the Gulf Stream, Kinsale is a warm water port, an enclave that never freezes over. Situated on the wide River Bandon that led to the Celtic Sea, Kinsale proved to be an ideal setting for Anne. Here, the sea and the people, whose livelihoods were mostly connected to the ocean, were part of Anne's daily life, and this experience stayed with her. Especially if she lived in a fine house on Compass Hill that overlooked the "sinuous, sheltered harbour," Anne often viewed the white canvas sails of ships that roved the world's oceans. Such sights long remained deeply implanted in Anne's heart and mind long after she grew to adulthood. As a youth, she walked the shoreline and wharf area, while flocks of noisy seagulls circled above the port, catching sights of sailors and the seafarer's world. Anne early witnessed a seafaring environment that left a deep imprint in her psyche.[23]

But the natural beauty of County Cork masked a host of ugly realities, from murders in the dark taverns along the Kinsale wharf to the threat of piracy. At some point, Anne almost certainly learned of the horror stories about when "Turkish," "Algerine" (of Algiers), or "Moorish" pirates from north Africa (today's Morocco, Algeria, and Tripoli) sailed into the Irish Sea and even raided County Cork's coastline in 1631. Partially inspired by the Koran, which sanctioned slavery of non-Christians or infidels, and as part of a jihad against non-believers, one such pirate raid had swept through the port of Baltimore, Ireland. Here, Muslim pirates had rounded up more than one hundred Irish men, women, and children—the village's entire population—who were taken back to Algiers as slaves. Likely from her father or mother, Anne first learned of piracy by hearing about these raids in her own home county, where so much blood had been spilled in Ireland's history.[24]

As Anne grew up, the people of Kinsale eventually realized that William's young boy, who was living in his home and supposedly being groomed as a law clerk, was his own child, Anne, the daughter of Mary Brennan. Time passed and gossip increased, and the townspeople were eventually no longer fooled by the artful attorney, who made a living from overturning facts, when necessary, to win cases for wealthy clients.[25]

But an unkind fate was about to forever alter the course of Anne's life. The rising tide of gossip about Anne's true identity finally reached Mrs. Cormac. Anne's secure world in Kinsale with her doting father by her side was destroyed, after self-righteous members of the community began to suddenly turn on her father. Once his estranged wife learned the truth, she promptly cut off William's annual allowance. But then, the "husband enraged, in a kind of revenge, [took] the maid home and [lived] with her publicly" thereafter.[26] As could be expected, Mrs. Cormac turned vindictive. She directed her wrath not at her husband but the source of her troubles, Anne, threatening to have Anne banished from Kinsale without a penny to support herself in the future.[27]

But more discord between William Cormac and his wife provided an unexpected boon for Anne, and she was not exiled as Mrs. Cormac wished. Instead, the child was now permanently united with her mother and father, who no longer had anything to hide. Clearly, as he now realized, William's love for Mary and Anne was deeper than what he had ever felt for his wife. Consequently, this period was the happiest time of Anne's young life, as well as for her reunited parents.

However, just when it seemed as if all had been finally settled satisfactorily, this domestic bliss for the new Cormac family proved to be short-lived. Gathering momentum that might have been partly fueled from the pulpit, by Protestant ministers, Catholic priests, or both, more people of Kinsale turned against William Cormac, who was still legally married to his wife in the eyes of the church. He, therefore, was living in sin with his former maid of dubious morals and their illegitimate love child, and this unconventional mixed Protestant/Catholic relationship resurrected old religious prejudices and hatreds.

This common-law marriage in a strict, conservative environment came at a high price for William Cormac. His life with his mistress and child was personally rewarding, but his reputation and professional life now began to suffer. He had finally found true love and an unprecedented happiness with Mary and Anne, which had nothing to do with moving up the social ladder. Clearly, William was an independent-minded man who had charted his own course in life. But the public knowledge that he was living in sin resulted in a social backlash that damaged his legal practice.[28]

Like other Irishmen who faced the wrath of intolerant communities for violating strict social norms in an ultra-conservative environment, William's now-happy home life was made intolerable by an outraged public. In the 1750s, fellow Irishman William Gilliland faced a comparable situation: He was literally "run out of the old country by the family of a woman with whom he was in love," because his social status was much lower than the respected lady. For Gilliland, an escape to America offered the only solution.[29]

Left without any realistic choice, with clients dropping and his business spiraling toward ruin, William Cormac was forced to make the same drastic decision as William Gilliland. He was now determined to embark upon a fresh start in life, in a new land with those whom he loved the most in life. Instead of simply abandoning them to their fates as many upper-class members would have done in comparable situations, William defied convention by charting a new course with Mary and young Anne.

In this regard, William Cormac now allowed his true character to rise to the fore. What stemmed from the Cormac-Brennan scandal was an early lesson that Anne would never forget. And as so many past generations of Irish immigrants learned, the best place to start anew lay beyond the sea, in America. The Irish had often emphasized the fact that the next town to the west of their isle was Boston, Massachusetts. But, of course, sizable port cities along America's eastern seaboard—New York City, Philadelphia, and Baltimore, as well as smaller cities like Charles Town (now known as Charleston), South Carolina, and Wilmington, North

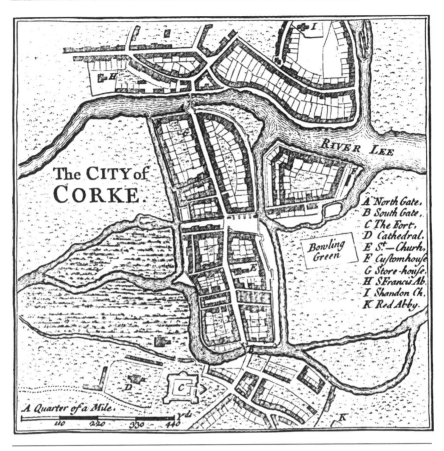

The CITY of
CORKE.

RIVER LEE

Bowling
Green

A North Gate.
B South Gate.
C The Fort.
D Cathedral.
E St.—Churh.
F Cuſtomhouſe
G Store-houſe.
H S.Francis Ab.
I Shandon Ch.
K Red Abby.

A Quarter of a Mile.
110   220   330   440   yds

Above: The town of Cork, County Cork, was built on the site of a Viking trading center and was the largest port in south Ireland when Anne and her family sailed for Charles Town, South Carolina.

Carolina, or even Savannah, Georgia—offered possibilities for a capable Irish lawyer to practice law. William, determined to make a fresh start, sold what little remained of his legal practice and home in Kinsale, liquidating and concentrating capital. He then made arrangements to journey northeast to the city of Cork with Mary and Anne.[30]

William's ultimate solution mirrored that of many other Irishmen who have fled to the New World because of scandal.[31] By this time, William possessed knowledge about the increasing stream of Irish who had migrated to Charles Town, South Carolina, including those hopeful souls who had departed Kinsale, and Cormac very likely knew some of these

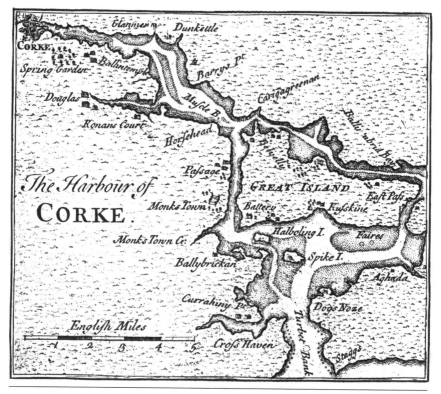

Above: The excellent harbor of Cork made the city the finest port in the south of Ireland.

settlers. As early as 1669, a ship of immigrants from England "stopped at Kinsayle [sic] [about] the first of September."[32] Here, the sailing ship took on a load of Irish immigrants and set sail for Charles Town.[33]

William planned to depart from Cork, because he was not known there. In addition, no one in Cork knew that Mary Brennan was not his wife and that the child with them was not legitimate. By traveling to Cork, William may also have been escaping creditors, or perhaps even community leaders and church officials who sought to persecute him as a moral example. William Cormac had learned the meaning of an Irish witch hunt, and he planned to depart the Emerald Isle with no regrets.

In addition, the possibility existed that the incensed townspeople would try to prevent the family's migration from Kinsale, as they, of course, knew the local sea captains. Thus, Anne, who was already experienced in duplicity, as she had been long disguised as a boy in her father's household, was involved in a clandestine escape not just from Kinsale but from Ireland itself. Most importantly, she never forgot the invigorating feeling of personal rejuvenation that came from the promise of a fresh start, when she, her father, and mother departed for a new life in a faraway land across the Atlantic. The family's hopes and ambitions were high when they sailed without incident out of the scenic "Cove of Cork, which is perhaps the most spacious and commodious haven in the world," as one impressed Englishman wrote.[34] For the hard-luck Cormac family, who could not live in peace in Ireland, America—and Charles Town, South Carolina—beckoned as never before.[35]

II

THE NEW WORLD
AND
CHARLES TOWN,
SOUTH CAROLINA
1708-1718

FEW PORTS in the Western world were more culturally divergent than Charles Town, the capital of the South Carolina colony. William, Mary, and Anne had left a mostly Catholic country and were resettling in the Proprietary Colony of South Carolina, colonized by Protestants—however, all sects found Charleston the bustling "London of the Low Country," a safe haven to worship as they pleased. Hopeful Irish immigrants had poured into South Carolina since at least 1669. Likewise, South Carolina, which was still a frontier region beyond the coast, also served as a refuge for people who were running from the law.

Some of the first Englishmen who settled in South Carolina had migrated from the prosperous English colony of Barbados, part of the Lesser Antilles, in the eastern Caribbean. Barbados had been early transformed into England's first lucrative Caribbean island, founded on sugar cane production and slavery: the successful blueprint for

Opposite: Modern view of Eighteenth-Century Charleston courtyard, a known pirate gathering place.

future English development of the Caribbean islands as well the American mainland.

But even more than the warm climate, religious tolerance had long been the magnet that drew immigrants to South Carolina. Dissenters made their way there from across western Europe, especially from Ireland and Scotland. Huguenots, devout French Protestants who had been persecuted by the government at home, were the leading dissenters who migrated to this new land after King Louis XIV had declared Huguenot Protestantism illegal in France in 1685. Huguenots, mostly from Normandy, had captured the Spanish island of Port-Margot, in what's now Haiti, during August 1640; unsurprisingly and as if in retaliation, a good many Huguenot buccaneers waged a holy war against Catholic Spain in the Caribbean.

Charles Town and its planter society was a world apart from Southern Ireland. The semi-tropical Low Country of eastern South Carolina was an alien terrain for the Irish immigrants, who'd come to the humid coastal plain from a land of green mountains, lush valleys, and clear streams. Charles Town, which possessed a small French Quarter like New Orleans, Louisiana, was considered "the most culturally British city in America."[36] Here, thanks to the growing demand in Europe for rice, the planters of the gentry class grew wealthy and began to imitate the gentry of England, embracing upper-class values and belief systems. In this booming economy, which used the vibrant slave trade to provide a limitless supply of workers for the expansive rice fields of the lowlands, these planters became some of the richest men in North America.

By the time that Anne and her father and mother had arrived in Charles Town around 1708, when Anne was about 10 years old, it was a relatively new settlement. The town had been established barely 40 years before, in 1670. Built on the palmetto-lined banks of the lazy Ashley River by wealthy absentee landlords from Barbados, Charles Town was a thriving commercial community. In 1708, the town's population stood at 9,580, and more than 4,000 of these residents were slaves. Here, in South Carolina, the hard-working settlers and their slaves successfully recreated a little Barbados on the mainland, which was less vulnerable to hurricanes than the Caribbean island. Here, rich fields of sugar, rice, and indigo spread for miles along the fertile coast, unlike in Barbados,

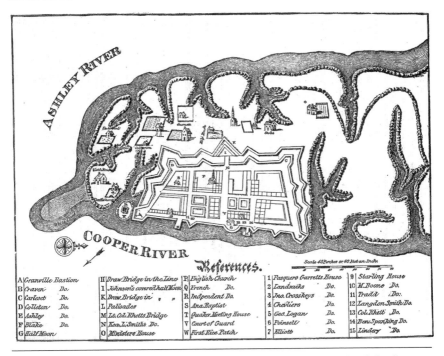

Above: Anne arrived with her immigrant parents in the port of Charleston, South Carolina.

where expansion had reached its limits, as large planters had early secured most of the island acreage. Anne and her parents discovered that Charles Town offered an appealing mixture of West Indian culture and Irish culture. Most dissimilar from Ireland were the forests of giant oak and cypress, with Spanish moss hanging down from massive limbs that touched the ground, which lay just outside the town's limits: the antithesis of the manicured agrarian landscape of the County Cork farmland around Kinsale.[37]

The dangers of life on the Atlantic's low-lying coastal plain had been evident to Anne's father upon first sight. When their ship entered the wide expanse of Charles Town Bay, they saw that the city had been walled with brick to protect the inhabitants from the Yamasee confederation of native tribes as well as from French, Spanish and pirate attacks. In 1706, French warships, carrying Spanish troops, had appeared in the harbor, demanding the town's surrender, but the threat was repelled by the militia.

Located at the confluence of the Ashley and Cooper Rivers and facing the wide harbor that fueled its commercial prosperity, low-lying Charles Town was laid out in neat lines, with narrow streets crisscrossing the southern end of the peninsula. In 1700, not long after Anne was born, Charles Town was described in complimentary terms by immigrant John Lawson: "The Town has very regular and fair Streets, in which are good Buildings of Brick and Wood."[38] Close ties between Kinsale and Charles Town had long existed by Irish and South Carolinian merchants and traders, and this connection explained the steady stream of hopeful migrants from the Emerald Isle. This Celtic-Gaelic exodus had been fueled by the crushing of each Irish rebellion by the English. Large numbers of displaced Irish, especially former Jacobite revolutionaries, fled to the West Indies, and Barbados in particular. Irish immigrants from Kinsale had first landed in South Carolina as early as 1670, as part of the resurgent migration more to the mainland than the sugar islands of the West Indies. As one early South Carolina historian emphasized: "No country furnished the province with as many inhabitants as Ireland."[39]

The fundamental South Carolina Constitution of 1669 had bestowed freedom of worship not only to Irish Protestants (mostly Presbyterians) but also Quakers, French Huguenots, and Jews.[40] South Carolina also offered "cheap land, free tools and seed" to lure Irish Protestants—but not Irish Catholics, who were initially banned—to settle on South Carolina soil.[41]

Around the time that Anne and her parents arrived there, in 1708, the population of Charles Town consisted of just over 4,000 whites, with 4,100 black and 1,400 native slaves. Significantly, slaves outnumbered the free citizens in the town. Of course, Anne and her family hailed from a land without slavery, where a black person could only occasionally be seen, perhaps on a New England ship that stopped at Kinsale. Therefore, she must have been shocked by the sight of so many people of African descent in Charles Town. But doubtlessly, what was most shocking for Anne and her family was the realization that these unfortunate people were entrapped forever by slavery, which guaranteed lavish profits for the planters who lived like feudal lords.[42]

But most of all and as reflected in the large slave population, Charles Town, "a place of beauty and pathos," was in essence little more than a Caribbean port town on American soil, thanks to early immigrants from

Barbados. In South Carolina, cash crops of the plantation system controlled the bustling economy, beginning with the cultivation of rice in the 1690s. Unlike the pious Catholics of County Cork, the culture and society of Charles Town and South Carolina reflected Caribbean values, lifestyles, and belief systems that were closer to those of the French and Spanish Caribbean islands than to England's. Consequently, men of God from the north, especially from New England, were shocked to discover that the people of Charles Town were so unlike those in other parts of America, because of the lively, free-spirited Caribbean lifestyle in which "the people seemed wholly devoted to pleasure." The town's culture was distinguished by formal balls, bouts of heavy drinking, and other social activities held by the Low Country elite, and Anglican minister Alexander Garden was stunned by the realization that South Carolina's hedonistic "gentleman planters are above every occupation but eating, drinking, lolling, smoking and sleeping."[43]

But the minister could have more correctly criticized the Charles Town merchants, who had first grown rich from the lucrative deerskin trade with the Cherokee and Creek tribes in the South Carolina interior, before the sugar boom. The Native Americans became dependent upon this trade, because they acquired firearms, lead, and black powder, and dependence upon it grew so strong that one British general, Thomas Gage, admitted that the Native Americans had "disused to the Bow [and arrow], and can neither hunt nor make war, without Fire-Arms, Powder, and Lead."[44]

But life on the coast was entirely different from South Carolina's unruly back country, where large numbers of poor Irish and Scotch-Irish had settled to scratch out a meager existence. One fundamental, but often overlooked, reason why the ties between Charles Town and the Caribbean remained so strong by the time the Cormac family arrived there was its deep economic links to piracy. Due to South Carolina's vulnerable location, at the eastern end of a vast wilderness that extended inland toward the Appalachian Mountains, merchants and residents early became dependent upon the flow of goods stolen by pirates. Here, at the colony's largest port, pirates early found an ideal market to sell their wares at a much lower price, because South Carolinians purchased normally expensive imported goods from England. Therefore, the close economic connections between Charles Town and piracy had existed since the first days of settlement, and they stayed robust through the early 18th century.[45]

However, this situation was not entirely unique to South Carolina, because this thriving "corporation of pirates" extended far and wide along the East Coast. By the 1690s, New York City had replaced South Carolina and Rhode Island as the trading location of choice for pirates along the Atlantic coast. Self-serving governors and other government officials had turned a blind eye to these illegal activities, especially the sale of stolen goods in merchant shops, and the sight of the pirates in their midst. Pirates strutted up and down Broad and Wall Streets in open daylight as if to mock the authorities.[46]

In regard to the fundamental differences between Kinsale and Charles Town, the latter community was essentially located on the Caribbean's northern edge in terms of overall demographics, cultural ways, and economics. Charles Town still reflected the planter class ethos, and as the Cormac family discovered, these migrants had faithfully replicated the culture, society, and slave regime of their West Indies island. Although the two busy commercial ports on opposite sides of the Atlantic shared the same seedy elements along the shorefront and wharf areas, with busy taverns, hard-drinking sailors, bordellos, narrow streets, and ramshackle houses crammed together, the two distinct societies possessed strikingly different value systems. While Kinsale and County Cork consisted of white people who looked and acted fundamentally the same, the most striking difference was that Charles Town appeared in many respects almost like a community in western Africa. The community consisted of large numbers of African Americans, mostly slaves, many of whom spoke the distinctive creolized patois of the South Carolina Low Country known as Gullah, but also many free black people as well. In time, one of the household servants of Anne's father would be a Gullah woman named Bacu.

A wealthy class had early emerged with planters improving thousands of acres on plantations that extended up the fertile bottoms on both sides of the Cooper and Ashley Rivers and north of Charles Town in Berkeley County, where many Irish immigrants had settled. Taking their distinctive Celtic-Gaelic culture with them, Scotch-Irish immigrants, impoverished and of modest means, created their own ethnic communities.

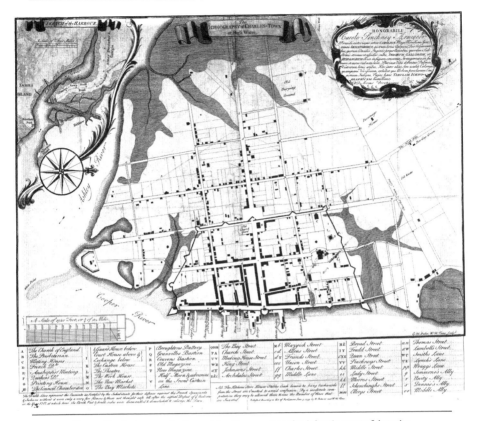

Above: Charleston was the largest Southern port on the Atlantic coast of America.

They established "little Ulsters," and tracts with names such as "Lymerick Plantation," on the Cooper River in Berkeley County, in honor of the Irish city of Limerick. But the vast majority of settlers who trekked inland into the uncharted Piedmont region of South Carolina were poor Irish and Scotch-Irish immigrants in search of cheap land and fresh starts.

Benefitting from an expansive bay and heavy commerce, Charles Town became the wealthiest port city with the highest per capita income of any residents in America. Mirroring those of the English upper class, the luxurious lifestyles of the South Carolina gentry were supported by large gangs of slaves working in the lowland fields of rice and indigo, both cash crops that produced fabulous wealth. In the words of one South Carolinian, "Negroes were our wealth, our only natural resource."[47]

William Cormac must have been delighted by the tolerant, less religious environment of bustling Charles Town, compared to his native County Cork. As an attorney who knew how moral laws could be perverted for self-service, he detested the hypocrisy of the excessively pious: a lesson no doubt learned by his daughter, Anne, at some point. Perhaps best of all, because smuggling and other criminal activities were so common, Charles Town needed good lawyers for honest men—as well as for criminals.

For William more than Anne, therefore, Charles Town was a very good place for an enterprising person with a troubled past and a good education to start anew. Because South Carolina was governed by English laws, William continued to practice law in South Carolina as if he were still in Kinsale. He ostensibly married Mary in Charles Town to initiate the family's fresh start at a promising place that was sufficiently removed from Old World biases and prejudices, after their ordeal in Ireland. Consequently, for the first time, and most importantly for her own personal development and self-esteem, Anne was no longer to be called a bastard, as she was in Ireland, where the dark stigma doomed her to a lower rung on the social ladder.[48]

The refined Charles Town gentry and planter class also differed from the English gentry in another significant way, in that they continued to emulate Barbadian traditions, including widespread miscegenation, which thrived more in Charles Town than any other city in the English colonies. Here, an unbridled racial intermixing flourished among all classes of men, leading to a large mulatto class, the "new people" of America. Miscegenation thrived for successive generations, resulting in an overall whitening of the black population. Rather remarkably and to a degree unseen elsewhere in America, Charles Town "was the one place in the Carolina world where whites and blacks came together all through the generations."[49]

Even the town's leading newspaper, *The Gazette*, recorded the widespread extent of the relationships with black women, from casual liaisons to serious relationships that lasted decades. The newspaper even revealed a duel fought between two leading white men over "a certain Sable Beauty." Meanwhile, another cautionary article lamented the open displays of love-making: "Certain young men of this Town are desired to frequent less with their black lovers in the open Lots . . . ."[50]

Because he was an Irish immigrant, William's entry into a newly minted society, which mimicked that of England, was not a seamless one. However, he succeeded in creating a new life for Mary and Anne in relatively short order, thanks to his legal practice—he was experienced in British law, which governed both Ireland and South Carolina. After accumulating profits, the opportunistic attorney eventually tired of law and instead aspired to become a merchant, where more money could be made, because commercial activities in a vibrant Low Country economy were booming. Like so many other Irishmen, William was able to take the leap and switch careers, discovering that he could, in fact, reinvent himself in America.[51]

Without the monopolistic competition from British merchants, as in Kinsale, William embarked upon a lucrative profession at exactly the right place and time. He acquired a small fortune in a relatively short time because of the heavy volume of business, in both legal trading and smuggling, which included slave trading. As well, Anne might have first seen pirate leaders on the streets or heard of pirating activities in regard to her father's business, which may have benefitted from the selling of stolen pirate goods. Eventually, William accumulated so much money that he was able to fulfill another South Carolina dream: He established himself as a rice planter and part of the gentry when he purchased "a considerable plantation" north of Charles Town in Berkeley County, South Carolina, where many Irish immigrants had settled. Rice cultivation was now becoming more profitable and spreading gradually north, and William also grew indigo, used for blue clothing dyes.[52] Here, in the humid subtropical climate of coastal South Carolina, there were riches to be made.

Sixty miles northeast of Charles Town, Cormac operated his plantation in the Black River country near the little port of Georgetown, South Carolina.[53] It is not known, but perhaps William decided to move out of vice-laden Charles Town, something of a modern Sodom and Gomorrah, in an effort to provide young Anne with a more wholesome environment. The Black River area, a primeval wilderness of swamps and tropical-like forests, was still a remote frontier region at the time, and the wooded lands of the coastal plain were cheaper than the city. There, just above where the Black River joined the Big Pee Dee River and where the ever-widening waterway became tidal, William, Mary, and Anne began their new life on a sprawling rice and indigo plantation. William had accomplished what was impossible for him to have achieved in Ireland, where great tracts of land were owned by English and Anglo-Irish landlords. The Cormac plantation consisted of hundreds of acres along the dark river that snaked slowly through the pine forests to the sea. With the help of a good many slaves, William shipped harvested rice that was then transported by boat down the Black River, which flowed to Charles Town, where ships sailed for the markets of Europe.[54]

Anne most likely received a decent education from a private tutor in the large planter tradition. Amid an unspoiled countryside, Anne also led an active outdoor life, including horse riding, shooting, and hunting small game. Here, she learned about firearms and how to use them—a necessary precaution for self-protection in case of attack from the native tribes. Because South Carolina was the adopted homeland of many European political refugees, especially those from Ireland, Anne might have been taught at the family's plantation house by a French Huguenot teacher. Protestant Huguenots had migrated to Charles Town as early as 1680, fleeing Catholic France, where they long had been persecuted by church and state, and in such large numbers that they were able to establish their own church. Many found work in South Carolina as private tutors, and like other children of leading planters, Anne likely benefitted from these educated individuals. Immigrant John Lawson described how planters with money, like William Cormac, "have Tutors amongst them that educate their Youth a-la-mode."[55]

DYNAMIC IRISH WOMEN

If educated by one of these French Huguenot tutors, then Anne might well have learned about one of the most remarkable women in French history, Joan of Arc. It's easy to see how an independent-minded girl like Anne could have identified with this dynamic young woman who had fought a war against the influence of the same enemies of the Irish— that is, the English—in defense of her native homeland. Joan was one of France's great heroines, who led French forces to victory against English invaders in the late 1420s, during the Hundred Years' War. What might have impressed Anne was the fact that Joan had accomplished her deeds of daring on the field of strife, while dressed in a suit of battle armor, like the French male soldiers. Known as "The Maid of Orléans," this young peasant girl inspired thousands of Frenchmen to rise up. These devout Catholics believed that Joan had been sent by God to vanquish the English and save France from conquest.

Armed with a heavy sword and mounted on a horse, Joan led the French to one victory after another, while carrying a battle flag, decorated with the Christian Cross of Lorraine, and shouting religious words of faith. Like no other French leader, she invoked God's assistance against the English and inspired fanatical support. From the village of Domrémy, in the Duchy of Bar, just outside the border of the Duchy of Lorraine, Joan achieved victories by following her own instincts against the advice of more cautious male leaders. She continued to wear men's clothing to defy convention after battling against the English imperialism: an inspirational lesson that would certainly not have been lost to Anne, if she had learned of Joan of Arc's exploits. This was a remarkable case of an ordinary woman of the peasant class rising up to defend her country with great valor, while leading large numbers of fighting men in action.[56]

But a far more likely early historical example of a bold woman who carved out her own destiny, legacy, and life and who might have inspired young Anne was one of her own fellow countrywomen: Grace O'Malley of County Mayo, Ireland. Born more than a century after Joan of Arc, Grace inherited her love of the sea from her father Dubhdarra (Black Oak), who took considerable pride in his only daughter. He was the leader of the seafaring O'Malley clan and their fleet of warships that roamed in Ireland's western waters. Known as the "Queen of the West," Grace was Ireland's pirate queen and the chieftain of the O'Malley clan during the late 16th century. She was also the most famous pirate in all of Irish history at the time, and she still holds a revered place in Irish folklore. One of the boldest sea captains of her day, Grace launched hard-hitting raids in pirate galleys from Clare Island upon both Spanish and English ships. Grace O'Malley was known for her outstanding leadership ability, military skill, and fighting spirit, which included battling on deck with flintlock pistols or a cutlass in hand—skills later displayed by Anne Bonny as well.

Grace O'Malley, or Granuaile as she was known to the Irish people,

Above: Clew Bay, Ireland, served as the home base of female pirate Grace O'Malley.

was born around 1530 to the Gaelic aristocracy around Clew Bay in County Mayo, long a sanctuary for the O'Malley ships. Like no other Irish pirates or even any women of her day, Grace became a legend in her own lifetime, commanding large numbers of sailing ships and Irish fighting men against the English, while raiding the unprotected coasts of Ireland and Scotland and even Spain. Grace was not only a fellow Irishwoman, but also went to sea at a young age in a martial role, while defying not only tradition but also an ancient foe—almost certainly an inspirational legacy to a young Irish girl as she was growing up in Kinsale.

Because the O'Malley clan derived most of its income from fishing, Grace was not as much of a pirate in the traditional sense of raiding for financial gain. Nevertheless, she was widely feared as the bold leader of highly mobile galleys of the O'Malley fleet, which had evolved from the Viking long ships that had paved the way to Ireland's invasion. Dark-featured with gray eyes that sparkled in the heat of combat, Grace first raided English shipping with her hair cut short, blending in to a degree with male crew members. She appeared much like her fellow countrymen, who manned her raiding ships and fought with a typical Celtic-Gaelic ferocity against invaders. Like her seafaring ancestors whom she revered, Grace's safe enclaves were Clare Island, in Clew Bay, and the rocky lands of western Connaught, in County Mayo, northwest of Galway.

In a rugged land of hardy seafarers and O'Malley castles, English warships found that Grace's stronghold was untouchable. A cagy and bold "she-king" who spoke Latin with a smooth ease, Grace earned a fearsome reputation among her enemies as the "nurse to all rebellions" against England. Less experienced than the Irish raiders, the English were unable to safely navigate these tricky waters—known well only to the O'Malley clan—in order to attack Grace's ancient sanctuary. In 1576, Englishman Sir Henry Sidney, Lord Deputy of Ireland, described Grace with respect in official correspondence as "a most famous feminine sea captain called Granny Imallye [who] was a notorious woman in all the coasts of Ireland."[57]

Most importantly, an inspirational lesson almost surely not lost to Anne was that Grace's life represented "the most transgressive role to which a woman could ever aspire . . . a rare woman who claimed freedom as her birthright" in an age in which women were essentially slaves.[58] Indeed, Grace's bold example became an enduring "symbol of freedom in an oppressed time" in Irish history, and to young Irish women like Anne.[59]

Anne had almost certainly early learned about Granuaile from the local people of Kinsale, or from her father and mother, who perhaps passed down the oral tradition about the Irish heroine. In command of her own fleet of pirate ships, manned by mostly male clan members, Grace O'Malley had occasionally sailed past Kinsale or perhaps even stopped at the port to obtain supplies, at a time when she referred to herself in writing as "Grany ny Mally of Conaght." Therefore, Grace O'Malley became a local folklore legend of not only the people of Ireland but also of Kinsale, because she had often sailed the waters of south Ireland. Like Anne's story, the romantic mythology about Grace's life has most often overlooked the fact that she was also an average person in some ways, a loving mother who married twice. However, she was destined to be disregarded by many male historians in large part because she was "a woman who overstepped the part of womanhood."[60]

Because she was an Irishwoman like Anne, Grace O'Malley provided the most inspirational example to Anne of a pirate queen who survived by her wits and resourcefulness. She long defied the day's conventions and restrictions to create a new identity for herself by excelling far beyond expectations for women in a man's world. The story of Grace O'Malley would have provided an inspiring—even nationalist—example of battling against the ancient enemy of the Irish people through attacking English commerce, almost as if a payback for Ireland's subjugation.

Consequently, it's possible that young Anne was exposed to inspirational female role models—women of courage and character like Grace O'Malley and Joan of Arc who had dressed as men, which allowed them to earn a rare bit of respect in their strict patriarchal worlds. Both dynamic women owed their fame largely to their own intellects and achievements, independently of men, rather than mythical accomplishments fabricated from the pens of latter-day writers and historians. As well, both women fought specifically against the English, a role destined to be later reenacted by Anne herself in the Caribbean.[61]

SOUTH CAROLINA TEENAGER

Anne's teenage years in the region north of Charles Town, which was still a frontier, were a dangerous time. In November 1693, Charles II of Spain had first declared black runaways to be free if they reached Spanish soil. As such, slaves sought refuge by fleeing south from South Carolina toward Spanish Florida, especially the city of St. Augustine on the Atlantic coast. South Carolina's slaves revolted in 1711, when Anne was 13. But the ravages of disease were far more deadly in this area than slave revolts were.

Anne's life changed forever at age 15, when her mother, Mary, died of typhoid fever, which had taken so many lives in the coastal lowlands. At this time, the Cormac family had only lived in South Carolina for about five years.[62] Still a teenager, Anne was suddenly thrust into the adult world and its responsibilities and now replaced her mother in keeping up the household and helping her father operate the extensive plantation, where work continued from sunup to sundown. Saddled with more responsibility than ever before, Anne also managed the daily operations of the entire house, not unlike her mother's original responsibility as a maid at the Cormac house in Kinsale.

Above: The example of heroine Joan of Arc might have inspired Anne Bonny.

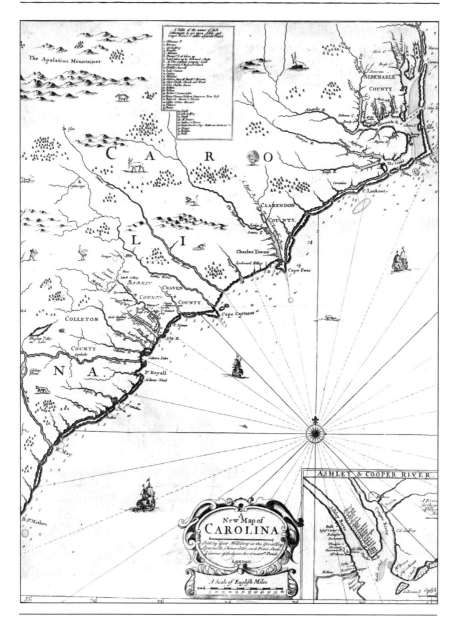

Above: The lengthy coast of the South Carolina colony.

In the immediate wake of her mother's death, Anne bonded with her grieving father. Out of practical and emotional necessity, the two at first became "inseparable," working more closely. He most likely had been responsible for teaching Anne how to use a flintlock and a sword.[63] However, Anne never completely recovered from the shock of Mary's sudden death. Mary's demise came before she and Cormac had had another child and so Anne remained an only child—a privileged position that was relatively rare in the 18th century. As could be expected, she became somewhat spoiled as a result. Already precocious, Anne early developed into a high-spirited young woman, and operating her father's house and plantation made her all the more willful in regard to getting her own way.

But Anne's bond with her father eventually turned to disillusionment. This may have stemmed in part from her mother's death, which she evidently blamed on William, as he had brought them to the remote plantation. Burdened as well by the considerable responsibility of running a large household, Anne allegedly lashed out—including one incident toward an English maid, which was much exaggerated by Captain Johnson, who deliberately emphasized any kind of rage for the sake of sensationalism. But in truth, because her own mother had been a house servant back in Ireland, Anne very likely felt some empathy for such women in this role. Allegedly, Anne turned a knife upon the servant girl in a fit of rage, but an unrestrained murderous intent, as suggested by Johnson, cannot be substantiated.

If the incident did occur, however, then Anne's behavior might have stemmed in part from troubles at home. After the death of Anne's mother, her father may have found a sexual replacement in the form of the English servant maid or even a black female slave in the planter class tradition—a possible source of Anne's growing anger toward her father. Even more, after Mary's death, William began to drown his personal pain in bottles of Irish whiskey. (Alcohol was safer to drink than Low Country water, which was almost brackish and likely to cause illness.) Whatever the exact cause, the divide deepened between father and daughter.[64]

During this period, William Cormac not only owned his rice plantation on the Black River but still maintained a house in Charles Town, where he continued to operate his merchant business and perhaps even practiced law. Therefore, Anne frequented Charles Town too. She might have stayed longer periods at the house in town, especially if the fissure between father and daughter deepened. She also became disgruntled with the mundane existence and burdensome responsibilities of her isolated plantation life. Williams Cormac's plantation household was operated by a trusted slave in Anne's absence.

By this time, Anne was 16 or 17 and desired a normal life with young people of her age, without the burden of almost limitless adult responsibilities. Additionally, as a healthy teenager, she naturally became interested in young men, who were relatively rare on the plantation. But another overlooked factor could have explained why Anne departed the plantation and headed back to Charles Town. Most likely, she relocated with her father in the city because of the slave revolt of 1714 and then the subsequent outbreak of the Yamasee War in 1715. The relentless wave of white settlement was pushed back by the Yamasee confederation of native tribes, who were the most effective allies of the Spanish in St. Augustine, Spanish Florida. Liberated slaves also joined in the fight against the settlers. William Cormac's only child would have been safer with him in Charles Town than on the plantation.

By this time, Anne was growing into a young woman and naturally began to draw suitors from Charles Town. In city society, she was seen as worthy wife material who carried a good inheritance.[65] However, especially now without a mother, Anne was more vulnerable in emotional and physical terms, and in Charles Town, ample opportunity existed "for a young woman with a wayward streak and an inheritance to get into trouble."[66]

At this time, no one possessed higher aspirations for Anne than her doting father, who had grown wealthier over the years and had bought a sugar plantation in Jamaica. As could be expected, Anne's looks, personality, and background drew all types of men, including unsavory characters from the rowdy port city. Unfortunately, most young men were more interested in fulfilling their lustful desires in crude fashion in a dark Charles Town alley, or by presenting a façade and attempting to marry her in order to get their hands on her father's wealth. In the beginning of her stay in Charles Town, she accepted respectable suitors—the well-educated, mannered sons of planters and merchants—in accordance with her father's high social standing. One of these aristocratic types was too aggressive, and "she beat him."[67]

Such indications revealed that Anne's sense of self was character-ized by independent-mindedness, willfulness, and feistiness—some of the same qualities which would soon lead her toward a most unconventional life in the Caribbean. She was somewhat selfish, because of her young age and the fact that she was an only child from a rich family. However, with each new experience in Charles Town, Anne became wiser, if not a bit cynical, in dealing with artful suitors of a freewheeling port city that was known for its vices and liberal ways. She was virtually surrounded by debauchery and sinful behavior of almost every imaginable variety.

The open sexual relationships between white men and slave women grew to such proportions that the alarmed editor of the *Gazette*, Charles Town's leading newspaper, warned that this lascivious phenomenon was "spreading worse than smallpox" in Charles Town. In Anne's case, it must have seemed as if the loose morals and licentiousness of these aris-tocratic planters' sons, who had long had easy access to slave women on plantations, where "every slave cabin was a house of ill repute," had been projected upon her. But Anne held her own against the wiles of expert seduction techniques, rejecting the advances of fellow teenagers as well as experienced older men.

Rarely for a teenage girl of the era, the high-spirited Anne possessed a strong sense of self and independence that served her well against the evils of this unruly port city. She refused to be taken advantage of by men. At a time when female docility and submissiveness were expected as proper behavior, she was not one to fall prey to misuse at the hands of an artful male manipulator. Clearly, in rejecting all unsuitable suitors in the city, Anne refused to be intimidated by those who had only their own selfish interests at heart and not her own.[68]

However, quite unlike any other place in America, Charles Town was a place where all sorts of trouble were brewing, regardless of how hard Anne tried to avoid and dodge it—a situation not unlike her father's when his life was changed forever by the intolerant environment of Kinsale.[69]

AN EXCITING NEW LIFE IN THE CARIBBEAN
1718

BEYOND THE PORT of Charles Town and the swamps and pine forests that surrounded the town on three sides, a new world of opportunities, both legal and illegal, lay in the Caribbean for enterprising individuals. All that Anne had to do in order to escape South Carolina's provincial confines was to board one of the sailing ships in Charles Town harbor, to be carried away by a stiff breeze—just as her family had done when they left Ireland—and embark upon a new life. As the city maintained close commercial ties with ports in the Caribbean, Anne heard many tales of the distant Caribbean islands and they evidently offered, if only in romantic terms, many more exciting possibilities than South Carolina. While scanning the horizon to the east, Anne perhaps began to realize that only the expansive harbor and the outlying sea provided an escape out of a provincial existence, to the larger world that lay beyond. Even the romantic names of Caribbean islands sounded enchanting and mysterious, such as the English islands of Jamaica and Barbados, the French colony of Saint-Domingue, and the Spanish colony of Cuba.

Opposite: View of Montego Bay, Jamaica.

Anne's eventual decision to leave South Carolina for the Caribbean has been portrayed primarily from a traditional male perspective because of Captain Johnson's 1724 book. As could be expected, he stressed how Anne simply followed her man, James "Jim" Bonny, to the Caribbean in the time-honored tradition of subservient women, who were unable to chart their own course in life: the stereotypical expectations of a patriarchal society. In historical terms, this standard explanation of women as mindless followers driven solely by uncontrollable love, rather than intellect or reasoning, has long been applied to women transgressing into a man's domain.

Of course, such a convenient excuse offered by male writers and historians—even though separated by centuries—conforms to their male-centric belief systems that bold decisions by women can only be explained as them mindlessly following a man's example, primarily that of a lover or husband. In this way, the woman's decision-making process has been systematically reduced to low ambition, in which a woman's free will and intelligence was second to her supposedly uncontrollable emotions. This caricature of a woman would do whatever was necessary, even at great personal risk, just to be beside her man, who made all major decisions as dictated by prevailing sexual politics.[70]

But was Captain Johnson's simplistic male-centric formula actually the case in regard to Anne? Although it cannot be documented, the probable scenario, long overlooked by historians who have too closely followed Johnson's fantastic narrative, was that Anne did not meet a young, lower-class sailor named James Bonny in Charles Town and then follow him dutifully to Nassau, Bahamas. Instead, she might well have departed Charles Town entirely on her own, and then met Bonny in Nassau, which is perfectly possible, considering that Bonny was a pirate and Nassau was the greatest pirate haven in the Caribbean at this time. Because much that was written in the Johnson book has been either grossly exaggerated or is just plain wrong, this theory should not be dismissed, especially because Anne was increasingly disgruntled with her life in South Carolina.

Instead of following young Bonny wherever he decided to go, Anne may have first just decided to run away from home, her father, and the so-called respectable—but hypocritical—Charles Town society based upon

England's hierarchical model. She detested the snobbish, class-oriented society of the Low Country Planters, where place of birth and family background meant everything, and she may have encountered arrogant disdain from her gentry-class peers as well, especially if her illegitimate birth became common knowledge among South Carolinians.

There were a host of other reasons that Anne may have wanted to create a fresh start in life, as when she and her parents departed County Cork and crossed the Atlantic.

She could have received a dose of snobbery from the planters' sons and daughters because she still spoke in an Irish brogue—perhaps she and her family were still seen as foreigners from the "old sod." Also, despite being an only child, in purely economic terms, Anne was left without bright prospects if her father remarried, in a patriarchal society in which only the eldest son inherited the family farm or business.

A teenage girl of the upper class would have encountered difficulty in developing a romantic relationship with a pirate as well. Anne's watchful father would not have allowed her to frequent the seedy parts of the notorious Charles Town waterfront, because the family reputation had to be maintained, especially after the Kinsale scandal. Clearly, Anne's desire to flee all that she knew was actually more complex than what was presented by Johnson, and the only route by which to flee from her world was by way of the sea, which symbolically represented a new start.

Another contributing factor to Anne's dissatisfaction in South Carolina could be that, because the Cormac clan were Irish immigrants, the nurturing familial environment of the Celtic-Gaelic homeland was absent on the Black River Plantation and in Charles Town. Consequently, Anne's life was less full in traditional Celtic-Gaelic terms. Most Irish immigrant families, especially lower-class and Catholics, were relatively isolated in South Carolina and remained in insular ethnic communities, where Irish Catholics—a minority—found safety and security in numbers.

Add to this the fact that Charles Town was an isolated enclave, and the heavily forested Piedmont region where the Cormac plantation was located was lightly populated. Because Charles Town was cut off from the rest of the English colonies except for links by the sea, the Caribbean was the nearest and most readily available outlet for Anne to embark upon a new life.[71] Anne also already possessed some knowledge of the

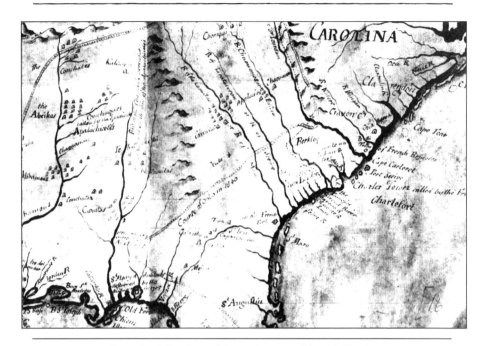

Above: South Carolina and the northern part of Spanish Florida.

Caribbean, as Charles Town was essentially an extension of the Caribbean, with Caribbean cultures, folkways, and lifestyles as well as strong links to the major Caribbean ports, especially British possessions such as Jamaica.

Other psychological factors also set the stage for Anne's departure from all that she knew in South Carolina. As mentioned, the father-daughter bond continued to suffer from severe strain. But this might not have been Anne's fault, as historians have long claimed. If only subconsciously, it was perhaps natural if William somewhat resented Anne because she was a lovechild, whose existence had torn him away from his beloved Celtic-Gaelic homeland, his family members, and a secure place in society. In addition, William had brought his wife to America as a result of Anne's birth, and now she lay in her grave. Therefore, perhaps if only subconsciously, William might have blamed his daughter for the loss of his wife, even though it was his own lack of adherence to society's conventions that forced the family to depart from Ireland.

For Anne, no escape on American soil seemed possible, and few options were open to her. After her mother's death, she had no other immediate family members in South Carolina besides her father. And she obviously could not return to Ireland more than 3,500 miles away; her father's scandals had burned all bridges and ties to Kinsale. Perhaps Anne only found peace of mind when away from her overbearing father, her boring life on the Black River plantation, and a bleak existence as a proper lady of the planter class in Charles Town. Compared to her troubling life at home, Anne no doubt felt a sense of freedom whenever she was alone, including while viewing the sea that historically represented escape and now seemed to beckon her. Flowing endlessly to the distant eastern horizon, the Atlantic Ocean represented the very essence of freedom, partly because its vastness had already freed her and her family from Ireland's unforgiving environment only a few years before.

While looking at the peaceful waters of Charles Town, Anne might have watched the effortless ease of the disciplined formation of pelicans, the breeze behind them, without flapping a wing in their lengthy glide. If so, Anne may have felt that she was like one of those graceful birds—ugly and awkward on land but so beautiful in flight—and dreamed of journeying far away from whatever was troubling to her, to a new place without pain and confusion brought by vexing family matters, and a more complicated world than she had ever imagined.

A Pirate Named Jim

By late 1718, at age 19, at some unknown place and time in Charles Town, Anne first met the young sailor named James "Jim" Bonny. The handsome seafarer was captivating to her, although as far as she knew, he was a common seaman without money, influence, or social connections of any kind: the very antithesis of the type of young man to whom Anne's father would have given his approval. But by this time, Anne had already decided to leave her life in South Carolina, so she could have seen Bonny as a way out of her situation, and her rebellious spirit could have played a role here—by choosing to associate with Jim Bonny, Anne directly defied society's expectations. William Cormac, therefore, was naturally enraged when Anne told him about her choice.

Also of Irish descent, full of blarney, and literally a man of the world, Jim Bonny told her about his life at sea. As Anne readily noticed, the jaunty sailors of Charles Town were a distinct "race apart" from colonial society at large. Independent and individualistic types not unlike Anne, these men used a distinctive seafaring value system and jargon. In the Age of Sail, transient seamen thronged the streets, taverns, and brothels of Charles Town, roving like prowling wolves, and Jim was one of them. However, he was not actually a common seaman, as he told Anne—in truth, he was a pirate. With his connections in Charles Town, William Cormac almost certainly knew this and realized that his hard-headed daughter had made a big mistake.

Jim Bonny was also charming and good-looking—in fact, the word "bonnie" means pretty or attractive in Ireland—and his attentions were flattering to a young woman who was still naïve about the world's devious ways. Another part of his appeal was the fact that Jim was an Irishman. He and Anne shared a common ethnic heritage that led to mutual interests and perhaps memories of their native homeland, maybe even the port of Kinsale. Anne was still only a teenager, and she was also preconditioned in many ways to become enchanted by a dashing young man with good looks and colorful tales of the Caribbean. Anne was thoroughly enchanted by Jim and the sea, becoming what people called "sea struck," and he had intensified her youthful obsession.

Clearly, William had reason to be upset by the match of his beloved daughter, who had been groomed for upper-class status, to a sea rover with no future. In fact, William became so incensed that he disowned her. However, the social gulf between Anne and Jim was sufficiently wide that this fact likely presented a perverse appeal to her, because she knew that her choice antagonized her father. Anne and Jim were also birds of a feather because they were both natural rebels and shared a contempt for society's hypocritical values, inequities, and injustices—not unlike the common bond once shared by Anne's parents, which had bonded them together back in Ireland, when it was them against the world.

Aside from their intensifying romantic liaison, this mutual disdain for an unjust society, abusive power structure and hypocrisy, especially among the upper-class elite, forged a common bond between Anne and Jim: something that William was unable to understand. Although seafarers usually disliked landlubbers, whom they looked upon with contempt, the ties between Anne and Jim were firm. As their relationship became more serious, Anne became increasingly eager to dispose of the detested label of landlubber.

To fuel her father's anger to new heights, Anne became as passionate about Jim Bonny as her father had been about her own mother, and the love affair was destined to change Anne's life forever, just as William's love for Mary had altered the course of their lives. It seemed almost as if something within the Cormac family genes and biological makeup ensured that intense passions generated by love were monumentally disruptive to their lives. William Cormac had lived in the most unconventional possible manner for an extended period, doing things his own way, according to his strong will, and Anne had inherited these distinctive headstrong qualities, which guaranteed ongoing personal conflicts between the two. For a variety of reasons, Anne held tight to her own distinct ideas about her personal choices that not only ran directly contrary to those held by her father and patriarchal society in general, but also mocked his lofty ambitions for his daughter.[72]

Falling for Jim Bonny came at a high price for Anne and the little Cormac family. Her behavior broke her father's heart while at once fueling his wrath—not unlike the reaction of his high-bred first wife, back in Ireland, when she had first learned of his relationship with Mary Brennan.[73] Anne and Jim soon had plans to marry, and the reputation that William had steadily built up by so much hard work and respectful behavior in Charles Town, after it had plummeted to an all-time low in Ireland, would once again become stained. Because his daughter was so much like him, William Cormac was about to gain a pirate for a son-in-law, while inheriting yet another family dilemma and scandal.

By this time, word had filtered through the pirate's grapevine at the busy wharf, taverns, and brothels of Charles Town, which was much larger than Kinsale, that new opportunities were being presented at Nassau, the capital of the island of New Providence in the Bahamas. Here, a new day had dawned for those criminal seafarers, who were engaging in an ancient profession that defied the strongest empires and navies in the world, by taking advantage of the hapless merchant vessels.[74]

However, Anne almost certainly didn't make a premeditated decision to leave South Carolina for the express purpose of becoming a pirate. Anne and Jim defied her father's wishes and eloped, just as her own parents had done, and as a consequence of her youth and relatively sheltered background, she evidently believed that her husband was an honest seaman, not a pirate. But her father had disowned her and had expelled Anne from his home, and as never before, Anne was probably more than ready to leave behind a provincial world in which she had never quite fit.

Like her young husband, and especially now that she was married to someone whose livelihood was not rooted in South Carolina, Anne may have found some solace from her own ever-increasing personal troubles in the sense of freedom in Jim's invigorating tales of the sea and the enticing promise of departing Charles Town. Even more than in her patriarchal society, however, life on the ocean was exclusively a male's world, and a tough one at that. But for this woman born in Ireland, the sea possessed more enticing possibilities than insurmountable obstacles and dangers. While most ladies in Charles Town could only gaze upon the sea with regret, or fondly dream about what life might be like on the sea were they not women, Anne looked at that vast expanse leading to mystical and exotic places much differently, because it was something that was already familiar to her. Anne had never forgotten the long journey across the Atlantic that provided a new lease on life to the Cormac family. Consequently, Anne's most intimate sense and instinct began to evolve around her growing, novel belief that the sea's unlimited promise should not be denied to her because of her gender—an idea that was heresy in late 1718.[75]

Already, a strange destiny had set its course for Anne Bonny, and in ways that she could not now understand or imagine possible at this time. Anne had no way of knowing that a dynamic pirate named John "Calico Jack" Rackham now served as a leader of the hardened crew under Captain Charles Vane, who had only recently sailed the Atlantic's waters just outside Charles Town during the summer of 1718. One day in the future, Anne Bonny would sail the Caribbean under Captain Rackham, not only as a crew member but also a trusted top lieutenant, once he became a pirate captain. Fate was already shaping the future of young Anne Bonny in mysterious ways entirely unknown to her.[76]

A REPUBLIC OF FREEDOM-LOVING PIRATES

AT THIS TIME, Anne Bonny was unaware that piracy was a most dangerous profession, and even older than the ancient land of Ireland. Piracy had existed in cultures and civilizations around the world, thriving as an omnipresent part of the human experience since times immemorial, dating back 8000 years—practically to the first time that man took to the sea. By the time that Anne Bonny was born, piracy had been refined and perfected into a highly effective art form.

As a young man, before he became the most famous emperor in the ancient world, Julius Caesar was captured by pirates who raided Roman merchant ships plying the Mediterranean in 78 B. C. As such, there was nothing unique about the eventual spread of an especially vibrant form of piracy in the Caribbean Sea by the early 18th century, where it was fueled by the intensity of European imperial rivalries, which were no longer focused on the traditional power struggles in the Mediterranean. Instead, these heated rivalries were resumed in the New World by the major European powers, led by Spain, which had benefitted from a head start by arriving in and exploiting the New World before its neighbors did. Among the tropical islands of the Greater Antilles, first claimed by Spain, the power struggles of the greedy European monarchs were played out like the maneuvering of the mythical Greek gods on Mount Olympus. The

---

Opposite: Englishman Edward Teach was the feared pirate captain better known as Blackbeard.

first English buccaneers, or privateers, sailed slightly later, during the age of Elizabeth I. They waged war on longtime religious and political rivals, especially Catholic Spain, across the Caribbean.

While Spain was pocketing gold, silver, and gems from the Aztecs in present-day Mexico as early as 1517, it wasn't until the 1570s that England joined the high-stakes game of crassly exploiting the New World's bounty. Nevertheless, the British were determined to get their fair share of the spoils in the name of God, country, and imperial destiny. English sea raids descended upon the Spanish treasure convoys departing from New Spain during the first leg of the journey back to Europe. Sea routes were well-known by the opportunistic English buccaneers, who proved to be master predators in the Caribbean's waters. Slow-moving Spanish vessels were ambushed by these experienced English seamen, whose skills became legendary. Spanish convoys sailed principally sent out of the deep bay at Havana, Cuba, which served as Spain's Caribbean headquarters, by way of the Straits of Florida, to expedite their passage across the Atlantic.

Covertly dispatched by Elizabeth I, who denied the existence of a wide-ranging fleet that served English interests so well by waging war against Catholicism on the sea, daring English buccaneers, the "unholy offspring of the Caribbean frontier," and then later-day pirate captains descended upon Spanish ships. The pickings were easy because the Spanish ships were slowed not only by their weight but also by the prevailing east-west winds in their return to Spain. The Caribbean Sea flows north along the Yucatán Channel into the Gulf of Mexico, and then past Havana and through the Straits of Florida, before entering the Atlantic; Spanish ships sailed east to Europe while benefitting from the strong currents of the Gulf Stream. With Havana serving as the great commercial hub, the Gulf Stream, known as a "river within a sea," carried the annual Spanish treasure fleets from the New World.

Ironically, the buccaneers and later pirates only took from Spain what she herself had taken from the New World and its indigenous people: a double theft propelled by an insatiable greed. The Catholic Church officially had bestowed upon the Spanish conquistadors and explorers the sacred right to vanquish the native Aztecs in the name of religion. In much the same way, the devastating buccaneer raids of the English sea rovers also stole slaves from the cargoes of slave ships. Led by audacious captains such as Francis Drake, the son of a Protestant preacher, the buccaneer attackers on the Spanish fleets fit neatly into the overall tradition of Protestant England's long religious struggle against Catholic Spain. Once again, raiding and killing became a religious duty at sea.

The English buccaneers had served Queen Elizabeth I extremely well in damaging Spanish shipping and commercial cities on the mainland, reducing Spain's wealth and power in a lengthy war of attrition. These astounding successes placed England "on the road to empire," fabulous wealth, and greater power. Buccaneer activities were centered at Port Royal, Jamaica, which had been captured from the Spanish in 1655 as part of Oliver Cromwell's Western Design project to conquer the Spanish West Indies. Jamaica was the first colony in the Americas captured by a state-sponsored British military expedition—ironically, it had been taken after the expedition had been thwarted from achieving gains on the island of Hispaniola, which is divided today between Haiti and the Dominican Republic.

This unprecedented conquest and annexation of a major Spanish island and colony had initiated a new era in Caribbean history. With the Royal Navy far away protecting England against European enemies, the granting of letters of marque—which authorized a British privateer to capture vessels—from the Jamaica governor became widespread. Buccaneering now became the primary means to protect what eventually became England's wealthiest sugar island. Jamaica was strategically positioned for the launching of sea raiders to strike at the Spanish sea lanes, and it gave rise to the golden age of buccaneering, hence Port Royal's importance.

By the late 1600s, however, English policy had turned from plundering to focus on protecting a safe, free flow of trade, where more riches, including slaves, could be gained from lucrative legitimate commercial enterprises, even while piracy was reaching its zenith. Therefore, piracy began to be more widely perceived by the major powers as the greatest threat to commerce and national wealth. Sugar cultivation garnered great riches in the Caribbean colonies, far more than what relatively little was agriculturally produced by the thirteen English colonies—that is, the future United States—from the rise of the planter class.

And all of this economic development and progress was based upon a robust system of slavery that could no longer be disturbed to ensure massive profits, especially with the price of slaves rising ever higher, by buccaneer raids that had long netted large numbers of black slaves held by the Spanish. Africans had replaced the inefficient use of Native American slaves, who were prone to European diseases and had died off quickly, unlike the laborers of African descent. Slave ships, lightly armed and relatively small, were easy prey for pirate raiders. After the sack of Veracruz, Mexico, the English buccaneers sailed away with 1,500 slaves in May 1683, and English buccaneers carried off more than 3,000 slaves from the French Caribbean island of Martinique 10 years later. Of course, whenever possible, the French returned the favor, stealing 1,300 slaves from the British colony on the tiny island of Nevis in 1706. For this reason, merchant ships carrying sugar back to European markets, as well as the slave ships that were supplying larger numbers of slaves to the sugar plantations, had to be protected.

Ironically, the buccaneers eventually became victims of their own successes, which swelled their ranks to more than 3,000 men and 16 warships by 1685: a formidable threat that had to be eliminated by the British government because reduced profits from these raids threatened overall national wealth and prosperity. In conducting this unofficial brand of foreign policy, the English sea rovers had already fulfilled their national purpose by this time, having raided major cities and inflicted considerable damage to the Spanish economy, while acquiring wealth to fatten the national treasury. However, because of changed circumstances, the buccaneers' day in the sun had already passed. Consequently, they now became expendable because they represented a potential threat that had to be negated by the leading European powers. Bowing to the demands of the wealthy, politically influential sugar planters who called for the end to the buccaneers as part of an ongoing power struggle to control Jamaica, England's new anti-buccaneer policies, such as the Jamaican Act of 1683, began the process that eventually brought a permanent end to the greatest pirate haven of all, Port Royal.

In true Machiavellian fashion, even the greatest English buccaneer, Henry Morgan, had turned against his own freewheeling brothers of the sea. When he took office as Jamaica's governor, it brought about the demise of buccaneering in Jamaica, until his death in 1688—a de-

Above: Captain Henry Morgan, Famed Buccaneer of the late 1600s.

cade before Anne's birth in Ireland. The powerful Royal Navy increased its efforts to suppress the pirates, because they had already served their overall national purpose in the intense international power struggle in the Caribbean.

Therefore, with the age of the buccaneers/privateers coming to an end in Jamaica around 1697, the center of pirate activities shifted away from Jamaica, which was ideally situated near the heart of the primary shipping routes in the Spanish Main. Thanks also in part to the 1692 earthquake that destroyed two-thirds of Port Royal, by the century's end, the buccaneers were absent from what had been the vital center of buccaneering. Port Royal had long wallowed in excess, as the notorious "Sodom of the New World:" Second to none in debauchery, the port was home to manifold brothels, grog shops, gaming houses, and taverns (at least 44) with colorful names like the Sugar Loaf, the Cat and Fiddle, the Cheshire Cheese, and the Green Dragon.[77]

After Port Royal faded from its glory days, the pirates needed a new base of operations and general headquarters for their future operations. Perhaps Sir Thomas Lynch, the governor of Jamaica, said it best in 1672 regarding the effort in the Bahamas to replace Port Royal as the center of pirate activity: "This accursed trade has existed so long [in the Caribbean] and is so widespread that it shoots up again, like weeds or the Hydra's heads, as quickly as we can cut it down."[78]

And no place was more favorable for the rise of a new Hydra head of piracy than the port of Nassau. The Bahamas were strategically located on the Caribbean's north and near the all-important sea lanes that led back to Europe. On the island of New Providence, one of the largest islands in the Bahamas at around 80 square miles and an ideal sanctuary for defense or for launching raids, Nassau was a natural "pirate's paradise, a harbour for the down-trodden from the New and Old Worlds."[79]

Indeed, something menacing was happening at the port of Nassau. Early Spanish settlement on the flat, sandy New Providence Island had languished because of its dangerous reefs, shoals, and rocks, which became a graveyard for the large Spanish ships, unlike the smaller pirate ships. Finding no riches in the Bahamas, Spanish interests then turned to focus on the American mainland, and the Bahamas were not colonized. However, the Spanish left behind one of the Caribbean's finest natural harbors, which could accommodate as many as 500 pirate ships, mostly light draft sloops and schooners, although its waters were too shallow for the entry of pursuing large British warships. Nassau was a perfect replacement for Port Royal as the new center of English pirate activity in the Caribbean.

Nassau shortly evolved into the principal "Nest of Pyrates" after it had shifted away from Port Royal. Unlike other Caribbean islands that featured high, forested mountains, such as Saint-Domingue (today's

Haiti) and Jamaica, the Bahamas are mostly flat and without rivers and streams, making the soil poor for cultivation. Thus, English development of these islands had been early stunted as well, because sugar cane had failed to thrive there as it had on more fertile islands, and as a result, only a small population of hardscrabble Protestants settled in the Bahamas.

But more importantly because of circumstances, a new type of society, more egalitarian than anything ever seen by these young men, was gradually taking shape in Nassau. Pirates from Jamaica flocked there, as did hundreds of unemployed seamen—primarily from England's vast merchant fleet but also from the Royal Navy. Others were freed slaves or indentured servants, many of them Irish and Scottish, whose terms of servitude had expired. Beyond the reach of the major European powers still aware of these stealthy developments in the Bahamas, this great gathering of mostly lower-class individuals became known as the "Brotherhood of the Coast" and the "Confederacy of the Brethren of the Coast." In the hope of reaping riches by striking at Catholic Spain, the seasoned members of this rough-hewn brotherhood concentrated at Nassau to create a new version of Port Royal. Naturally at odds with all forms of authority and especially with forced labor systems that had exploited the two lowest classes—black slaves and white indentured servants—opportunistic individuals of both races bonded as one, creating a solid front against an oppressive capitalist system that had long abused them.

These pirates also banded together over a desire for revenge and riches: desires cemented by a longing for greater freedom, which Anne Bonny could identify with. Already, the largely Irish indentured servant class of England's Caribbean islands, especially Jamaica, had been excluded from upward mobility and permanently relegated to the lower rungs of planter society, even once they were no longer servants. The large sugar cane planters already had acquired most of the island's acreage to create vast estates at the expense of small farmers.

For this reason, slaves who had escaped from this same plantation system formed a united front at Nassau with the poor white lower class, who had left for many of the same reasons. Emboldened by the presence of so many gathering black and white pirates, and with the planter's once-secure world starting to collapse around them, escaped slaves joined the pirates in their war against the abusive power structure, which had

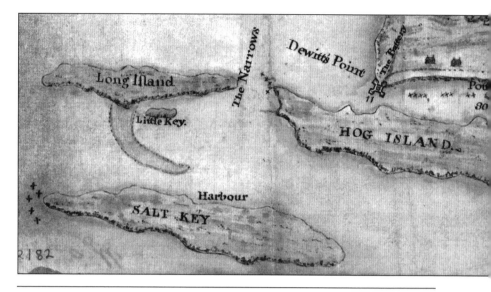

Above: Nassau, Bahamas, and its ideal harbor for pirate ships.

brought them and their ancestors from West Africa to the New World in chains. These slaves united with black and mixed-race (known then as mulatto) free men at Nassau.

Some scant evidence exists that even Edward Teach, also known as Blackbeard, was of mixed black and white ancestry. His hometown of Bristol, England, had early thrived on sea trade and benefitted economically from strong commercial ties to the Caribbean, especially Jamaica. Because of ocean commerce, including the lucrative slave trade that had populated the West Indies' sugar plantations with millions of unfortunate Africans, Bristol was England's second-largest city in Teach's day. Eager to destroy the entrenched exploitative systems that had long profited from their ceaseless toil in the sugar cane fields, these former slaves were committed to waging war against the power structures of Europe's elite, especially slavery. Described as "truculent as game cocks," they also proved to be ideal pirates with excellent fighting skills. It was no coincidence that many pirate crews liberated the unfortunate Africans when they captured slave ships, regardless from what nation.[80]

Another reason that Nassau evolved into the principal headquarters of an outlaw or pirate state, or republic, is because of the end of the war

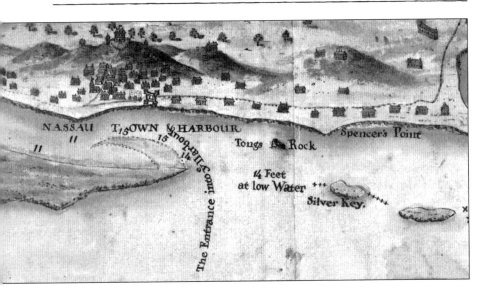

between England and her two great Catholic rivals and ancient enemies, France and Spain. With the signing of the Peace of Utrecht, the War of the Spanish Succession concluded in 1713 and peace was restored, after a dozen years of religious and economic conflict. The conflict's abrupt end had thrown thousands of seamen from Great Britain's large navy and merchant fleet out of work. This mass of mariners still simmered with resentment against their former opponents and were conditioned to wartime excitement and challenges on the sea—something that, due to human nature, could not be easily set aside. Large numbers of unemployed men needed to make a living with no real skills other than waging war, and the growing pirate haven of Nassau called to a significant number of them.

The particular skill set of these men pointed to only one possible option: once again embarking upon an old occupation that was a mere continuation of privateering, itself an inexpensive government means of sanctioning piracy, made official by a "letter of marque" to attack the opponent's vessels. It was a talent that many of these men had honed during more than a decade spent wreaking havoc on the merchant fleets of Spain and France. Besides the steady flow of commerce along the vulnerable sea lanes, targets were also lucrative for the sea rovers when they operated out of Nassau, because Spain held additional isolated mainland possessions in North and South America.[81]

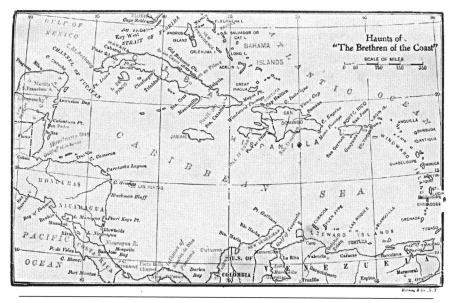

Above: Pirate haunts throughout the Caribbean.

To resume their former wartime occupations, these seamen found a secure staging area and good harbor far from Port Royal, which ironically now served as a center of British naval power. Most of all, they required security from which to not only attack Spanish vessels but also to find safe refuge in a number of possible anchorage points that were nestled among a vast chain of islands covering a wide area in the Bahamas. As these veterans of years of naval warfare realized, only one location best met all the much-sought set of requirements of a perfect base, ideal harbor, and staging area of wide-ranging pirating operations for these veteran seamen: Nassau.

It was an ideal sanctuary. First and foremost, protecting the wide harbor at Nassau was an uncharted maze of narrow channels, surrounded by coral reefs and sandy shoals. This prevented easy entry from English pursuers without intimate knowledge of these tricky, dangerous waters. And to the pirates' delight, this secure natural port was sheltered amid the expansive archipelago of the Bahamas, which consisted of more than 700 islands and keys.[82]

Most importantly in overall strategic terms, the western end of the vast Bahamas archipelago—extending nearly 600 miles northeast, from near the coast of Florida almost all the way to Hispaniola—was within easy striking distance of the Straits of Florida. By this time, this vast expanse of water was the most lucrative targeting area in the world, because a relatively narrow channel served as the main shipping route between Europe and the New World. Spanish ships from Cuba, Mexico, and South America, along with vessels from France's Caribbean possessions and English ships from Jamaica and other British sugar islands, passed through this strategic shipping channel.[83] The string of hundreds of tropical islands sprinkled over a wide area made the "Bahamas seem almost to have been created with piracy in mind."[84]

Separated from the North American continent by the Florida Straits, the Bahamas enjoyed a mild climate, which was balmy and cool in summer from the northeast trade winds. And because no rivers descended from any inland hills to send dark sediments into the sea, the waters around the coral islands of the Bahamas were the clearest in the world. The abundant sunshine and crystal-clear waters then promoted rapid coral growth, resulting in lengthy reefs in the shallow waters, which formed a natural barrier around New Providence Island, especially on the northern ocean side. Therefore, only the most knowledgeable ship's captains and navigators could safely negotiate Nassau Harbor and pursuers, including the Royal Navy, were discouraged to enter. Even Christopher Columbus had been deterred by the "great coral reef of rocks" in this area. Quite simply, these waters were "murderous to uninformed navigators."[85]

The omnipresent dangers of Bahamian waters were well known, but they were navigated expertly by pirates thanks to their superior seamanship, stemming in part from the prior Royal Navy and merchant marine experience of many crew members. The low-lying island of New Providence, formerly known as Sayle's Island, was settled only a few years later. In 1651, George Gardyner wrote in his *A Description of the New World* how in regard to the far-flung islands of the Bahamas: "the coasts of most of them are dangerous [but] with a wary Pilot, and care in giving the Islands a fair birth," sailing vessels could pass unscathed. These dangerous waters were strewn with rocks, reefs, and shoals that seemed created by a pirate-loving God.[86]

ACCIDENTS OF HISTORY

The early history of the Bahamas' settlement also made Nassau an ideal haven for pirating activities. Because of generally infertile soil, the Bahamian settlers had endured a difficult existence on the flat, sandy islands. Imports were relatively few, with even fewer exports. The nascent economy foundered, and settlers—mostly English and Irish immigrants—struggled simply to survive. But there were never enough immigrants or prosperity in the Bahamas, unlike Jamaica. Revealing the early close connection between the Bahamas and Charles Town, the settlement's founders had turned to South Carolina in 1670 and officially requested the Proprietors of the Carolinas to include the Bahamas in their grant, in order to ensure future support during hard times.

Isolated and without sufficient support from England, the American colonies, or other English West Indian Islands, especially Jamaica, the Bahamas had been vulnerable to Spanish reprisals like no other colony in the far-flung Caribbean. The island of New Providence had been first sacked in January 1684, taken by surprise by Spanish raiders. Not only slaves but also women and children were taken into captivity and brought to Havana. Such devastation resulted in the abandonment of the hard-luck colony and the island of New Providence itself, with most survivors relocating to Jamaica, but also to New England, especially Massachusetts.

Tentatively, English settlers then began to return two years later from Jamaica. The people of New Providence once again requested annexation by Jamaica to ensure future protection and security—an elusive dream that was never realized. Meanwhile, ever larger numbers of pirates had continued to infest Bahamian islands and waters, finding refuge and security. Governor Cadwallader Jones, who arrived in 1690 and was in league with the pirates, took official action. He bestowed privateer commissions, while receiving kickbacks in prize money in return, in a cozy governor-pirate relationship. With the additional spurt of growth, a new governor then gave the city originally called Charles Town—the same name of Anne's adopted hometown in South Carolina—a new name, Nassau, in 1695.

With pirates continuing to utilize the Bahamian islands as secure bases to attack English, Spanish, and French vessels, the inevitable occurred, especially when England went to war with France in 1702. Revenge-seeking adversaries in tall ships delivered a hard-hitting preemptive strike, so that New Providence and its excellent harbor would not become a base for English privateers if the governor presented additional commissions to the pirate captains in the Bahamas. With the colony vulnerable without assistance from England and other neighboring English islands, especially Jamaica, this devastating French and Spanish attack from Havana in October of 1703 destroyed the struggling colony, including the town of Nassau. Showing no mercy to heretics, Spanish Catholic soldiers put Protestant inhabitants to the sword. As could be expected, they then once again took prisoners and slaves back to Cuba. However, neither the colony nor Nassau ever fully recovered from this devastating Spanish raid. The Spanish struck again in October 1706 to complete the work of destruction. Thereafter, the Bahamas were now without a government and only a few people remained on New Providence Island: the necessary vacuum to bestow an ideal setting for the establishment of a new outlaw state, a pirate republic.

Not only was the local population of the Bahamas sufficiently small to minimize any possible resistance or complaint about the flow of unrestrained pirating activities, but many colonists, sick of farming and starving, became pirates themselves. All in all, New Providence Island perfectly fit all necessary requirements for an ideal pirate haven in Anne Bonny's lifetime. Given this situation, ever opportunistic pirates became the undisputed masters of the Bahamas, filling the void. After the Peace of Utrecht was signed to end the conflict between European powers in 1713, an estimated 1,000 pirates, in three main groups, were situated in the Bahamas.

This ever-increasing force of pirates served as the core foundation of "this colony of rogues," desperadoes, and malcontents, who had plenty of scores to settle with the ruling powers. Two of the main groups were led by popular pirate commanders: Blackbeard, who had previously sailed out of Jamaica, and Charles Vane. Captain Vane sailed with a young and ambitious quartermaster, Jack Rackham, who was second-in-charge of the pirate ship. At this time, Blackbeard was relatively new to the profitable game of piracy. He had not yet acquired a reputation as a daring leader who led bold raids that became the talk of Nassau's whorehouses and taverns. Meanwhile, so thorough was their control of Nassau and New Providence Island that pirate leaders styled themselves as governors, while flaunting their elevated status and ill-gained wealth for all to see.[87]

Large numbers of escaped slaves from Spanish, French, and English islands in the Caribbean, especially Jamaica, became part of this vibrant egalitarian community of pirates at Nassau. Although racial animosities and prejudices still existed, they were far less common than on land, and an unprecedented amount of racial unity developed because only the best and most qualified seamen sailed forth as crew members: ability, and not skin color, became paramount. Most of these lower-class individuals, both white and black, were former seamen from the British Navy and extensive merchant fleets, which had so recently engaged England's enemies.

In fighting for king and country, these sea rovers had already experienced some of the harshest discipline, brutal punishments, and horrid living conditions as seamen, while enduring low wages and bad food. Consequently, hundreds of these young men and boys were now turning to something entirely new: the creation of a truly revolutionary society for renegade and disenfranchised seamen, based upon fairness, equality, and democracy. The new society was the antithesis of the old abusive system and the gross inequities of English and European society, based on wealth and class.

For the first time, the average pirate now sailed forth from Nassau with a rare measure of respect and dignity in a self-created democracy at sea. An unparalleled development in a harsh hierarchical world where true egalitarianism was utterly lacking before America's novel experiment, beginning in 1776 with the Declaration of Independence, the pirate crew operated as an onboard democracy. Basically, the pirates had declared the first independence from the European monarchies before the Americans did. Common agreement among the pirates led to the choosing of captains, missions, and objectives by popular election in the democratic tradition. By popular vote, pirates retained the power to make major decisions, including the power to elect a captain who would lead them on pirating excursions. And they also had the right to vote the captain out of his position if he failed to live up to their expectations, including in regard to securing prizes. For the average pirate, distinctive individual rights, signed on paper to create a respected permanent document, flew in the face of the traditional absolute and abusive power of captains, who ruled like kings in the world's navies: a defiant reaction to the arbitrary, bleak existence of the much-abused British seamen in the Royal Navy and in the merchant fleets.[88]

This egalitarian pirate society pulled lost souls, adventurers, outlaws, indentured servants, ne'er-do-wells, ex-slaves, the disenfranchised, and the oppressed from around the world, including Anne's adopted hometown of Charles Town. They were natural radicals, revolutionaries, and rebels, who relished the opportunity to strike back at what they most hated. Occupying the lowest rung of society—outsiders of a "floating population" with nothing to lose—these desperate seamen wanted payback.

Nineteen-year-old Anne Bonny was about to make Nassau her home, which was a port town quite unlike anything that she had previously seen. She and her new husband reached New Providence Island in late 1718, at a time when it was windy and rainy in the South Carolina Low Country— a good time to leave—but their ship entered the blue expanse of Nassau Harbor under sunny skies. Even though she failed to realize it at the time, Anne's life would never be the same afterward. She entered through the "Gallant Harbour for shipping," one that she eventually came to know like the back of her hand.

Charles Town had its seedy underbelly along the waterfront, but nothing like what Anne would see in Nassau. It was an environment that was entirely new to her and other landlubbers—the world's most unconventional fraternity, consisting mostly of lower-class people who were united as one. With Jim Bonny by her side, she became part of an anti-authoritarian way of life and a freer community, where the common people ruled themselves. The town was considered an impossible social experiment, where individuals of initiative and intelligence utilized their own God-given abilities to create reputations and careers for themselves, far outside of restrictive societal bounds and government control. And most astonishingly, the key to this success was the simple concept of like-minded individuals working in harmony without racial, social, or class restrictions. This egalitarian environment that offered a greater personal freedom and sense of independence than Anne Bonny had ever experienced—a dream come true for a young woman who had been raised with an excessive amount of strict, arbitrary authority.[89]

The Bahamas never had been transformed into one of the profitable sugar islands that were some of the richest possessions of the European powers, such as Jamaica for the English and Saint-Domingue (today's Haiti) for the French. To reap the fantastic wealth from sugar cane production, armies' worth of slaves were imported from Africa to the Caribbean, fueling production at astronomical rates to create even greater profits, and from 1689 to 1714, the slave population of Jamaica nearly doubled. But on New Providence Island, Anne saw relatively little of slavery's horrors, compared to her life in South Carolina—only later would plantations become a central foundation of the Bahamian economy. Instead, Anne must have been shocked by the sight of so many free black men and women, who were treated far more fairly by whites than in Charles Town and the Low Country.

In this "brotherhood," men of African descent enjoyed the same crew member rights as white pirates from England, France, Spain, Ireland, Scotland, and the Caribbean Islands. What had been created by this novel Republic of Pirates was not only a transnational but also a transracial society. Here, the usual all-important factors of color, class, and family background no longer mattered—an extensive social makeover of a hierarchical society's value systems, especially the class-, religion-, and race-based artificialities that determined one's fate and future. Therefore, black, Jewish, and Native American people—who were also mostly former slaves—were accepted as equal members in Nassau's culture.

The indigenous people of the tropical Bahamian islands had been either killed off or enslaved by the Spanish, beginning when Christopher Columbus first emphasized how these easygoing native people would make "good servants." The Bahamas had been early depopulated of the Lucayan people, who succumbed to European diseases to which they had no immunity. After the native people died off, the Caribbean sugar islands were then replaced with tens of thousands of African slaves, who had been brought from highly efficient slave "factories" along Africa's Gold Coast, to fuel the plantation system and sugar cane production.

FORGOTTEN IRISH LEGACIES

Given the fact that Irish people, especially Catholics, had long known underdog status and oppression from English conquest, this multiracial free society of pirates was likely uplifting to Anne, who had faced so much inequality in her own life. The distinctive Irish character and empathy for other peoples, especially the downtrodden, had been forged by a lengthy history of adversity and subjugation by a foreign invader. In consequence, a well-honed sense of humor characterized by irony, biting wit, parody, self-mockery, cynicism, and satire, as well as compassion for the disadvantaged and an innate ability to poke fun at life, had evolved among the Irish people. In this sense, Anne's background had also preconditioned her for becoming a full-fledged member of this democratic experiment that was unmatched anywhere else, more than a half-century before the American Revolution's beginning.[90]

Anne was a natural fit into this new society and democracy among the lower-class pirates for another reason as well. As an Irishwoman, Anne likely would have nursed some latent or perhaps even overt animosity toward Great Britain. Not surprisingly, then, many pirates were of Celtic and Celtic-Gaelic descent, especially Jacobite Scotsmen, and also a good many were specifically Irish. (Caught and executed in 1715, Scotland-born Captain Alexander Dolzell was one such Jacobite.)

The vast majority of Caribbean pirates, though, were Protestant English. However, Irish Catholics were as likely to become pirates as Irish Protestants, who had recently battled against the Irish Catholic Jacobites of James II and until the Jacobites were crushed at the battle of the Boyne in County Meath, Ireland, in 1690.[91] These Celts held a deep-seated hatred against England for having conquered Ireland and Scotland, and in this sense, a large portion of the pirates at Nassau continued the Jacobite tradition of fighting its historic oppressor.

AN ENTICING POSSIBILITY

After having escaped her South Carolina confines, only one chain was left to be broken for Anne to fulfill her dream of complete liberation and personal redemption, which had always been nothing more than a dream for her: the high-handed patriarchy, which enforced the societal concept of alleged female inferiority that had long made Anne's personal life miserable and her future bleak.

By what Anne saw around her in Nassau, she at some point recognized that her status as a woman—this final barrier to achieving a greater sense of true equality, which she had never previously experienced—would be relatively easy to overcome. All that Anne had to do was to utilize her own intelligence and resourcefulness to don male clothing when the time and right opportunity came. Such a stratagem would result in the most radical of personal transformations—from a woman to a man—and would help her to fit smoothly, if the ruse could be successfully maintained, into the overall flow of this "Brotherhood of the Coast."[92]

Most importantly, an even rarer opportunity existed for Anne, if she could prove herself skillful, resourceful, and intelligent enough, while disguised as a man, to win sufficient respect among a pirate crew to be voted in as a leader. This may have seemed possible, as some African Americans had been elevated to positions of authority by white crew members, who appreciated outstanding personal qualities more than skin color. But Anne's decision to masquerade as a man was still in the future.

BLACKBEARD

Born Edward Teach, the pirate captain Blackbeard was an Englishman from the port of Bristol, which had grown rich from the slave trade. Blackbeard's rise as a pirate captain came relatively late, around 1716, and just in time to coincide with Anne Bonny's entry onto the Nassau stage. It was said that half of Blackbeard's hundred-man crew consisted of black pirates, who worked together with whites for the mutual benefit of each other—one sailor, Caesar, had even been personally "bred up" by the captain.[93] What has been often overlooked, however, was that Blackbeard himself was rumored to be "a light-skinned mulatto."

By the time of Anne's arrival on New Providence Island in late 1718, Blackbeard had earlier made Nassau his home base, along with other seasoned pirate leaders like Captain Charles Vane.[94] Before he returned to his North Carolina haunts, Anne might well have seen Blackbeard on the sandy streets along the low-lying Nassau waterfront. If Anne had not seen him in the town, she would have very likely heard the name of Teach, Tach, or Thatch, as the Englishman was widely known in the pirate community—although "Blackbeard" was the most popular name for the strutting captain with a distinct British accent. In 1724, Teach "assumed the cognomen from the large quantity of hair which, like a frightful meteor, covered his whole face and [his] beard was black, which he suffered to grow of an extravagant length."[95]

When Anne arrived in Nassau in late 1718 as a teenager, she entered a lively environment, but ironically, most of Nassau's pirates had taken the king's pardon, or amnesty, with the arrival of the new governor. Woodes Rogers had arrived the same year as Anne, in July of 1718, having been sent to Nassau by the English government to clean up the town. Upon Governor Rogers' appearance, many pirates who had taken amnesty now returned to sea roving for prey, because it was so lucrative. However, around 2,000 pirates still remained in the Bahamas that summer, practicing their old trade with renewed vigor as if Governor Rogers had never landed.

A YOUNG MAN NAMED JOHN "CALICO JACK" RACKHAM ON THE RISE

Charles Vane had been centered in Nassau, until he became the only pirate captain to defiantly sail out of Nassau in late July 1718, after refusing to take Governor Rogers' pardon. John "Jack" Rackham served as Vane's quartermaster—basically a lieutenant— a rank just below captain that entailed important duties, such as leading boarding parties onto prizes at sea, aboard the pirate ship *Kingston*.[96]

Unlike Captain Vane, and seemingly miscast among a crowd of unruly seamen, the handsome Jack Rackham was not known for a ruthless or murderous nature. Despite his chosen profession, Jack stood apart thanks to his superior education and refined ways—personal qualities not usually seen on pirate ships. Generally, captains of pirate vessels made deliberate efforts to create terrifying personas and spread a fearsome reputation to gain a faithful following and ensure less resistance among victims, guaranteeing that prizes could be more easily taken. But instead of the usual Robin Hood stereotype, Rackham was far more of a dandy than a murderer, psychopath, or criminal. Having carved out a distinct but atypical persona among the rough and uncouth crew, he stood apart as a gentleman pirate. Despite being an aberration among hardened pirates, though, Rackham retained the respect of his men and remained popular.

No doubt like Anne Bonny, the dashing Jack Rackham was more concerned about the style and color of his fancy clothing rather than cutting throats and torturing captives to force them to reveal the location of their concealed gold, silver, or diamonds. But he was no typical dandy who could be underestimated. Jack was ambitious, and he was also mentally and physically tough enough to defy his own captain in a high-stakes gamble. He had headed his own recent mutiny of disgruntled pirates, who had unseated Captain Vane by democratic vote.

Jack Rackham's rise stemmed from unusual circumstances. On November 23, 1718, off the East Coast of North America, Vane's pirate brigantine, a durable double-masted vessel, encountered a larger ship. However, the targeted ship was not intimidated by Vane's raising of the black no-quarter flag meant to force a hasty capitulation. More than just a taunting banner, the black pirate flag proclaimed that there would be no mercy for the crew if immediate surrender was not forthcoming. Instead, much to Captain Vane's surprise, his pirate ship suddenly received a broadside from what was now obviously a fearsome French man-of-war. Therefore, Vane wisely refused to take the considerable risk of battling a larger opponent, which he correctly considered much too formidable, in a lengthy slugfest, especially when easier prey was available. Even if the French ship was eventually overwhelmed by boarding, casualties among the Vane crew would be high, and it was simply not worth the cost.

In regard to the taking of this French prize, however, Jack Rackham thought differently. He now saw a golden opportunity in addition to just taking the ship—he made a calculated bid to become captain. Of course, this was a risky maneuver that might well backfire on Rackham, if the crew failed to support his bold attempt to unseat Vane. Openly challenging his captain, and based upon his wise tactical evaluation in regard to the crew's prevalent sentiments, Rackham casually dismissed the obvious fact that the French man-of-war possessed far more cannons and a

Above: Captain John "Calico Jack" Rackham, a dapper and well-dressed
leader of the pirate crew that included Anne Bonny and later Mary Read.

larger crew—around 2 to 1. Appealing to the men's courage, greed, and
egos, he then boldly proposed that "they might board her, and then the
best boys would carry the day."[97]

The quartermaster's bid to win over the crew to his side paid off. The majority of the crewmen backed Rackham and opted to board the French man-of-war, aiming for a rich payday. However, Captain Vane exercised his authority according to the pirate code and written agreement, refusing to waver in his decision. But by this time, Rackham already had the crew's support, and he knew that most of his followers were motivated by the old buccaneer adage, "No prey, no pay."

The following day, after the French man-of-war had been allowed to escape due to Vane's passivity, which heightened disgruntlement among the overeager pirates, the crew officially voted to replace Vane with Rackham. Then, the humiliated Vane, infuriated by Rackham's treachery, was allowed to leave in a captured sloop, along with 16 pirates who had supported him.

Rackham then went on the offensive. Clearly, the young man knew exactly what to do to consolidate his new leadership position, having learned his lesson well from Vane's abrupt fall from grace. On the very first day as captain, he captured and plundered several ships. Then, to the west of Jamaica, the Rackham crew captured a ship out of the Portuguese island of Madeira, around 400 miles off the northwest African coast. For two or three days, casks of the dark, sweet, fortified wine that had made Madeira famous were hurriedly loaded into the *Kingston*.

The ransacked vessel was then given back to its master, who had lost everything but his life. Then, Hosea Tisdell, who operated a tavern in Jamaica and had been made captive on a previous prize, was allowed to accompany the captain on the now much lighter ship, called a Madeira-man, back to Jamaica. Evidently, Rackham, who was also a savvy businessman, and the pirates made a covert business arrangement with Tisdell to sell the fine Madeira wine at his tavern, in either Port Royal or Kingston. As was often the case, the calculating Rackham was thinking ahead—he knew that a small fortune could be reaped from selling the wine. The pirates preferred their traditional rum punch to Madeira's exquisite wines—much stronger spirits than wine could be later acquired by the crew from future captured prizes—but Madeira was the wine of choice among aristocrats and the elite, especially in colonial America.

In preparation for celebrating their success, Rackham and his crew retreated to a small remote island, most likely in the Bahamas. Here, they began the laborious process of cleaning the *Kingston*'s hull of barnacles and wood-eating naval shipworms, which thrived in warm waters, to ensure swifter movements, sharper turns, and faster speed of their vessel on the next cruise. Such nautical advantages were critical for running down prizes and escaping swift pursuers. Then, the new captain, proud of his recent exploits at sea, and his now-happy crew finally relaxed. Crew members drank excessively to celebrate their success, while mocking the dethroned Captain Vane. After setting sail toward Jamaica, Captain Rackham continued to lead his men with a newfound aggressiveness. He soon took a ship headed for the large sugar plantations of Jamaica.

Then, while sailing toward Bermuda, he captured two more ships: one from South Carolina, very likely from Anne's own Charles Town, and the other from New England, probably Boston. Rackham, now captain of the swift double-masted brigantine—the "sturdy workhorse of the day"—was coming into his own. He was beginning to make a name for himself by the time that he returned to the Bahamas with his two prizes.[98]

A FATEFUL CHANCE MEETING

When Captain Rackham walked onto the wooden wharf that led to the heart of Nassau in the Caribbean heat of May 1719, he enjoyed widespread popularity for commanding his own vessel, the *Kingston*, which had become a terror to merchant ships. After having deposed Captain Vane in a democratic manner instead of cutting his throat, Jack Rackham had suffered few losses while reaping extensive gains. The newly anointed captain strutted down the sandy streets of Nassau, and although he basked in his position, he still remained more of a gentleman pirate than a cut-throat. Like an aristocrat, Jack's personal style was distinguished by proper manners rarely seen in the pirate community, and his charm seemed to contradict his growing reputation as a daring pirate captain. But, of course, his crew members knew better.

With Governor Rogers still cracking down on piracy—those who had continued their trade after taking amnesty had been hanged as recently as December 10, 1718—Jack wisely landed his two prizes at a remote point in the Bahamas. Here, the prizes were systematically looted, while his own vessel, the *Kingston*, was cleaned and re-tarred for waterproofing. Along with these two prizes, his respect among Nassau's pirate community had been enhanced by his advancement to captain.

Blessed with good looks and winning ways, young Jack Rackham had a way with the ladies, appealing to women of all classes and races. He was tall and well built, a striking figure among the motley crews in Nassau, and wore his dark hair long, to his shoulders, in the flamboyant style of the day. He enjoyed the caresses of a number of mistresses, including some hidden at a sanctuary in Cuba; he'd had several children by several of these Spanish women. Of course, Rackham's growing list of bedroom conquests only additionally enhanced his reputation among his envious peers—amid the throng of unwashed pirates in Nassau, the young captain stood out as a rare dandy who "sprinkled scent on himself." Throughout his pirate career, he defied romantic stereotypes, and although successful in both pursuits, Captain Rackham proved to be more of a lover than a fighter.

At one of Nassau's popular taverns, on east-west-running Bay Street that curved along the sparkling blue waters of the harbor or perhaps one of the perpendicular streets that met Bay Street from the south,19-year-old Anne Bonny first caught sight of Captain Rackham in either late April or early May 1719. At this time, he was in Nassau to take the governor's royal pardon, which he gained apparently because he included the governor in a cut of the hefty profits, or because he had taken a Spanish vessel, or both.

Compared to Anne's husband, Jim, who had revealed an overall lack of character if not abusive ways—a tragic price paid for her youthful imprudence and innocence that had resulted in a hasty marriage—Jack Rackham was altogether a much different kind of man, both on the inside and outside. The contrast between the two men was now especially striking to Anne. Jack was a widely respected leader of an experienced pirate crew, and he was not ruthless or cruel like practically everyone else in Nassau. Captain Rackham even treated captives with a measure of kindness, like a proper gentleman would. Rough and uncouth compared to the pirate captain, Jim Bonny was an ordinary seaman of the lowest order with no leadership ability. Perhaps for the first time in her life, Anne took interest in an authority figure, such as her father, and soon became smitten with Jack Rackham.

Above: Bay Street ran along the waterfront of Nassau, Bahamas.

Now far removed from his home port of Charles Town, Jim Bonny was now certainly out of his element. Only a low-ranking pirate without expectations or prospects of any kind, Bonny had few, if any, of the bold characteristics of Captain Rackham's. There at Nassau, Jim Bonny's increasingly obvious deficiencies as a man, a companion, and especially a husband became more noticeable and clear to Anne, and her once-burning love for him began to fade.[99]

Jack stood out not only because of his commanding presence, leadership qualities, and handsomeness—it was also due to what he wore. Unlike other pirate captains who sported fine embroidered silk, velvet, and satin, taken from their rich captives, Jack preferred light cotton clothing, made in India and printed in bright colors and patterns: calico. Practical and more durable than finery, this material was much more comfortable in the tropical climate. Calico was the first fiber to be mass-produced, which helped to jumpstart the Industrial Revolution in England. At Nassau, Rackham's brilliantly striped trousers made him a unique figure in the pirate port. Captain Rackham's clothing also made a personal statement in keeping with pirate tradition of defying societal norms: by wearing calico, he was making his own unorthodox choice, following his own personal preferences that were more practical than fashionable. By refusing to wear fancier upper-class apparel—colorful frock waistcoats and knee breeches—he additionally stood out from his peers.

Clearly, the pirate captain knew how to look his best, and the esteemed leader who took pride in his appearance soon earned a sobriquet that lasted his lifetime—to one and all, Jack Rackham was known as "Calico Jack."

Captain Rackham's flair went naturally unappreciated by the pirates, but not by Anne. During the spring of 1719, Anne fell in love with "Calico Jack" Rackham, not long after his arrival in Nassau. Although she was already married to a pirate, Anne perhaps experienced a typical crush of an average 19-year-old, and the pirate captain began to bestow special gifts upon Anne, some quire extravagant. She felt no desire to resist his charm or advances as she had in Charles Town, when ardent young men had attempted to force themselves on her. Conversely, Jack was not at all intimidated by Anne's good looks, intelligence, or lively personality. After having rejected all suitors except Jim Bonny, whom she had likely married in part to escape Charles Town and her father, Anne was ready for a significant change.

No one knows exactly when their love was consummated, but it was evidently a whirlwind romance at Nassau, after Captain Rackham had forsaken piracy upon taking the king's pardon in May 1719. At this time, Anne's husband was conveniently absent from Nassau, sailing as a pirate on a lengthy cruise. But this new relationship was not only a case of lust on Anne's part or meant to be just a short-term fling to satisfy basic physical needs in her husband's absence. Nassau was a dangerous place for a woman without her husband nearby, and Anne also immediately needed a strong male protector with clout, lest she become fair game for roving gangs of drunken pirates. In a wide-open town like Nassau, if a young woman was not known to belong to one particular man, then she risked belonging to all of them.

Therefore, Jim Bonny's lengthy absence created a perilous environment for Anne, more so than she may have originally anticipated. And for all his young wife knew, Jim was running around with another woman at some port in the United States or even in England.

And, of course, what available woman in Nassau could possibly resist the handsome Captain Rackham in his bright clothes, long scented hair, and winning ways? He simply did not look, act, or smell like the other pirates—or her husband, for that matter—who never bathed, practiced poor oral hygiene, and wore dirty, smelly clothes. Quite simply, the captain was more appealing to Anne than any other man in Nassau. Captain Rackham soon "found means of withdrawing her affections from her husband, so that she consented to elope with him . . . ."[100]

As in Blackbeard's case, little evidence has survived about Jack Rackham's background. But nothing has been found that indicates that he demonstrated any savage traits or extreme violence in his work. Like many pirates, Captain Rackham hailed from one of the major ports of England, such as London, Liverpool, or Bristol (like Blackbeard). Despite the romantic stereotype of the pirate captain, he was probably not a former member of the aristocracy, which partly would have explained his burning ambitions to rise up the ladder in pirate society, but he was almost certainly at least a middle-class product, unlike his lower-class crewmen of the *Kingston.*

Because Anne was bound by English law by way of marriage, she reverted back to the ways of her ancient homeland as a solution to her personal dilemma. In Ireland, women are empowered with the ancient legal right to end a marriage—that is, a divorce—by way of her own decision, "with no repercussions" whatsoever: something that did not exist in paternalistic English law, in which women were treated as little more than chattel. This legal system of the common people of early medieval Ireland was called Brehon Law and had been formulated in the 7th century, but the legal system of Ireland's common people was based upon a collection of ancient texts known as the "Great Collection of Ancient Learning," which were completed between 650 A. D. and 750 A. D. Some of these laws ran contrary to Christianity's teachings, and as could be expected, Brehon Law had been early eliminated by the English conquerors of Ireland, because of its dangerous egalitarian legacy, especially in regard to women's rights.[101] Anne might have known that Brehon Law imparted a host of legal rights to women, unlike English law, from her attorney father.

It is not known for sure if Jim Bonny had been abusive, alcoholic, or a womanizer, or perhaps all three, but he was certainly immature and poor marriage material. Belatedly, Anne realized that Jim was a very poor catch in every way.[102] Even before Captain Rackham's arrival, Anne had become disillusioned with her and Jim's ill-fated union after having been married for a short time, perhaps only a few months. If Jim had been abusive either verbally or physically to her, then Anne certainly felt no moral or legal obligation to remain with him. Demonstrating some of her father's same ambitious qualities, she also wanted more in life than a hand-to-mouth existence spent hanging out in smoky, noisy taverns full of rowdy seamen.

But most of all, Anne Bonny was in love with Jack Rackham—or thought she was. She naturally wanted to be with her captain at all times, after deciding that her marriage had been a mistake. She needed a new start, and one without Jim Bonny. Anne believed that Jack, as he no doubt emphasized to her, had no wife in Nassau, which was the case, and the former object of his principal affections was now far away in Cuba, which was about 300 nautical miles from Nassau. But the feeling that Captain Rackham had held for his Cuban mistresses had faded away like a South Carolina summer upon October's arrival—like the feeling that Anne had once felt for her husband. There, in freewheeling Nassau, Jack became not only Anne's lover but also her protector, and perhaps even her savior, depending on the exact circumstances.

Anne was yet married to Jim Bonny and legally obligated to him by English laws on land, but she made a long-term personal and solemn commitment to Captain Rackham, in regard to a new life together at sea once the captain set sail on his next voyage, by invoking the traditional "ways of the Irish people." And this decision was so bold for a woman of the era that Jack might not have believed her when Anne first declared that she would go to sea with him.

A MASTERFUL DISGUISE

Anne had fallen in love not only with Captain Rackham, but also with the idea of becoming a pirate along with him, if he returned to his old profession in cruising the Caribbean's waters. Indeed, "she consented [to] go to sea with Rackham in men's clothes [and] She was good as her word."[103] But wearing men's clothes was nothing new for Anne. As a young girl, when her father wanted to keep Anne's identity a secret from his first wife and the gossipy townsfolk of Kinsale, he had disguised her as a boy. Thus, posing as a man in order to join Captain Rackham's crew would not be a difficult task for Anne, who already knew how to play the part. Significantly, seamen's cotton clothing was exceptionally coarse and baggy to enhance the performance of typical duties at sea—ideal for disguising the female form.

An opportunity to be at Jack's side for an extended period at sea as common-law husband and wife wasn't Anne's only motivation by this time. By joining Jack at sea, she was seizing a golden opportunity that was unavailable to her on land. If properly exploited, Anne would finally be able to achieve what she had always wanted and longed for in her life: a rare measure of equality, respect, and elevated status beyond the confines of a repressive patriarchal society.

Indeed, Anne Bonny was one of the few women of the 18th century who developed a solution to the greatest dilemma faced by common people, especially women, of the day: How and where could a single individual find a measure of equality and sense of personal dignity in an entirely new environment, beyond traditional constraints and arbitrary barriers?

Anne decided to boldly seize the moment—and she would never look back. By acting on her innovative and bold idea of serving as a man "before the mast," Anne would accomplish a great deal in personal and psychological terms. Donning seamen's clothing to become a respected member of a hard-working crew of equals in the "Republic of Pirates" offered her not only the possibility of a more independent and fulfilling life, but also a chance to embrace new challenges. From her father back in South Carolina, she had learned how to use a sword and firearms for self-protection, while living in the frontier-like environment on the plantation north of Charles Town, and so she was now presented with an opportunity to learn more about herself through utilizing other such latent abilities and strengths, while proving her worth not only to others, including Captain Rackham, but also to herself. Undertaking a male pirate's role as a young lady would present the teenager with the stiffest challenge of her young life.

But unlike other women who disguised themselves as males, Anne did not have to reject or subvert her sexuality or feelings as a woman, because she also could still be herself when with Rackham in the secluded captain's quarters. Thus, Anne could fulfill both male and female roles aboard ship, and such an experience could have been equally liberating to her, to enjoy the luxury of living dual lives of both genders on the same day. This also allowed her more personal freedom—essentially a liberation of spirit and soul—than any previous time in her life.

Given this situation, Anne had to feel a certain sense of exhilaration (and of course anxiety) about the new possibilities and challenges, after undertaking an entirely new course in life, whenever she went to sea with the Rackham crew while dressed as a sailor. Serving as an equal crewman aboard Captain Rackham's ship at considerable risk to herself, engaging in battle whenever necessary, and boarding a prize all "symbolize[d] the ultimate liberation."[104]

By this time, Governor Rogers had heard all about Jack Rackham's recent exploits at sea, where he was taking prizes with impunity. Along the waterfront and taverns in Nassau, Captain Rackham or his crew members, probably after drinking too much rum, had evidently been boasting about their activities. Additionally, Captain Rackham had made the mistake of spending too much time in the same place collecting new crew members, while waiting for his favorite sailing ship to be thoroughly cleaned. As such, Governor Rogers learned of the location of Jack's two prizes on one of the uncharted Bahamian islands.

Jack's new relationship with Anne might have been a factor that explained why the captain had unwisely let his guard down and remained too long in one place. Eager to scoop up the spoils for himself, the governor dispatched a fast sloop and an experienced crew to take possession of the two vessels stashed at the remote location. After learning of the governor's plans, however, Captain Rackham and his men laid their own plans to quickly escape the trap with a fresh crew—one that included Anne Bonny.

HARSH REALITIES

By taking to piracy once again, Rackham was reneging on his pardon from the governor. This meant that if he was caught, he would be unceremoniously hanged, along with his crew.[105] Times had changed in regard to piracy, and Anne Bonny was unknowingly caught in a time warp; because of her youth and inexperience, she might have had no idea that a grim fate awaited her if captured. At this time, even before her career as a sea rover began, a new, ugly reality lay ahead: The celebrated Elizabethan heyday of the buccaneer had already passed like a daydream, having peaked more than a century before.

Unknown to Anne at this time, this harsh new reality was made more obvious when a respectable New York sea captain, Captain William Kidd, was hanged in London. Had she been aware of this grisly fact, Anne might have been disturbed that this unlucky buccaneer was a fellow Celt, who had been born in Dundee, Scotland. Despite being presented with a letter of marque by King William III of England to chase down pirate ships as a privateer and confiscate their ill-gotten gains, so that profits could be divided among him and his supporters, Captain Kidd was ultimately executed in public on charges of both piracy and murder. In late May 1701, he dangled high from a hangman's noose over the Thames River, to showcase to all that a harsh fate awaited those who made the mistake of roving the sea in search of prey.[106]

More recently, and despite his good connections with North Carolina officials, including the governor, Blackbeard himself was finally cornered at an inlet on the inner side of Ocracoke Island, in today's North Carolina, by the British H. S. S. *Ranger* from the royal colony of Virginia on November 22, 1718. A vicious hand-to-hand combat resulted when Captain Teach boarded the *Ranger* with his men. Armed with a broadsword, a Scottish Highlander fighting for the English crown "gave Teach a cut on the Neck, Teach saying well done Lad, the Highlander reply'd . . . I'll do it better, with that he gave him a second stroke, which cut off his Head [and then] Teach's body was thrown overboard, and his Head put on the top of the Bowsprit" of the ship. The pirate prisoners were then taken back to Virginia.[107]

The systematic hunting down of pirates by English authorities was one of the great ironies of history, because it had been "the pirates who made England rich and great in her dawn of overseas expansion" in the New World.[108] In a classic case of bad timing, the life of a pirate had become much more dangerous by the time that Anne Bonny went to sea.

SAILING THE CARIBBEAN'S BLUE WATERS
1719

MAKING an audacious personal commitment that defied convention and tradition, Anne joined Captain Rackham in the exciting activity that she had heard all of Nassau talking about: the "sweet trade" on the high seas. This bold adventure was riskier than anything she had ever experienced. In almost a repeat of her escape from South Carolina, shipping out with the Rackham crew offered Anne a way out of a bad relationship and an effective means to exorcise past mistakes and lingering personal demons.

Life in the "Brotherhood of the Sea" also provided Anne with unprecedented economic benefits. Here was a rare chance for a young woman to make money by way of plunder. Most of all, piracy offered Anne a more independent life to gain what was extremely rare for any woman in the 18th century: a sense of autonomy, respect, equality, and the possibility of enjoying "the good life." Back in Charles Town only a short time earlier, she had risked everything in marrying a young pirate of dubious character and then departing her adopted homeland. Now she demonstrated even more initiative by compensating for her prior errors in judgment, refusing to pay a higher personal price for that indiscretion of youth and inexperience.

Opposite: One of the many pirate hideouts in thinly populated Cuba.

ANNE BONNY.

Firing upon the craw

Above: Portrait of Anne Bonny when she first went to sea disguised as a man.

Because few other opportunities were open to lower-class individuals to advance upward, this life was especially appealing to young men of society's lowest rungs. Even England's common seamen received abysmal food and treatment at sea on military and merchant ships. The profession of piracy provided better treatment and upward mobility and a chance for uneducated men with no family or social connections to reap a fortune and retire young to a small farm in England or a West Indies sugar plantation in comfort.

And now Anne embraced that same enticing dream, risking all on the belief that fate would finally turn in her favor, after enough hard luck and heartbreak for one lifetime. As mentioned, Anne's life had not been easy. First, she had been born illegitimate. Then her family had been forced to flee her native homeland, her mother had died, and her brief marriage to Jim Bonny had ended. Once again, and out of necessity in part because so much had gone wrong in her past, Anne was throwing the dice in the hope of a brighter future. Despite all the sharp setbacks in her life, she still thought in optimistic terms. Thus, she enthusiastically cast her future with a young pirate captain whom she loved.[109]

Anne's risky decision can be seen as an act of courage, because she refused to accept a dismal situation and fate. Rather than simply a case of breaking her marriage vows to jump in bed with a new lover, Anne was making a long-term commitment with Rackham. In the pages of history, other equally self-actualizing women had likewise demonstrated remarkable courage by refusing to remain with an ill-suited husband, deciding to change their lives for the better. Rather than becoming victims, they found emotional and spiritual refuges by "fleeing from a drunken and brutal husband in the safety of a male guise . . . ."[110]

In embarking upon a new career as a pirate, consequently, Anne was essentially invoking the ancient Celtic-Gaelic Brehon Law—that listed women's rights, unlike English (or, later, American) law—of her Irish homeland, i.e., the right to divorce her husband with impunity. Brehon Law also granted rights upon women to engage in wartime activities, including even "the power to participate in war councils" in defense of the Celtic-Gaelic homeland.[111]

Anne would be able to do just that also because of the democratic nature of the pirate society. And in carrying flintlock pistols and a cutlass like other crew members, Anne was emulating the combative roles of Irish women who had become legendary in the revered annals of ancient Irish history. One such legend celebrated the martial exploits of the warrior-queen Maev, whose "purpose was not only to inspire warriors but actually to participate in war as a fighter," while serving as an aggressive war leader of the Irish people. Anne might have heard the ancient sagas of this legendary Irish woman warrior from her parents as a young girl.[112]

Unknown to her at this time, Anne was also actually following in the footsteps of the first known and recorded female pirate of western Europe, Jeanne de Belleville of Breton, or Brittany, in France. As in the case of many pirates, like Anne in 1719, Jeanne had gone to sea in large part because of the hard luck and her ill fortunes on land. During the War of Spanish Succession from 1701 to 1714, Jeanne's husband was unjustly declared a traitor, whereupon he was decapitated, and his head was displayed to the populace in Nantes, France, as a grisly warning. Along with her sons, an enraged Jeanne swore vengeance on the responsible authorities.

She then raised a small army and battled against a more powerful opponent on land. Despite being overwhelmed by stronger forces, she refused to relinquish the struggle. Determined to fight to the bitter end, regardless of the odds, Jeanne then took to the sea to continue waging war on opposition shipping, striking at merchant vessels. In command of three warships, Jeanne led her soldiers and sailors by personal example. She was the first member of her crew to board a prize, like Blackbeard himself, leading her band of French warriors in hand-to-hand combat. After life's unpredictable tragedies had affected both Anne's and Jeanne's respective fortunes on land, at no fault of their own, the sea had provided not only a refuge for both women but also a place to fulfill their potential under extraordinary circumstances.[113]

Anne's fateful decision to leave everything that she knew behind to embark upon an exciting (or so it seemed) life at sea was not unlike hundreds of other Irish exiles, who had long fought against the British far from home. These exiles were Ireland's famed "Wild Geese." After having been defeated in their bid to create an Ireland free of British rule and signing the Treaty of Limerick in 1691, these Irish-Catholic revolutionaries, the Jacobites, had left Ireland to serve with distinction in armies across Europe, especially in defense of Catholic France and Spain.[114]

In preparation for going to sea with the charismatic Calico Jack and his pirate crew during the spring of 1719, Anne took extra precautions to make sure that her identity would not be discovered by her pirate comrades, whom she would serve beside in suffocatingly close quarters on the ship. Her challenge was stiff, because one of the stricter codes of the Caribbean pirates dictated that there was "No Boy or Woman to be allow'd amongst them."[115]

Therefore, not only was Anne taking a great risk by attempting to become a crew member, but so was Captain Rackham. In fact, the young captain was even jeopardizing his authority by demonstrating what could be perceived by the crew as a direct violation of the pirate code. If Anne's sex was discovered by the crew, then not only would this revelation cause dissension and trouble—perhaps even mutiny—but Rackham might lose his position as captain. He could also be voted out by an indignant crew.

The magnitude of the risk voluntarily taken by this young captain revealed the depth of Rackham's desire to be with Anne. Rackham evidently trusted Anne's artfulness when it came to keeping her secret from the other crew members. Naturally, he assigned her to the captain's personal staff so that she could sleep in the captain's quarters, as to raise no suspicion from the crew.

First and foremost, Anne needed to "pull on a pair of men's breeches," and hide any hint of her femininity. Worn for practical purposes, especially durability, seamen's clothing included short but oversized blue jackets, significantly large enough to hide Anne's breasts, and long, baggy canvas trousers (called "petticoat breeches"). As an extra precaution, Anne also wore a large "nondescript cap," which, if worn low, helped to hide her feminine facial features. Traditional pirate clothing was often fashioned from pieces of rough canvas—the same material that sails were made from—and proved to be highly durable on rigorous voyages.

As mentioned, perhaps the most important advantage that enabled Anne's ruse to succeed was the fact that wearing masculine clothing was nothing new to her. After all, her own father had disguised her as a boy in male clothing for an extended period, when he took her into his own house in Kinsale, so that the first Mrs. Cormac would not discover that this was the maid's daughter. Likewise, she almost certainly wore hats while managing and working on her father's plantation, such as a slouch or planter's hat, especially during the hot summers for protection against the sun. By donning sailor's attire, Anne had taken the clothing of a typical laborer to fit her chosen profession: not unlike the working-class women of Paris who delivered coal in men's clothes, including pants, for greater ease of movement.

As important as an effective male disguise on the upcoming cruise into the Caribbean, Anne would also have to flawlessly imitate and mimic the everyday talk, movements, loud bluster, and mannerisms of the ordinary veteran seamen, who had spent most of their free time in taverns, brothels, and other dens of iniquity. Fortunately, Anne had been around James Bonny and other seamen in Charles Town long enough to intimately know the rough ways and talk of seasoned mariners. She was familiar with seamen from both sides of the Atlantic and their mannerisms, even their distinctive walk: a rolling gait from maintaining balance for extended periods on a ship's rolling deck.

The most obvious difference between Anne and her fellow sailors was that she spoke with a slight Irish brogue, while most crew members, probably including Rackham himself, were from England. However, once aboard ship, if her ruse proved successful, then she could bask in a sense of community based upon a refreshing environment of egalitarianism and anti-authoritarianism. For Anne and other young seafarers far from family and home ports, the ship served as a surrogate home. But to become a full-fledged member of this unorthodox democratic community, Anne's disguise had to be flawless.

THE GODS OF THE SEA

In this era, a woman aboard a ship had been considered bad luck by superstitious mariners for centuries, because since ancient times, travels by sea had been the exclusive domain of men. In overall historical terms, however, this was ironic, because the sea and even the sailing ships themselves had been looked upon as essentially female in legends for centuries. Even more, the men and boys who made their livelihood on the treacherous waves had long invoked the protection of powerful goddesses. During the Golden Age of Piracy, the magnificently hand-carved and -painted wooden sculptures of women, such as the Roman goddess Minerva, on ship's bows were created to protect sailing vessels and their crews, especially on the "maiden voyage." As well, hurricanes, a whirlpool, or a dead sea—for calm waters were potentially fatal for crews during extended periods—were thought to have been invoked by angry female spirits and demons determined to destroy a male crew, because of their sex.

Thus, in the seafarers' world, where life was cheap and fate extremely fickle, the feminine represented both good and bad, as if symbolizing woman's incomprehensibly complex nature to many men. But when faced with a crisis, seamen depended not only upon God but also on the sea's maternal protection to provide divine shelter from raging storms, as the ocean was "the mother of all things." If English pirates, Protestant or Catholic, learned anything spiritual from their Spanish Catholic foes in captivity, it was the fact that Santa Maria served as the patron saint of all Christian seafarers far from home.

And as believed by Celtic pirates, perhaps including Scotland-born Thomas Jameson, age 20, and Ireland-born sailors like Walter Kennedy and Anne herself, female witches possessed supernatural power to sink ships and destroy male crews. Nevertheless, for the average pirate, a woman aboard a ship was considered bad luck that might doom a vessel and its crew to an unkind fate—a risk for Anne if she were exposed.

Seamen were naturally far more superstitious than landlubbers because their lives depended upon the capricious whims of the Gods of the Sea, winds, storms, and waves. At this time, almost every crew member aboard any ship believed that a voyage's success and simple survival depended upon a combination of good fortune and staying in God's favor, especially during hurricane season or when facing the fire of close-range broadsides from enemy warships.[116]

A RISKY UNDERTAKING

In overturning the conventions of her patriarchal world, Anne was flouting not only matrimony and traditional land-based laws by impersonating a male pirate but also the time-honored traditions of the sea. In the words of historian Marion Meinzer in regard to the historic role of female pirates, including Anne, which extended back to ancient times: "They move on the water, the element in which the primal feminine is at home. It seems that at sea, women have the home advantage. Women on board ships were either feared or regarded as bringers of luck. Pirate women were considered especially dangerous, and accepted as leading at a time when women on land had long been robbed of their rights and dignity. Pirate women were often compared to furies or sea snakes."[117]

Most significantly as part of her personal sojourn on the waves, Anne Bonny was destined to evolve from a nondescript woman disguised as an ordinary pirate to an almost solitary defender of Rackham's ship during the crew's greatest crisis. At that time, she would fight fiercely because it was her duty as an equal member of the ship's crew, while male crew members, including the captain himself, were either drunk or declined to fight against the odds. More importantly, Anne fought not only for fellow crew members, but also the freedom and equality that she had never known on land. Male cynics, especially those frustrated and hurt in love, have often said that the female of the species is the most lethal, and Anne Bonny proved an example on this memorable occasion. Clearly, the full extent of Anne's transformation from a young Irish lass to a self-assertive pirate in her own right represented a remarkable metamorphosis.[118] Indeed, "nobody was more forward or couragious [sic] than she" as a pirate in the crew's ultimate emergency situation when boarded by attackers.[119]

As could be expected, then, Anne's spirits soared higher, basking in the novel experience of entering a new life, after the canvas sails had been hoisted high and filled with a warm, fair breeze. Captain Rackham's sloop gained speed in cutting neatly through the calm waters beyond Nassau Bay. Feeling almost as if she were part of the sea herself, Anne rejoiced in the sound of the rhythmic slapping of the waves against the oaken sides of the ship, whose masts supported the billowing clouds of white canvas now filled with air.

Soaking everything in on her first pirate voyage into a new life, Anne felt the ship sailing easily through blue waters and heard the creaking sounds of its giant hull that would become so familiar to her. However, in her enthusiasm of serving as a crew member, Anne probably had no idea how slim were her chances of a successful undertaking, because the odds were so heavily stacked against her ruse. On her maiden voyage as a male pirate, perhaps she momentarily contemplated possibly drowning—no evidence has been found that Anne knew how to swim—if the caprices of the wind turned against the ship, or if her new home went down either by accident or by cannon fire.

Anne's decision to go to sea represented a symbolic escape like when she and her parents had to hastily depart Ireland to start a new life in America. But this time, everything was different. She was no longer escaping a hostile environment and scorn; instead, this voyage represented a brighter future. To Anne, the sight of the sea's vast expanse was now a liberating experience.

Most significant to gain a certain legitimacy that was denied her at birth, Anne's signing of the Articles of Agreement—stemming from the buccaneer pacts known as "articles of association"—marked a symbolic turning point in her life. Signing this document would promised her fair and equitable treatment in a free seafaring society of equal individuals on the high seas. Of course, this signing was calculated to ensure greater cohesion among crew members of varying backgrounds, races, and nationalities. Consequently, lower-class pirates, long familiar with upper-class abuses, signed this "charter" with their first names only.

Incredibly, among hardened and tough men who made thievery a profession, a disproportionate amount of integrity and honesty marked their dealings with each other, which solidified a sense of unity among the pirates. Aboard Captain Rackham's ship, this act now held more validity with longer-lasting significance than Anne's marriage license to Jim Bonny. With quill in hand and no doubt with a sense of pride, Anne used her new pirate name of Bonn—short for Bonny—in signing the most important document in her life.

RAPTURE

Anne never forgot her first cruise in the Caribbean, begun by the spring of 1719. For the rest of her life, she reflected upon this initial voyage with a fondness that was not unlike a new mother reminiscing about her first-born child. Her first voyage presented a rare opportunity to gain more confidence and a healthy dose of self-respect, while functioning as a crew member with assigned duties. All the while, she accomplished the necessary seaman's tasks and shouldered her responsibilities.

On the wide wooden deck of Rackham's ship, she early proved herself to be worthy of equal respect. She learned the importance of demonstrating endurance, fortitude, hard work, and honesty (a case of literal honor among thieves). Anne would have to risk her life in dangerous duty, including combat, just to bask in this new unprecedented sense of equality. She now served as an equal member of a pirate community that turned the rigid structures of not only society and gender expectations, but also the Royal Navy's traditions, completely upside-down.[120]

DISTORTED ROMANCE AND FICTION

Because Anne never recorded her life story in her own words (i.e., in a diary or journal), the true personal experiences of other women who also posed as males on ships are most revealing to understand Anne's situation. Indeed, she almost certainly experienced some of the same feelings, especially a sense of accomplishment, as other women who served in the British Navy and on English merchant ships disguised as men. With determination and skill that shattered the traditional gender stereotypes, these resourceful women proved themselves "as good a man as any other" of the crew.[121]

However, male historians and writers, especially Captain Johnson, whose reliance on the sensational aspects of Anne's story guaranteed a best-seller to a scandal-hungry (mostly upper-class male) audience, have overly sexualized her life, especially in regard to erotic speculation, including lesbianism. Unfortunately, from the beginning, Anne's life story on land and at sea has been deliberately constructed to feature blatant sensationalism in order to sell more books: a well-calculated marketing strategy that proved successful, paying nice profits to the author, who relied upon excessive fiction.

In psychological terms and in regard to the fundamental masculine requirements of a patriarchal society, Johnson emphasized the alleged romantic relationship between Anne and Mary Read, who later joined the Rackham crew also disguised as a man. He gave us a highly sexualized and dysfunctional portrayal of Anne that has been perpetuated by generations of other male writers for primarily the same purpose. In Johnson's vivid imagination, where much speculation has been long portrayed as fact, Anne was allegedly so morally loose that she immediately tried to seduce the good-looking young sailor (Mary Read in disguise), because her carnal desires were entirely out of control—not only a traditional male fantasy but also stereotypical to the caricature of a morally deprived and debauchery-prone woman who dressed like a man. Early historians even went a step beyond the alleged lesbian relationship to write about a highly speculative ménage à trois among Jack, Anne, and Mary.

In truth, and contrary to the caricature of uncontrolled debauchery and sexual excess on every level, the trio actually worked side by side and competently performed their assigned duties in the serious—but mundane—business of helping to sail a ship, because such moral lapses, errors in judgment, or mistakes would result in disaster. Therefore, clear judgment, discipline, sobriety, and a strict adherence to the pirate code and assigned duties were absolutely necessary for the ship's and crew's survival. In time, Anne rose up to a position of respect and some authority as one of Jack's lieutenants. Thereafter, she needed to maintain her established position by flawless behavior.

In explaining the common mentality of generations of male authors and writers who have focused almost exclusively on the most sensational aspects of Anne Bonny's life, historian Jo Stanley perhaps said it best in understanding "how and why myths of women pirates are permitted and perpetuated [but] one answer is that some men need to create highly coloured stories of women at sea became they find it difficult to believe that women can be ordinarily competent and ordinarily incompetent: simply seafarers."[122]

Women masquerading as men at the risk of their lives simply to gain the right to go to sea was nothing new in the annals of history. Anne was only continuing a lengthy tradition of so-called "she captains," who donned pirate garb and even took leadership roles to command their own vessels since ancient times. But a far larger number of women served as ordinary seamen. While almost all 17th- and 18th-century examples of females-turned-males (by disguise like Anne) depicted white British women for a European audience, at least one black woman was known to have served as a sailor before Anne Bonny's day. On October 18, 1693, Captain Thomas Phillips, who commanded the slave ship *Hannibal*, discovered from the ship's physician that sailor John Brown, who had become sick, was a woman of around age 20: about Anne's age when she embarked upon her first voyage in the Caribbean.[123]

Like Anne sailing with the Captain Rackham crew out of the Bahamas, these sailor women, black and white, "were known to run up the mast with expertise, could hold their grog [rum] like any other tar and never shirked the most arduous of duties," [and more importantly] "They proved that women were equally capable of excelling in the masculine sphere" of their maritime world. Quite simply, these resilient women in disguise became useful ordinary seafarers, who played an equal part in shouldering the ship's duties and responsibilities, just like the male crew members.[124]

One capable woman, Mary Anne Arnold, disguised herself as a man and served with considerable skill aboard a naval ship, the *Robert Small*. Her captain never forgot how well Mary faithfully performed her assigned duties, including the most dangerous ones: "I have seen Miss Arnold among the first aloft to reef the mizzen-top-gallant sail during a heavy gale in the Bay of Biscay."[125]

ANNE'S DUTIES ABOARD SHIP

Anne now wore baggy sailor's clothing, including either baggy "petticoat breeches" or canvas trousers, and with her reddish-gold hair either tied up or cut short and hidden under a hat or perhaps even a large handkerchief (a popular style among pirates). She functioned as part of a close-knit team—from which she kept her distance for obvious reasons—of varying expertise and experience levels. By working as one, the crew kept Captain Rackham's ship operating without a hitch on Anne's first voyage. Under the bright Caribbean sunshine and fair winds that brought a refreshing warmth, Anne worked hard in unison with other crew members in a wide variety of common seaman duties: the tasks of heaving the anchor up on deck; raising the great expanse of white canvas sails to provide ample wind power on gusty days; working the pumps to get water out of the ship's leaky haul if necessary; loading and unloading supplies aboard ship, maneuvering heavy hemp ropes and lines into their proper places to lift or lower the canvas sails, and countless other daily duties.

Initially, on her first voyage, her hands might have been raw from pulling the long ropes and handling rough sailcloth. While sailing, Anne very likely did not realize that the large canvas sails themselves, which she helped to raise with so much labor under a searing sun, consisted of coarse linen exported from her own native Emerald Isle.[126] Most demanding of all was the heavy lifting of the largest expanse of canvas, the mainsail, high up the mast to gather all available wind power. Perspiring heavily after so much hard work on the sun-scorched deck, she felt the triumph of jobs well done and in unison with other crew members, which helped to compensate for the daily fatigue.

Fresh water was in great demand for a crew during a long cruise on a pirate ship. For the pirates, securing adequate supplies of fresh water was even more difficult than keeping a supply of fresh foods aboard ship. Alerted by the distinct smell of land before any sight of green was spied on the distant horizon, Rackham's crewmen made preparations, because the ship had to slip and drift quietly into hidden bays and obscure inlets (where there were no large military garrisons) for parties to row ashore, fill large wooden barrels with water, and then bring them and other valuable supplies, including meat and produce, back to the ship. With muskets and cutlasses handy in case they met any of the king's soldiers who were the pride of Madrid or London, Anne might well have been part of one of these parties that ventured ashore to secure essential supplies.[127]

ANTICIPATING COMBAT

But the greatest test of all for Anne was that of combat, her baptismal fire in which she must have long wondered how she would fare. This crucial role in either defending the ship or boarding a prize was important for her complete acceptance by the crew, because if she were to display any stereotypically non-masculine qualities under the stress of combat (her first), then she might be exposed. Of course, Anne knew as much and took necessary precautions to some extent. Consequently, she was highly motivated not only to fight with an enthusiasm equal to the male pirates, but also to even outdo them by exhibiting martial qualities in a combat situation. Acting more fiercely than other crew members guaranteed that no one would suspect that she was a woman.[128]

As mentioned, demonstrated courage in battle was the most important test that Anne had to pass to gain full respect during her first voyage out of Nassau. She possessed a hot Irish temper, and this quality—a handicap in tranquil civilian life, especially in places like genteel Charles Town—might well have proved an asset in combat. She met every challenge. Thus, Anne was in the process of laying a firm foundation, both as an efficient crew member and a reliable fighter, for an eventual role as one of the top lieutenants of Captain John "Calico Jack" Rackham's crew.[129]

Combat has been one of the most rigidly enforced gender activities in human history, until masculinity and fighting were seen as one and the same, especially by male historians and writers who have traditionally viewed women warriors as nothing but mythical creations: a guarantee that Anne's story would long be routinely dismissed and ignored. But, in truth, Anne was every bit as capable as a fighter. One of the pirate articles of Captain Bartholomew Roberts' crew almost certainly applied to the Captain Rackham crew during the same period: "To Keep their Piece, Pistols, & Cutlash clean, & fit for Service."[130]

In regard to her first combat, Anne's personal experience was very likely comparable to the anguish felt by young Union soldier Henry Fleming in Stephen Crane's immortal *The Red Badge of Courage*. Before his first battle, Fleming long wrestled with the personal meaning of courage in a patriarchal society that viewed conflict as the very definition of masculinity: the supreme struggle in which a man's character and worth received their ultimate test. Therefore, in facing danger, this arena of mortal combat served as the decisive stage for Anne to demonstrate her highest moral qualities as not only a pirate but also as a young woman.[131]

As mentioned, 20-year-old Anne was also engaged in a masquerade to demonstrate that she deserved her status as an equal member of pirate society. She worked harder and served with more enthusiasm to prove that she was indeed worthy of equality, fair treatment, and respect among her rough-hewn comrades. Thanks to a familiarity with firearms from growing up on the South Carolina frontier, where her father had hunted game in the dense pine forests north of Charles Town, Anne was prepared for combat. She was determined to fight, not out of pathological bloodlust, homicidal rage, or greed for gold, but so that she could successfully meet the ultimate challenge of a man's world: a primary motivation of young, able-bodied men going back to the ancient Greeks waging war against Troy. In a symbolic showdown on the broad wooden deck of Rackham's ship, "Bonny's masculine clothes and mythical confidence with the cutlass are consistent with the pirate code that inverted all convention."[132]

Describing a situation that certainly applied to Anne, "In the military, women [disguised as male soldiers or seamen] experienced an individual liberation that dissolved any sense of sisterhood solidarity as they became 'one of the boys,'" or as one of Rackham's pirates, who were mostly young, unmarried, and uneducated males of the lowest class.[133]

ERASING THE OLD

Also dissolving for Anne were all the old patriarchal rules and hierarchies that had caused her past difficulties. To her delight, these were now replaced by egalitarian values and rules of pirate society, where every crew member had a voice and a vote. Despotic authority of sea captains in the Royal Navy, rigid class distinctions, and arbitrary privileges based upon birth, class, and social standing were noticeably absent on Captain Rackham's ship. Plundered booty as well as disciplinary actions were evenly distributed to these sailors. The rights and privileges enjoyed by pirates exceeded those of the average male citizen on either side of the Atlantic, and they far surpassed anything experienced by women in early 18th-century society. It was a sharp difference now fully appreciated by Anne, who basked in her newfound sense of freedom at sea.

Voted to his lofty position by the crew in true democratic fashion, the ship's captain in fact only enjoyed full authority in battle, when his orders had to be obeyed for unified action, either offensive or defensive. But if a captain proved an unworthy leader, a disgruntled crew did not hesitate to vote him out of his position. Second in rank in this floating democracy, one primary duty of the quartermaster was to enforce pirate rules. Aboard *The Royal Fortune*, the first written article that applied to the pirate crew of Captain Bartholomew Robert's pirate ship was that "Every man has a vote in the affairs of the moment; has equal title to the fresh provisions, or strong liquors, at any time seized, and may use them at please . . . ."[134]

But like most pirate cruises in the Caribbean, Anne's life aboard Rackham's sloop was mostly routine, even boring, with relatively little action when not encountering a prize ship. Cuts and bruises from the daily work were standard, and she almost certainly experienced seasickness. During these long periods at sea, the myth of the glamour and romance of a pirate's life was just that, having little to do with more mundane realities while serving on a dark, leaky, and damp ship.

"Land Ho!"

Other than combat, the most perilous assignment came whenever Anne served as a lookout in the crow's nest at the fore topmast, especially in bad weather. She strained her eyes to catch sight of land or an approaching ship on the heat-hazed horizon, while the tropical sun scorched everyone and everything on the ship's deck. Fair-skinned crew members, including Anne, would have become tanned while performing their duties hour after hour on the deck. The searing Caribbean heat also turned the ship below deck into an oven, especially when winds were calm—known as "slack winds"—and the ship barely moved over the still water.

A sense of fellowship and camaraderie was found on deck, where typical pirate humor was cutting sarcasm, most often directed at the aristocratic, wealthy elite, especially governors. Jokes and laughter often erupted from Rackham's sloop when far out to sea. In this way, the crew members, known for their sense of fatalism and stoicism, lightened the heavy burden of daily chores required for the functioning of the ship.

TROPICAL STORMS AND OTHER DANGERS

But Rackham's crew members were not laughing amid the ravages of harsh weather, which threatened to capsize ships, or when the bottom of the sloop's wooden hull scraped over the sharp coral reefs in shallow waters to create nerve-wracking tension, from captain to cabin boy. Deadly tropical storms and the high winds of August and September sometimes suddenly threw crew members overboard, or wrecked vessels in the blink of an eye. During hurricane season in 1712, one hurricane destroyed nearly 50 ships in Jamaican harbors.

The daily workload aboard ship—a mind-numbing, never-ending routine—consisted of an incessant effort required to keep the ship in good shape. The clothing that Anne and her shipmates wore became soaked from waves sweeping over the deck during storms, and working for long hours in wet clothing led to sickness of many already malnourished pirates, especially because no physician was aboard ship. During tropical storms, the risk of falling off of a swaying mast or being swept overboard from the violently rocking ship were omnipresent dangers for an inexperienced sailor like Anne.

As "Bonn" learned, the sea upon which the pirates depended for a livelihood was also a constant source of peril. Diseases, such as yellow fever (known as "yellow jack" by the pirates) and dysentery, could quickly spread among a closely confined pirate crew, and poor hygiene and sanitation also led to the spread of body lice. Fortunately for Anne, however, sailing in the Caribbean spared her the horror of working long hours on a slippery, ice- and snow-covered deck, which she would have been exposed to in a northern climate.

CAPTURING A LUCRATIVE PRIZE

When not laboring to maintain the ship that had become Anne's sur-rogate home, the sheer boredom of a lengthy cruise became an enemy to the average pirate, sapping one's vitality and energy. Weeks, even entire months, could pass before a sharp cry suddenly erupted from an alert crew member, stationed nearly 100 feet up the main mast in the crow's nest, upon sighting a ship. Sailing out of ports such as Kingston, Jamaica, these ships appeared as a mere dot on the distant horizon at around 20 miles. Once a ship was spotted, orders rang out for crew members to grab sabers, cutlasses, flintlock pistols, and smooth-bore muskets in prepa-ration for possible action, before ascertaining if the approaching vessel was a warship prowling for pirates or only a vulnerable merchant vessel far from the safety of its home port—that is, fair game.

Contrary to popular myth, actual combat was relatively rare on pi-rate ships, including Captain Rackham's vessel. Like other pirate cap-tains on the prowl for lucrative prizes, Rackham's strategy was based upon the use of intimidation to force the opposing crew to surrender their ship without a fight. When far away from a home port, a small pirate crew could generally not afford manpower losses from over-aggressiveness.

Most importantly, the capture of a coveted prize, such as a rich mer-chantman, was the easiest way to obtain a new ship—one that was larger than Rackham's sloop and in better condition. However, winning a prize could be negated by heavy combat losses. Therefore, in order to limit man-power losses, targeted vessels were not routinely pounded into submis-sion by close-range broadsides and then boarded by a horde of screaming pirates, contrary to myth. Given these considerations, the pirates' strat-egy for taking prizes was based primarily on a well-calculated game of bluff. And first and foremost, this meant presenting such a fearsome ap-pearance that a targeted ship captain would submit without firing a shot.

Instead of actual fighting for a prize, as so often depicted by Hol-lywood films, the pirates relied upon their grisly reputations and black flags with white skulls to unnerve already nervous ship captains and their panic-stricken crews and passengers and coax them into a quick, blood-less submission. Advertising their ferociousness, the pirates were es-sentially performers who shouted, screamed, and fired pistols to spread fear. Veteran pirate captains were masters at the game of psychological warfare. Because of these tactical and manpower realities at sea, great lengths were taken by savvy pirate captains to guarantee the quickest, easiest, and most painless possible capture of a prize.

Rather than actual combat, what was more often experienced by the average pirate was lengthy periods of sheer boredom. In truth, greater joy among crew members came from the routine playing of martial, lively, and festive music on deck. Pirate captains, who could be voted out of their positions, fully understood the importance of keeping up spirits with entertainment, and in the naval tradition, musicians almost always accompanied pirate crews on their cruises. After all, the captain knew that his fragile veneer of power was based upon the smooth functioning of this close-knit community, and crew members had to be satisfied as much as possible during the long weeks and even months at sea.

INTEGRATED CREWS

Because pirates from Africa, or of African descent, were represented among multinational crews, many musicians on pirate ships were black, and like Anne, these black crewmen, including former slaves, basked in their newfound freedom in the pirate fraternity. Musicianship was a customary role for black sailors, born in Africa or the Caribbean islands, on both British and American naval and merchant vessels throughout the 18th and 19th centuries.

As revealed in one written pirate article of agreement: "The Musicians to have Rest on the Sabbath Day, but the others six Days & Nights, none without special Favour."[135]

Popular music played aboard ship was not an indication of a merry and carefree life at sea, according to the romantic stereotype. Instead, the music acted as a tonic to bolster a crew's spirit and instill a measure of contentment during the repetitive days of boredom, hard work, and inactivity at sea. And, as the captain realized, higher morale led to greater overall efficiency in emergency situations, including combat. Most of all, music offered much-needed relief from the daily drudgery and dangerous work of common seaman duties. Before unleashing an attack on a floating prize, veteran pirate captains sometimes ordered musicians to play martial airs to inspire the crew, armed with cutlasses and pistols, to greater exertions. Musicians aboard pirate ships were so valuable that they received a fair share of the booty equal to that of all other crew members.

For such reasons, musicians both black and white were among the most popular crew members aboard a pirate ship. Because music was such an important feature of Irish life, Anne probably enjoyed the songs, jigs, and ballads played on board, especially if a musician happened to hail from her homeland.[136] In addition, the soothing effect of music might have eased the consciences of some pirates who had committed murders that still haunted them. This was not a concern for Anne, because she had killed no one on her first cruise out of Nassau, New Providence Island. No one knows if Anne had any moral qualms about having embarked upon a new life as a pirate. But at least the Rackham crew was not engaged in the atrocity of enslaving people, and this fact might have offered Anne a measure of moral consolation, if she was troubled about the crew's criminal activities that might have initially shocked her.[137]

The Sanctuary of Cuba

Benefitting from the brisk trade winds that blew warm and prevailed from east to west to propel the sloop at a good clip, Captain Rackham and his crew sailed the Caribbean for "some time" during her first voyage. However, no record was kept of their exact routes or what prizes they took during Anne's first sojourn as a pirate. During the spring and early summer of 1719, Anne certainly gained more confidence in herself and her abilities as a crew member. With new challenges and experiences, she became stronger mentally, physically, and psychologically, transforming from a landlubber to a seafarer.[138]

Captain Rackham's most likely area of activity during this period was in the waters located west of New Providence Island, where the rich convoys of Spanish ships passed through the Florida Straits on their way back to the bustling Andalusian port of Cadiz, in southwest Spain—one of the oldest cities in western Europe. The main bastion of Spanish power in the Caribbean, Havana, Cuba, lay on the northwestern side of the largest Caribbean island and just below, or south of, the Florida Straits. Rackham needed to avoid Havana at all costs.

Above: A typical pirate hideout in Cuba.

Here at the western end of the Great Antilles and just north of Jamaica, the lengthy Cuban coastline offered not only targets of opportunity but also secure places to disembark. The crew could land here on Cuban soil to pick up fresh water and supplies, and the underground network of trade, or illegal smuggling, was lucrative there. English pirates had early made their secure inroads into the Spanish Caribbean islands, including Cuba, creating their own personal trade networks that proved profitable. Indeed, the English buccaneers, with so many speaking Spanish as their first language, anchored and even cleaned their vessel's hulls on the relatively safe "southern side" (compared to the north, or Havana, side) of Cuba. The Englishmen had long gone ashore here to trade, whore it up, and sell recently captured booty.

Thriving in the West Indies and in the American mainland colonies as well, this robust illicit trade allowed the local Cuban people to purchase necessary goods cheaply (compared to the heavily taxed goods of legal state commerce), which the pirates had captured on prizes, unlike the trade goods governed by tight government regulations and endless bureaucratic red tape. Captured slaves from Spanish, French, and English slave ships were often smuggled into Cuba by knowledgeable and skilled English sea captains, going to the highest bidder, to labor for the rest of their lives on sugar plantations. From what they traded when stopping along the heavily wooded shoreline, pirate crews obtained invaluable supplies of food, liquor, cattle hides, and dyewoods from the Cubans. A vibrant contraband trade existed between the English pirates, including Captain Rackham, who was a longtime sea rover in Cuban waters, evolving into the largest single outlet for Cuban products. Anne benefitted from this illegal trade in both personal (health) and financial terms, because of Rackham's close connections.

An ideal location for smuggling because of its lengthy coastline, Cuba was an underpopulated island that still looked much like it did when it had been discovered by Christopher Columbus in late October 1492. Ironically, Columbus had informed Madrid that Cuba and other Caribbean islands, which he named for Catholic saints, would be ideal for sugar cultivation. Columbus' ambitious plans were based on the exploitation of cheap labor—the indigenous population, before dying off from European diseases—that eventually resulted in the enslavement of millions of Africans, who were viewed by the Church as having no souls and, hence, ideal for exploitation.

Cuba's small towns were surrounded by cattle ranges and sprawling tobacco and coffee plantations, before its transformation beginning in the late 18th century into an economy based on a vast sugar cane plantation and slave system. The coast provided numerous obscure bays and sheltered inlets, half hidden by thick tropical vegetation, which indented the expansive shoreline, providing safe pirate havens for extended periods. Also, more than 500 rivers poured into the sea; by comparison, no such waterways existed in the Bahamas. Cuba's rivers even provided sheltered avenues for pirate ships to move inland, if they were sufficiently deep and if the wind was blowing toward land. When Anne first showed signs that she was pregnant and needed to be hidden from the crew, Captain Rackham, who knew Cuba's hidden places, realized that the island would provide a good refuge for a new mother and child.[139]

ANNE'S FIRST CHILD

By the early summer of 1719, Anne was expecting a child. It was her first pregnancy, evidently conceived in the captain's quarters of the sloop during her first voyage.[140]

Anne was about to have a child out of wedlock, as her mother had when she herself was born. Although some debate among historians has existed in regard to if this was Jim Bonny's or Rackham's child, the best available evidence has suggested that Jim Bonny was either unable to have or did not want children. Despite youthful passion at the relationship's beginning, their marriage was as unrewarding for Anne as it was childless. In addition, Bonny had departed Nassau, going to sea for an extended period, even before Anne sailed with Rackham. This timetable all but guaranteed that Rackham was the father of Anne's child. The inability to have a child together might have also been a source of discord between Anne and Jim, adding to her desire to end the relationship.

In addition, Rackham's subsequent actions in regard to Anne's and the child's welfare also strongly suggested that the captain was the father. Indicating that he was not a typically ruthless pirate, Rackham wanted the best for Anne and his future child. Although the captain had not married her because Anne was already legally married and they were living a life as pirates on the open seas, he was still as solicitous as possible toward her. Under the circumstances, Anne was perhaps not unduly troubled about having a child out of wedlock, as she herself had been illegitimate and had still enjoyed considerable love from her parents. For Anne, this lack of a legal formality was only a relatively minor technicality and just another one of society's traditional rules that they had shattered as a pirate couple. All in all, the experiences in Anne's personal life and her new career guaranteed that the concept of matrimony, especially after the failed marriage to Bonny, was of relatively little priority or concern to either Anne or Rackham during the circumstances.

Instead of thinking of his own selfish desires, including close companionship and sexual needs, Rackham chose not to take the risk of allowing Anne to remain on ship. Anne now faced what was in essence a double jeopardy: a pirate's precarious existence, now complicated by pregnancy, along with the inherent risks of childbirth that often claimed the lives of mother and child during this period.

Developing a solution to the ultimate dilemma, therefore, the increasingly concerned captain had a special place in mind for Anne and her child: a safe, hidden haven in Cuba. She obviously could not serve much longer with the crew in her condition. Indeed, if any signs of pregnancy became visible to the crew, then Anne's ruse would be over. Women

Above: Anne Bonny became familiar with Cuba when she delivered her first child on the island.

masquerading as men on British warships were known to give birth, but Anne would not be exposed to this risky proposition. Rackham correctly reasoned that the safety of mother and child would be more probable in a secure, little-known location on land—even a Spanish island—rather than a ship. Rackham had already "kept a little kind of family" in Cuba, and even had his own house located in a remote area. Here, Anne could safely give birth to her first child without interference from the government or Spanish soldiers, who hunted pirates mostly on the water rather than land.[141]

For such reasons, Rackham considered Cuba more of a permanent home than Nassau, where Governor Rogers ruled with an iron hand, thanks to his house, friends, and his familiarity with the island and its Cuban local customs. Rackham had almost certainly planned to retire—a case of getting out of a dangerous profession before it was too late—in Cuba at some point in the future. If so, then he could turn a pirate's ulti- mate dream into reality before the law and the hangman's noose caught up with him and Anne. Most revealing, just before his capture in the months ahead, the captain identified himself as "John Rackham, from Cuba!"[142]

But the exact location of the captain's safe haven of domesticity in Cuba has long been the subject of dispute among historians. One historian has even speculated that Rackham's "family" was Captain Johnson's "polite way of describing his harem of prostitutes."[143] The same modern writer also penned how Rackham "kept several mistresses" in Cuba, assuming that pirate associations were almost always defined by an excessive sexual nature, in keeping with the popular stereotypes and romance. But to define motivations stemming from out-of-control carnal lusts has been a gross simplification of complex factors.[144]

In his 1724 narrative, Johnson merely described that Rackham's associates were "some friends of his" in Cuba.[145] More likely, these friends were just that: smugglers or pirates themselves, but almost certainly not a harem of women or prostitutes, as if the captain were also a part-time pimp—especially considering that he owned a house in Cuba where this "family" lived, including children. Rackham would not have wanted Anne to be around sexual rivals, former lovers, or prostitutes, due to his concern for the overall safety of mother and his own child.

For a young man in Rackham's risky profession, in which few people could be relied upon for obvious reasons, these Cuban friends, who detested abusive Spanish control, could be trusted. In essence, they were business partners, smuggling to outsmart the Spanish, and possessed a mutual interest in close cooperation to maximize profits. Rackham needed a safe, reliable market—the role formerly fulfilled by Port Royal, Jamaica, for buccaneers before the 1692 earthquake—to sell stolen loot far from government soldiers and officials.

Fortunately for Anne, Rackham had some trusty Creole Cuban friends who were apparently former crew members and their families. Whoever Rackham's close associates in Cuba were, they could be relied upon to take good care of Anne and her child. As was customary at the time, a black female slave may have been on hand to provide care as well.[146]

These friends were more of "a little kind of a family" to this roving pirate captain, who claimed no allegiance, country, government, or flag, except the black flag. Many pirates had homes and families in tropical hideaways across the Caribbean, especially in remote inlets and bays

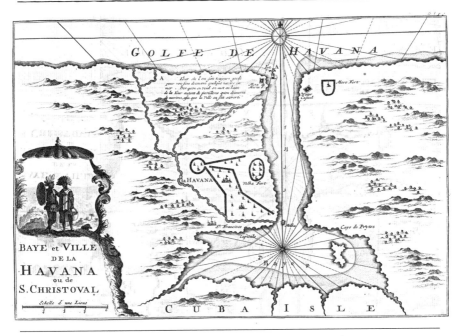

Above: The village and port of Havana, Cuba, in the early days.

that offered a safe sanctuary, and far away from the reach of ambitious colonial governors, who hoped to become famous by hanging as many pirates as possible.[147]

In the summer of 1719, with Anne "beginning to grow big" with child, Captain Rackham "landed her" at his "favorite cove" in "Cuba; and recommended her there to some friends of his, they took care of her" for an extended period.[148] Anne's safe placement has contradicted the romantic notion that Rackham possessed "a harem of prostitutes." But, of course, this sexually tantalizing view of Rackham's excessive lifestyle was in keeping with popular stereotypes that have continued to perpetuate the sensationalism surrounding pirate lives. Blessed with style and good looks, Rackham had little reason to focus his carnal desires on prostitutes. And if Rackham did want to secure prostitutes, he did not have to go all the way to Cuba, because Nassau was home to many brothels, as were other ports of call throughout the Caribbean. According to existing evidence, he had chosen Anne as his lover to enjoy a mutually satisfying and long-lasting relationship. He had decided that he wanted to be with only one woman, especially now that Anne Bonny was about to have his child.

And if the carnal business in the world's oldest profession was booming, which was usually the case with sailors and probably the Spanish soldiers around, Cuban prostitutes would have been too busy to care for Anne and her baby in this alleged prostitution ring scenario. Additionally, the possibility of Cuban prostitutes taking care of Anne would have been a high security risk, especially for an English-speaking female member of fair complexion who belonged to an English pirate crew and was far from her ship and captain. Rackham's "friends," consequently, were almost certainly located in the rural countryside, near a remote inlet or small bay to accommodate a pirate sloop, and not an urban area, where Anne's presence would have been noticed.

However, some historians have even speculated that Rackham boldly sailed into Havana's harbor—not a good idea for an English pirate in a major Catholic city teeming with many England-hating Spanish troops—and that Anne stayed with a family in Havana. But this fanciful scenario was almost certainly not the case. Far too many Spanish Navy ships and privateer hunters in search of English pirates were headquartered at Havana, Cuba's largest port. Instead of going anywhere near Havana and the imposing Spanish fortification known as the Morro Castle that guarded the wide harbor's entrance, Captain Rackham had sailed with the pregnant Anne to the safe "back side of Cuba" (south side), while Havana was located on the island's north shore.[149] Other evidence has suggested that Rackham often sailed from the port of Trinidad on Cuba's south central side, indicating that Anne was almost certainly landed at an isolated point on the island's south side. Nicholas Lawes, governor of Jamaica, wrote how Rackham sailed the Caribbean in "vessels out from Trinidado [Trinidad] on Cuba."[150]

Indeed, Cuba's port of Trinidad already had been a haven for English pirates for an extended period. Governor Nicholas Lawes wrote directly to the Spanish *alcalde* (mayor) of Trinidado, delivering a formal protest because of acts of piracy committed "on the King my Royal Master's Subjects, by a Parcel of Banditti, who pretend to have Commissions from, and Reality are sheltered under your Government . . ." Creating in essence a Spanish version of Port Royal, this included renegade Englishmen, or "Traytors," who had helped to make "the Port of Trinidado a Receptacle to Villains of all Nations."[151]

In reply to the governor, Trinidad's *alcalde* responded that Englishmen in the picturesque town were in fact now "Subjects of our Lord the King, being brought voluntarily to our holy Catholick faith, and having received the Water of Baptism." Captain Rackham might have been one of these individuals of English descent.[152]

The Trinidad area provided a secure location for Anne and her future child. Anne mostly stayed at some safe house either in or just outside the town of Trinidad, where Rackham very likely housed his little extended family and home. Located in the fertile agricultural province of Sancti Spiritus, Trinidad was an excellent port that possessed a lengthy pirate history. The port had long been used by English buccaneers, including by the legendary Captain Henry Morgan, as a good place to trade, especially for coveted Cuban tobacco.

Founded on December 23, 1514, the bustling town, framed by green forested hills that rose behind the mostly commercial and trading community, was distinguished by a central plaza in the traditional Spanish style. A magnificent Catholic cathedral stood in majestic fashion on the plaza. The buildings of Trinidad were dominated by exquisite Spanish colonial architecture, which was influenced partly by Spain's Moorish past and Spanish towns like Grenada—the last Moorish stronghold to fall in the resurgent Christian crusade known as the Reconquesta. These pastel buildings were topped with reddish-pink tiles with intricate designs, and their elegant second-story porches were decorated with elaborate wrought-iron railings, as in Spain, that overlooked narrow cobblestone streets.

Naturally, the foremost reason why Anne was placed ashore on Cuban soil this summer of 1719 was to continue to maintain her ruse as a male pirate, because Captain Rackham wanted Anne to eventually return to the ship and his own arms, after her pregnancy. Of course, when she first began to show signs of pregnancy, Anne was still in disguise as a man. Rackham was concerned about trouble developing, perhaps including sexual advances toward Anne once the crew knew she was a woman, while undermining the crew's overall cohesion and morale. As could be expected, a single female could cause all kinds of unintentional havoc among a crew of young, sexually deprived men far from their home port.

Also, the distinct possibility existed that Anne remained in hiding with Rackham's "little kind of [extended] family" relatively close to Trinidad, where she could readily benefit from medical care, perhaps from a Spanish physician, especially if unforeseen complications developed, at the time of her baby's delivery.[153]

It is not known but perhaps Rackham's Cuban "friends" might have included small Creole landowners in some not easily accessible area near Trinidad. With the average Creole settlers of Cuba struggling for a meager existence, smuggling presented an opportunity to earn a decent income. Many Cubans, therefore, relied more upon illegal trade and smuggling to survive, ensuring strong relationships and connections with pirates, including English ones like Rackham: an ideal clandestine environment that provided a safe haven for Anne.[154]

Here, on Cuba's more safe south side, Rackham's extended family of smugglers were bound together by mutual commercial interests and illegal activities that forged a bond of trust.[155] In addition, Johnson might have meant that Rackham had a former lover and a child of his own from a relationship that had cooled by this time. An ex-lover, especially if the mother of one of his own children, might have provided not only a secure refuge but also a familial environment for Anne and child once born. Here, in the southern part of Cuba, Anne now encountered a tropical land that was far more lush than New Providence Island and the Bahamas. Cuba was much more fertile, especially along the gently rolling plains, where fields of sugar cane spanned endlessly near the thick tropical forests that were untouched by man. Meanwhile, cool pine woodlands grew at higher elevations—ideal coffee country—on the island's eastern side, especially along the slopes of the blue-green mountains, where sparkling clear lakes were found.[156]

Cuba's pristine environment was more comparable to Jamaica than the Bahamas. Majestic royal palm trees grew, unlike in the low-lying Bahamas, where few palm trees were found on the less-fertile soil. Here, in her safe Cuban sanctuary, Anne no doubt felt more relaxed without the anxiety about her true identity being discovered. In her pregnant condition, Anne was probably not drinking rum—consumed in excessive amounts by pirates not just for the effects of intoxication, but also in the absence of fresh water, because unsafe, contaminated water was often lethal—when away from her captain and his raucous crew.

Anne's mother had been an Irish Catholic like most of the County Cork populace, so Anne possessed some knowledge of Catholic practices. In this sense, she was now reunited with Catholics—her maternal side of the family—in Cuba, as back in her native homeland. Catholicism likewise offered a spiritual sanctuary for Anne and her child. Other cultural similarities besides religious faith existed between the people of imperial Spain—Cuba, in this case—and Ireland, which helped to forge a stronger bond between Anne and Rackham's friends and associates.

If she was indeed Catholic, Anne might have had an opportunity to enter a cathedral in Trinidad or a nearby small town to worship at some point, perhaps in anticipation of a future baptismal for her child. If so, then she would have almost certainly prayed for the welfare of her captain, who was now out at sea and at risk from warships of the Spanish and English governments, and for her child about to be born. Contrary to stereotype, some pirates carried prayer books and the Holy Bible for comfort and spiritual renewal, while plying their destructive trade across the Caribbean. It is not known, but Anne Bonny might have been one of these types. Pirates offered prayers not only for personal safety of themselves and friends, but also for their capture of prizes.

In addition, attending Mass performed by a local priest in a small village with her Cuban "friends" would have helped Anne to more effectively conceal her pirate past and connections to English pirates, especially Captain Rackham, whose reputation had grown. Her time in Cuba was Anne's first experience with a Latin culture, although it was one with religious commonalities to the Irish people, and she almost certainly found some appealing comparable cultural aspects. For the first time, Anne ate Cuban food, such as local dishes like rice and red beans (arroz congri), black beans (frijoles negros), grilled chicken (pollo asado), and roasted goat. After so many months out at sea, she also very likely relished the abundance of local fruits, such as oranges, mangoes, and bananas. To keep up her strength, Anne probably also ate popular foods such as platanos (fried bananas), corn tortillas, or a Cuban kind of tamale, ayacas.

All in all, Captain Rackham had made a good decision in ensuring that Anne should give birth to her child in a secure location—literally a safe house—among his close "friends." These people treated Anne well, and no doubt better than she had originally anticipated in a foreign land among strangers of a dissimilar culture. As Rackham had envisioned, the Cubans, evidently both men and women, "took care of her, till she was brought to bed" to have her first child, which was destined to be delivered in early February 1720.[157]

Meanwhile, his landing on Cuba's south side to take Anne ashore had allowed Rackham an opportunity to acquire much-needed supplies. However, Rackham made a mistake by remaining too long at one location that initially seemed safe, as "they stayed for a considerable time," perhaps because of his desire to stay with or near Anne as long as possible.[158]

Meanwhile, now carrying Jack's child, Anne almost lost her captain and lover when least expected. Demonstrating a reckless streak that eventually proved to be his undoing in the end, Rackham was about to pay a price for having carelessly stayed too long in one place. When Rackham and his crew were finally about to depart his secluded cove on Cuba's south coast, most likely near Trinidad—where Anne was located near in a secure area and which served as a friendly port for English pirates who had converted to Catholicism to placate civil authorities—a Spanish coastal guard ship, with a small captured English sloop in tow, suddenly appeared. Rackham and his men were caught by surprise.

Fortunately for the vulnerable English pirates with little daylight remaining, Rackham had just weighed anchor and was setting sail when the Spanish suddenly struck. Rackham maneuvered in time to narrowly slip out of harm's way, gaining shelter behind a small island to bestow safety until the next morning's sunrise. With darkness having ended the pursuit, the Spanish ship laid anchor across the narrow channel, between the island and the Cuban mainland, that offered the only escape route for Rackham's sloop. The Spanish naval officers were confident that they could finish the job at first light and then capture the heretical English pirates, who could not escape, or so it seemed.

In such a desperate situation with seemingly no escape possible, Rackham hatched a clever plan. He led his men from behind the timbered island in a rowboat, gliding silently across dark waters, his men rowing with muffled oars through the humid blackness. Under the night's protective shroud and possessing the element of surprise, Rackham's men eased closer without detection. As quietly as possible, the pirates, with cutlasses and pistols in hand, then descended upon the captured English sloop. After overpowering the Spanish guards without shouting or making noise to alert the sizable crew of the nearby Spanish ship, the English pirates overwhelmed the vessel.

Doing exactly what was least expected, Captain Rackham's bold surprise attack "in the dead of night" succeeded as planned. Then, issuing hushed orders, Rackham's seamen "slipped the cable," setting the ship free. With a sign of relief, the captain and his joyous pirates then immediately headed out to sea in their new sloop, leaving his old one, the *Kingston*, behind. They then sailed away from Cuba's south side. When the confident Spanish of the "Guardia del Costa" descended upon the *Kingston* next morning, thinking that the English pirates were trapped there, they learned otherwise to their dismay. The ship was empty.

Rackham continued to prove to one and all that he was something more than a flamboyant pretty boy. This young ambitious captain continued to dispel another notion among the most established pirate captains: that he was an insignificant upstart with little tactical skill. Ironically, Rackham seemingly performed at his best when the odds were most stacked against him and when success seemed impossible. By any measure, Anne had chosen a most resourceful and enterprising man as her lover and her child's father.[159]

New Dilemma

Anne evidently knew nothing about her captain's close call with the Spanish military on the Cuban coast, which had almost placed him in the hands of a hangman in Havana. As the months passed in Cuba during her pregnancy, Anne now faced a moral dilemma. This initially seemed like an easy decision, but a host of complexities abounded for Anne. First, as a young expectant mother, she naturally wanted to remain with her first child when born, but that would have meant staying with Rackham's friends in Cuba and far from the ship.

But the fulfillment of this maternal instinct was impossible, because she was still considered an English pirate on a Spanish island, and she could be executed if her hideout were discovered and she were captured. Therefore, staying on a hostile island in a potentially dangerous situation, no matter how much she desired to remain with her child, was simply not a realistic option for Anne under these circumstances. She could not return to either her native Ireland or Charles Town, nor could she go back to Nassau. And, of course, she could not stay in Cuba. There was only one place where she could go: Rackham's ship.

Even more now because of the child, Anne still loved Rackham, and the life that she had left behind. Clearly, these were powerful motivations, because her ship and crew had become a surrogate family to Anne by this time. Not long after she gave birth to her first child in early February 1720, Anne prepared to resume the life that she had left behind. She could leave in good conscience because her child was under the good care of compassionate women, including a wet nurse. Anne knew that her baby would be safe and in a relatively nurturing maternal environment in Cuba.[160]

Captain Rackham deliberately sailed back to Cuba after about eight months—in the springtime of 1720—and after his narrow escape, as he knew that Anne had delivered her child. Then, from Cuba's south coast, he apparently dispatched a messenger to direct her to where his ship was anchored at some secure location along Cuba's southern coast. In this way, having gone back into disguise as a man, Anne was once again reunited with Jack and the crew and resumed her former life.[161]

After a long pregnancy and childbirth, however, Anne was a changed woman. She certainly missed her child who was left behind in Cuba and no doubt shed tears from the separation. Naturally, Anne felt the inevitable sadness and disappointment in a denied motherhood, but this situation was unavoidable under complicated and life-threatening circumstances. She now possessed a new motivation: to provide the kind of good life that she envisioned for her child, as it meant reaping a fortune for an early retirement from the "sweet trade." All in all, then, leaving her child behind in Cuba was not a case of unfeeling abandonment, as some male writers have claimed, in adhering to the stereotype of the ruthless Amazon warrior. Or if her child had died at birth, as some historians have speculated, then Anne would have no longer possessed direct personal ties to Cuba or her firstborn.[162]

For a host of reasons, the alluring appeal of the sea, and a pirate's egalitarian life as a respected member of the democratic "Brethren of the Sea" on a ship that had become a surrogate home, remained strong to Anne Bonny. Now offering a stable familial refuge to this young woman, the pirate society's "instinctive egalitarianism" aboard Rackham's ship matched her own personal needs and innermost longings. As in her past departure from Charles Town or Nassau, Anne's sojourn was "tantamount to departure into a life that begins anew, and knows nothing of rules . . . Class society, hierarchy, oppression, exploitation, national chauvinism, breeding and order—all the conditions of rule that people could not escape in 18th-century Europe—are merely laughed off and ridiculed in the Pirate Caribbean."[163]

Last but not least, the love of Captain Rackham for Anne also remained strong, along with her wish of uniting the couple with their firstborn child at some point in the future. Shelley Klein explained the captain's mixture of charm and distinctive personal style that made him popular: "Captain Rackham's regime was hardly a tough or harsh one [because he] wasn't a Blackbeard or . . . even a Henry Morgan. Instead, he was the equivalent of a petty thief—he was a minor crook, a man who preferred to restrict his raids to fishing boats and other small vessels. Without doubt, he struck terror into the hearts of his victims, but perhaps found the threat of violence to be as effective as actually perpetrating atrocities on those ships he looted. This may also go some way to explaining his undoubted success as a ladies' man—far from endeavoring to capture as many ships as he could, far from attempting to slaughter and torture every other sailor in sight, he appeared to prefer a gentler way of life, a life that included women. This is what ultimately made him so famous—his relationship with Anne Bonny . . . ."[164]

Forgotten War Against Slavery

In addition, Anne might also have seen another redeeming, but forgotten by historians, quality of Rackham's: He was a liberator of slaves. Rackham proved himself much different from the abusive slave owners, planters, merchants, and slave traders (types known by Anne in South Carolina, especially Charles Town) who had acquired massive fortunes based on human misery.

At this time, slavery was big business in the Caribbean world, serving as the central economic foundation of the islands. Slavery provided the fuel that generated the mass profits from the island's agricultural production, especially sugar cane, based upon the toil of thousands of Africans.

The endless European power struggles over the possession of the lucrative Caribbean islands would not have been fought without the vast profits derived from slavery. Even the Anglo-Dutch wars waged in the Caribbean were fought primarily over slave trading. Symbolically, the first great English buccaneer, John Hawkins, was a slave trader, who stole hundreds of slaves from the Spanish to reap massive profits.

Port Royal, Jamaica, became not only the center of buccaneering but also a leading slave trading center, where thousands of slaves were bought and sold. During its peak, Port Royal served as the largest slave port in the West Indies. On almost every level, from the pirate to Jamaica's governor—especially Sir Thomas Modyford, who presided over Port Royal when it reached its zenith from 1664 to 1671 as a buccaneer haven—the link between piracy and slave trading was so close as to be essentially one and the same. In dividing the rich spoils from attacking Spanish, French, and Dutch ships as well as mainland towns and cities, large numbers of captured slaves represented massive wealth for the buccaneers and privateers.

Sugar cane production was the key to the vibrant economy of Jamaica, England's most prosperous colony, which served as the longtime commercial center for the English slave trade. Founded after the Restoration and led by King Charles II of England's brother, James, Duke of York, the Royal African Company was a relentless money-making machine. The company had issued hundreds of licenses for English ships to transport slaves from West Africa to the New World. As a large shareholder in the company, even the king himself enjoyed lavish profits derived from robust slave trading. Clearly, a vibrant institution of slavery was the key to reaping wealth for the crown, planters, and the Royal African Company, which brought at least 100,000 slaves to the New World during its 80 years of profitable existence.[165]

In 1698, when Anne was born, the monopoly of the Royal African Company on the slave trade was officially abolished and opened up to private enterprise, in the capitalist tradition. This development ensured greater prosperity with the fantastic growth of slavery and sugar cultivation, fueling England's rise as a world power and eventually its industrial revolution to transform the nation into a superpower in time. Thereafter, private merchants and shippers across England, including the port of Bristol, which served as the "home for Britain's slave fleet," reaped huge profits from slave trading and by transforming "the pipeline from [west] Africa [into] a flood plain." What resulted in spectacular fashion was the "triumph of sugar-capitalism in the West Indies," especially in Jamaica.[166]

Quite naturally, black pirates gained considerable satisfaction from taking the slaves, monies, and ships from the most lucrative slave cartel in the Caribbean. No one knows the exact numbers of black pirates who sailed the Caribbean, but they were certainly far more numerous than the percentage of black sailors on commercial or naval vessels of the European monarchies' navies. The greatest English buccaneer, Henry Morgan, who was known as the "scourge of popery" in the Caribbean, had relied heavily upon black buccaneers from Jamaica and elsewhere to attack Spanish shipping and major towns. French buccaneer captains had likewise utilized former slaves to strike Spanish merchant vessels and towns during the day's greatest international rivalry for imperial supremacy.

Piracy represented serious (and growing) threats to the European economic system, based on slavery that made the Caribbean sugar islands so profitable, especially to the wealthy slave-owning class, in three fundamental ways: 1) the large number of black free men who were accepted members with equal rights in this Republic of Pirates, 2) the increasing number of pirate attacks on slave ships that resulted in the liberation of thousands of slaves, and 3) the legal, incredibly profitable English slave trade, which long controlled the market by royal decree. Indeed, because of stipulations in the Peace of Utrecht in 1713 that ended the War of Spanish Succession, the English won the most lucrative prize of all by gaining exclusive rights—the highly profitable Asiento—to sell slaves to the Spanish colonies in the Americas, with the English Crown profiting even more extensively from the slave trade.

With roving pirates controlling the Caribbean sea lanes, these lightning strikes at sea not only chipped away at the foundation of the slave system but also represented the greatest threats to one of the principal sources of wealth. An estimated flow of 36,000 slaves were transported annually by slavers from West Africa to the New World. And most importantly, this wealth-generating pipeline was the key to economic development and prosperity across the Caribbean. Therefore, pirate raiders who captured slavers were comparable to the Caribbean maroon communities of escaped slaves and their descendants, from which attacks were launched against the tentacles of the plantation system, resulting in "one of the gravest threats" to the plantation economy. Both revolutionary developments were guerrilla-like activities—one on land and the other on water—that struck at and reduced the enormous profits generated by the slave trade and the plantation systems. Clearly, for the planter elite and merchants across the Caribbean, these ever-growing threats—especially piracy, which was far more widespread—to the economy's very foundation needed to be eliminated as soon as possible.[167]

Many pirates, very likely including the Captain Rackham crew, liberated an unknown number of slaves on captured ships and then set them free. Symbolically, Anne would have partly identified with the slaves' precious moment of liberation, because women and slaves were equally oppressed victims of an unjust system. As pirates, however, black people and women—if disguised as men, like Anne—gained a newfound and long-sought equality among the sea raiders.[168] Most of all, the mere presence of this rogue state and "nest of pirates," in the words of Virginia's Governor Alexander Spottswood, was even "destabilizing the slave societies around it," which supported the vast wealth of a sprawling imperialistic empire and most profitable labor system.[169]

But in fact, there were not one but two distinct threats to the power structure. The pirates were not only striking a blow at the slave trade and the peculiar institution itself but also at the entire social structure of forced labor, both black and white, which supported the disproportionate wealth enjoyed by the aristocratic elite. Like aroused proletariats rising up to wage a people's revolutionary struggle for basic rights, the two lowest forms of white workers (indentured servants on land and seamen on the water) united with former slaves against their wealthy masters, employers, and the abusive economic and commercial systems that had exploited them for most of their lives. In righteous rage, they were inflicting damage on the economic support system of the western European ruling class, stretching from Spain to England, and the greatest profit-generating machine in world history. Mostly lower-class whites pressed into British Navy service as well as the white slavers—sometimes with the unsavory assistance of Arabs and African kings—"played prominent roles in maintaining British power," and the British Empire's prosperity that was unmatched.[170]

Thus, because of the sea rovers' successes, the Caribbean had been practically transformed into a pirate lake, for all practical purposes. Indeed, during the Golden Age of Piracy, "the pirates in the West Indies have been so formidable and numerous, that they have interrupted the trade of Europe into those parts, and our English merchants in particular have suffered more by their depredations than by the united force of France and Spain, in the late war," referring to the War of the Spanish Succession that ended in 1713.[171]

Another serious piracy-related threat also existed to the British Crown at this time. Because many pirates were from Wales, Scotland, and Ireland, they were naturally anti-British and pro-Jacobite. Walter Kennedy was one such Irish pirate captain, who roamed the Caribbean with impunity. When George I became King of Great Britain on August 1, 1714, the Bahamian pirates were also targeted because they were viewed as Jacobites, who supported James III, and revolutionaries who transformed Nassau and Providence Island into a Jacobite bastion. As such, these multiple threats posed by the pirates to the existing social, economic, and political order of the western European powers needed to be crushed at all costs. In a belated attempt to eliminate these growing threats, George I dispatched half a dozen warships to patrol the Caribbean in 1715. And he sent Governor Woodes Rogers to the Bahamas in February 1718, to take on the task of purging the pirates' breeding ground.

Governor Rogers was not a typical aristocratic politician, but a resourceful leader and man of action. In fact, he had been a former privateer captain and a savvy old sea dog. A Bristolian like Blackbeard, Rogers was competent and capable, and his first step in the process of cleaning up the pirates' nests of Nassau and the Bahamas had been to issue pardons to all Bahamian pirates—the one that had been accepted by Captain Rackham in May 1719. In a classic case of divide and conquer, the ambitious governor then planned to destroy all free spirits who refused to submit to his authority.

DARK RETRIBUTION

Clearly, the "greatest outburst of piracy in all the annals of seafaring" that was the Golden Age of Piracy was doomed once England and other European powers turned their wrath on those pirates who had the audacity to steal their own ill-gotten gains. But as the elite realized, future power, wealth, and prestige now rested upon England's ability to protect its lucrative trade, especially the slave trade. If this invaluable flow of commerce remained under siege on the world's waters, then the English Empire and its international economy were in peril. Consequently, the full force of imperial power struck back with a vengeance to forever destroy the threat. Between the years of 1716 and 1726, at least 400 and perhaps as many as 600 pirates were captured and executed by the orders of "imperial officials and vengeful colonists intent on responding to terror with terror."[172]

Now that the most powerful nations on Earth had declared war on piracy, Anne was destined to be caught in this backlash of vengeful retribution against all pirates. For an entire generation of pirates, the high cost of defying the power structures and governments of Europe and the Caribbean Islands was a quick death with little formality or protocol. Clearly, the cost was frightfully high for those proud members of the freest republic on Earth, who risked their lives for its preservation against the mightiest empires. During the time that Anne sailed the Caribbean, a price had to be paid in full for individuals who served with a cocky impunity "under the banner of King Death." Ironically, the meaning of these terrifying black banners, with their grinning skulls and crossbones of white or red, waving in defiance from fast, rampaging vessels across the Caribbean, had finally now come full circle. Because of the fierce backlash from the powerful elites, these emblems were being hauled down from flagstaffs in ever-increasing numbers by victors, ensuring an unceremonious death for large numbers of pirates by the hangman's noose.[173]

Although Anne was not aware of the grim reality that now stalked the Caribbean pirates, her days spent enjoying this new, freewheeling way of life were already numbered. A ruthless hand of vengeance and hard-hitting retribution from the combined wrath of thousands of outraged merchants, slave owners, slave traders, planters, shareholders, investors, bankers, speculators, and officials on both sides of the Atlantic was fast descending with a brutal finality on the Caribbean's sea rovers, who mistakenly believed that this rebellious life in defiance of authority would go on forever.

One pirate crew after another was systematically eliminated by those who enforced the will of kings and their well-paid followers. Refined Captain Stede Bonnet, a former planter of Christ Church Parish, Barbados, was the first well-known pirate leader to go down, but not in a blaze of glory as anticipated. Caught by surprise in the shallow environs behind the headland known as Cape Fear, North Carolina, by two swift South Carolina sloops on September 27, 1718, Bonnet and his crew, from mostly Jamaica, England, Scotland, Ireland, and Charles Town, were forced to surrender after a sharp contest. He was the first pirate leader captured by British authorities, who had declared a no-mercy war on pirates and were determined to demonstrate their far-reaching power with ugly examples. Thus, the shackled captain was carried into Charles Town on October 3 for execution.

Anne's father, the aristocratic William Cormac, might have been among the crowd to witness Bonnet's entry into the town in a carnival-like atmosphere. The resourceful pirate captain briefly escaped confinement, but was recaptured by authorities in early November, and in the end, he went out with his usual style at the gallows. While clutching a small bouquet of flowers, Bonnet was hanged on December 10, 1718, before a crowd of gawking onlookers and at a prominent place, Oyster Point—now called White Point Garden—in order to send a warning. The "Gentleman Pirate," as Bonnet was known on both sides of the Atlantic, was unceremoniously buried "below the water mark in the marsh."[174]

Anne's world was not only unforgiving, but also excessively hypocritical. Indeed, the respected government officials—upper-class representatives who were sending so many pirates rapidly to the gallows—often deserved a comparable fate for greater crimes that went undiscovered. Slavery exposed this glaring hypocrisy like no other single factor. In conjunction with African kings, who likewise profited, English slave traders often promoted warfare in West Africa in order to gain a cheap supply of new captives "to fill the slave market."[175] Ironically, one pro-slavery minister of Jamaica, John Lindsay, even excused these English slave traders of fueling war by convincing one West African leader to attack neighboring tribes (known as slave raids), because in truth, these brutal activities were no different from what "more polished kings [of western Europe], *do every day*."[176]

BLACKBEARD MEETS A VIOLENT END

Besides the harsh lesson provided by the hanging of the so-called "Gentleman Pirate," Anne might well have reconsidered her decision to become a pirate had she known of Blackbeard's fate. On November 22, 1718, he met an especially ugly demise less than six months after he reached the zenith of his pirate career by audaciously blockading Charles Town harbor without firing a shot. Here, he had taken eight or nine merchant ships while holding one of America's richest port cities at his mercy for an extended period.

With typical daring, Blackbeard also captured one of Charles Town's leading citizens, Samuel Wragg, who was a member of Carolina's Council of the Province, as a hostage. After the city fathers met Blackbeard's demands, Wragg and other privileged members of the wealthy aristocracy were sent back to Charles Town in the nude, which brought howls of laughter from the pirates. These audacious pirates loved both the fine embroidered clothing of the wealthy aristocrats as much as a good joke played at the expense of the city's pampered elite: two characteristics that led to Wragg's humiliation and to the shock of the good people—including Anne's father—of Charles Town.

Knowing that he had created a firestorm amid the South Carolina government after "having pulled off one of the greatest coups of his career" in blockading the busiest southern port on the Atlantic coast, and learning of the ruthless mission of Governor Rogers, who had become "a feared pirate hunter," to sweep the Caribbean clean of the pirate scourge, Blackbeard then made his getaway. He sailed north up the Atlantic coast, heading northeast for North Carolina's more friendly waters, in order to find a safe refuge among the remote inlets behind a protective screen of barrier islands.[177]

Realizing that he would have to pay a price for his Charles Town antics, Blackbeard wisely secured a pardon from his friend, North Carolina's governor, Charles Eden. Blackbeard had the governor officially commission the ship *Adventure Command* so that he could continue to raid under a legal guise. As in the past, Blackbeard, the governor, and his cronies were working together in order to share the spoils. Out-of-control greed at all levels, especially at upper echelons, had over-whelmed caution and prudence, especially in regard to the opportunistic Blackbeard.

These sizable, easily garnered profits led to Blackbeard's ambitious plan of establishing a new pirate base of operations on the North Carolina coast. Situated immediately behind the low-lying Outer Banks islands, located just below where North Carolina's easternmost point juts out into the Atlantic, Ocracoke Inlet with its shallow channels was Blackbeard's chosen lair.

Surrounded by a dense expanse of virgin woodlands and heavy timber, including towering cypress trees, the inlet waters of Ocracoke were tricky even for a savvy seafarer. With unseen shallows and sand bars under dark waters, the waterways around Ocracoke presented a formidable challenge for captains and pilots unfamiliar with their elusive secrets. Only a wily captain like the experienced Blackbeard, who knew the area very well, could successfully navigate through the maze of channels without running the ship aground.[178]

Blackbeard's arrangement with North Carolina's governor, wherein he received the governor's protection in exchange for a share of the loot, only added to the pirate captain's heightened sense of security. Feeling perfectly safe from the wrath of the infuriated people of Charles Town and the South Carolina governor, who lusted for revenge, a confident Blackbeard was not expecting any trouble from the more incorruptible governor of Virginia, another English colony located just north of North Carolina. Knowing that the odds were against him as times were rapidly changing, Blackbeard now planned to retire as a proper gentleman in northeast North Carolina: a classic case of cutting his losses and keeping ahead of an increasingly deadly game. Then, fulfilling the ultimate pirate fantasy that was shared by Captain Rackham, he planned to live off his ill-gotten gains like a feudal lord.

As if in preparation for this leisurely life as a landed gentleman of the North Carolina aristocracy, the pirate captain even married a 16-year-old girl. But she was not a well-tutored planter's daughter of Bath County,

North Carolina, as long assumed by historians. In fact, the girl was a prostitute chosen by the captain, who had an eye for beauty. Blackbeard found her a busy brothel at Bath; despite her youth, the teenager could drink as much rum and curse as well as Blackbeard himself. During the summer of 1718, she became his 15th or 16th wife. Meanwhile, Blackbeard's real wife and children, abandoned by their wayward father, were attempting to scratch out a meager existence back in the slums of London.

Blackbeard's tactics of seduction involved sending rounds of drinks to serving girls in taverns, instead of simply demanding more rum for himself, as a chivalrous gesture that masked more sinister designs. He often utilized an effective but cynical system to bed the best-looking women for extended periods: finding the prettiest girl in town and then taking her to his ship for sexual frolicking, as she had no way to escape his clutches once aboard.

Such was the case with the teenager. The ship's first mate, evidently wearing the disguise of a preacher's cloak, had married the pirate captain to the girl, and Blackbeard then thoroughly enjoyed the young lady's charms until his passion was spent, while his soon-to-be-discarded new wife believed that she had cleverly gained not only a new husband but also a wealthy one. But in fact, the ever-calculating Blackbeard was only buying time while evading society's religious and moral conventions and pretending that he had forsaken piracy, because he planned to once again resume his former career.

Taking to sea once more, Blackbeard then sailed to Philadelphia, where he soon learned that the Pennsylvania governor had issued an August 1718 warrant for his arrest, which resulted in his flight to Bermuda. There, he took some merchant ships and then sailed back to North Carolina, to share the ill-gotten gains with Governor Eden and his cronies. After a number of narrow escapes, Blackbeard soon returned to the friendly waters at Ocracoke Inlet and began in earnest to transform this hidden sanctuary into a base of pirating operations. He then sailed forth to systematically pick off one merchant sloop after another, including vulnerable ships sailing from the nearby Virginia Colony just to the north. After losing a great deal of money, victimized sloop owners appealed to Virginia's governor Alexander Spottswood for immediate assistance to parry this growing threat from Ocracoke.

Consequently, the enterprising Spottswood issued a 100-pound reward for Blackbeard's capture—or his head. Spottswood also dispatched two royal men-of-war to track down Blackbeard and his crew, commissioning two shallow-draft sloops, the *Ranger* and the *Jane*. Lieutenant Robert Maynard commanded the fleet. Unfortunately for Blackbeard, these pirate-hunting vessels were manned with experienced seamen and soldiers from two ships of the Royal Navy.[179]

Thanks to prior intelligence about Blackbeard's location, Lieutenant Maynard and his small convoy reached Ocracoke Inlet on the chilly evening of November 21. He soon heard drunken revelry echoing across the dark inlet, long before he saw the outlines of Blackbeard's sloop, the *Adventure Command*. As quietly as possible, Maynard ordered his men to drop anchor into Ocracoke's calm waters relatively close to the unwary Blackbeard, and then waited for dawn, when he planned to unleash his attack on the pirate ship.

Blackbeard and his relatively few men—only 18 desperate "Knaves" as the pirate captain described them in his journal—had plenty of reason to drink their troubles away. First, because the captain was evidently intoxicated, their sloop had run aground. They now had no choice but to wait for the arrival of the morning's rising tide to set them free from the sand bar. Throughout the night, Blackbeard passed the time by drinking to his heart's content and made no effort toward any necessary defensive preparations, despite knowing that the two sloops were on the way to attack him at this very time.

During the height of his power, before he was forced to seek protection in his obscure inlet, Blackbeard had once led a small fleet and more than 400 pirates. By this time, one pirate ship after another had been lost to the king's vengeance, poor quality or drunken seamanship, and navigational errors, until only the *Adventure Command* and a relative handful of pirates remained to carry on the fast-dying tradition of piracy. In addition, most of his men had died or deserted, which also contributed to Blackbeard's lack of preparedness at Ocracoke.

A cynical fatalist for good reason, Blackbeard had seemingly accepted his ultimate fate by this time. After all, he and his men well knew that Governor Spottswood was determined to destroy them, after having been already warned by Governor Eden's own emissary. Nevertheless, Blackbeard and his crew continued to enjoy themselves on this dark night as long as the supply of rum lasted, as if they instinctively knew that the end for them and the Golden Age of Piracy was drawing ever closer.

The chilly autumn morning finally dawned and the pirate ship remained silent in Ocracoke's dark waters. By this time, the Blackbeard crew was asleep after the night's revelry. Meanwhile, Lieutenant Maynard ordered anchors quietly weighed just before the first light of day illuminated the hidden inlet. Then, the lieutenant ordered a small boat lowered with his best fighting men inside. Maynard planned to take the pirates by surprise. However, the element of surprise was lost when Maynard's *Pearl* became mired in the same muddy bottom that also gripped Blackbeard's sloop like a vise. Fortunately for Blackbeard, to compensate for his negligence, the rising morning tide finally freed his *Adventure Command*. But Maynard's two sloops were likewise lifted by the tide. Once the ships were freed, the pursuers now headed toward Blackbeard's ship with cannons loaded.

Never having slept and still drinking rum, the pirate captain was now up on the wooden deck. Ironically, his Ocracoke sanctuary was about to be his undoing in the final act of his legendary pirate career. Partly shaking off his drunkenness with the adrenaline rush that helped compensate for the overabundance of rum, Blackbeard went into action.

After shouting to awaken his crew and then hurrying them into battle stations to defend the ship, Blackbeard's cannons were quickly loaded to greet the interlopers. The groggy pirates belatedly opened fire, shattering the eerie stillness of Ocracoke and raking both Maynard's ship and the other sloop, the *Lyme*, with broadsides until no one was left standing on the deck of the *Pearl*. Blackbeard believed that the day was won after his broadsides were unleashed at close range. Thanks to the rum, however, he had not realized that Lieutenant Maynard had placed his surviving men in hidden positions on and below deck, out of sight. Maynard had his men ready when the pirates boarded what they believed was an easy capture, as they had so often in the past.

Knowing how best to effectively exploit not only the pirates' recklessness but also their greed, Maynard's trick worked perfectly. With Blackbeard leading the way, the pirates boarded and were unexpectedly greeted with a volley that exploded in their faces. With most of his followers cut down, including his quartermaster Thomas Miller along with seven other crewmen, Blackbeard boldly met his attackers head-on. Bleary-eyed and still drunk, Blackbeard dueled Maynard with a flintlock pistol and a cutlass, gamely fighting back as if hoping to compensate for his tactical errors that had led him to this dramatic showdown.

In the hazy early morning light, Blackbeard never had a chance with so many of his men lying dead at his feet, including carpenter Owen Roberts and gunner Phillip Morton. Maynard's men soon closed in on the defiant pirate captain. Just when Blackbeard was about to finish off Maynard, he staggered from pistol shots and saber slashes from seamen converging on him, missing his mark. Then, from behind Blackbeard, who still faced Maynard, one man reached around and cut the throat of the pirate captain with a long dirk. Captain Blackbeard and the daring exploits of his *Adventure Command* had come to an abrupt end at Ocracoke.[180]

Upon Maynard's order, Blackbeard's head was cut off in celebration. To his shock, Maynard then discovered official correspondence in Blackbeard's cabin from the North Carolina governor and his emissary as well as letters from New York merchants, which fully revealed their close business relationship with Blackbeard: Merchants had long purchased stolen goods from Blackbeard at low prices and to avoid taxation, which were then sold to customers at a higher price.

Blackbeard had so confidently utilized Ocracoke Inlet as his private sanctuary because he was in league with the corrupt governor, who was becoming wealthy in consequence. All in all, the distinction between pirate and governor became not only blurred, but almost invisible. But in fact, the relationship between Blackbeard and the North Carolina governor was only the tip of the iceberg: merely a hint of the close-knit collusion between black-market profits and pirates and colonial officials, including even the most respected governors of the American colonies such as New York.

From the governor to the common people, seemingly almost everyone had a common interest to work in league with pirates for their own benefit, as well as to protect them. In this regard, mutual profits united one and all in these highly profitable criminal activities. Of course, this illegal transfer of wealth was no different from the practices of many longtime world leaders, from the King of Spain sending forth the Conquistadors—the first real pirates in the New World—to conquer the Aztec in Mexico and the Inca of South America to Queen Elizabeth I relying upon the buccaneers to steal Spain's ill-gotten wealth. Thievery on a grand international scale was not limited to a single religion, race, class, culture, or nation.

Nevertheless, common pirates like Anne were caught in a thoroughly corrupt system. A good many of England's colonial governors and leading officials, merchants, and respected members of the gentry class along the East Coast mutually benefitted from illegal trade. Much of the lavish profits derived from pirating went to the already rich and powerful, rather than to the average pirate—still another case of the old formula of the rich getting richer and the poor getting poorer, while risking their lives in the process.

Merchants from New York City to Charleston sold tons of gunpowder to the pirates so that they could continue their raids unabated, while setting up clearing houses for apparently endless amounts of booty. This illegal collusion had a lengthy tradition: Even Henry Morgan and his English buccaneers had been supplied with ammunition and weaponry from Virginia and New England colonies in a shrewd investment in stolen booty. The popular image has been that the governors of leading colonies, like New York, and key government officials were moral, upright protectors of the laws, but this idealized scenario was very much of a sham. Acting under a hypocritical façade of righteousness, they were seemingly ardent in their efforts to hunt down pirates, allegedly for the overall public and imperial good, presenting the sea rovers as the epitome of evil. All the while, the North American colonies provided a busy marketplace for the pirates' stolen goods, which could be bought far more cheaply than the same goods imported from England.

In return, the governors and colonists supplied homegrown products, including flour and other provisions for long voyages, to the pirates. During three decades of the Golden Age of Piracy, this massive corruption blurred all moral distinctions between good and bad or right and wrong. The corruption easily flowed from the deeply entrenched system of colonial governments having long employed privateers, which reached a high point in the 17th century, to protect their New World possessions by taking as many prizes as possible, in part to share in the profits.

Above: A grim trophy, Blackbeard's severed head.

And now in the early 18th century, these same governments that once had sent hundreds of privateers forth to decimate their enemy shipping had decided that far greater profits could be reaped from legitimate trade, which now needed to be protected. Consequently, the sea raiders of the Caribbean had been declared the foremost enemies of the state— and for doing exactly what the former privateers had done for previous decades to save their king's colonial possessions during a great international power struggle for control of the Caribbean.

To fulfill the king's wishes, the Royal Navy grew more powerful to protect what was now considered the most vital to England's prosperity: a free flow of trade that could no longer be interrupted or threatened by pirates. Because of the changing priorities of the ruling elite, those engaged in attacking commerce had been officially and legally transformed from national heroes into the worst criminals on Earth. These pirates now had to be exterminated by mass public executions, for the public good. In consequence, a much more formidable Royal Navy now sailed the high seas in a vigorous campaign to wipe out the last remaining bands of pirates in the Caribbean and along the Atlantic.

Ironically, pirates of Anne Bonny's era were now declared enemies of the state by many of the same colonial officials who had acted as their unofficial sponsors. Maybe Anne and her crew members were correct in waging war against the repressive system of wealthy merchants, government officials and governors, bankers, and other privileged members of the aristocracy. After all, it was they—and not the pirates—who had long crassly exploited the lower classes for profit and personal gain. Perhaps in part for this very reason, the government and power structures of Europe had turned against the same kind of adventurous seamen, whom they had once praised for waging war against the Spanish by way of piracy, masked by legitimate privateering. Unleashed by the governments of all nations, Catholic and Protestant, in wartime to plunder enemy shipping, the privateers were basically nothing more than pirates operating under the guise of so-called patriotism. The only difference between privateers and pirates was in popular perception and a single piece of paper, when the government officially issued a letter of marque.[181]

Even the rapid growth of America's leading commercial center, New York City, during the Golden Age of Piracy was in part attributed to close connections with piracy. Top leaders and the general populace tolerated piracy because of its financial benefits. The governor, who served from 1692 to 1698, established the custom that "any pirate, or any New York merchant taking a flyer in piracy, was entirely secure in his business provided he was willing to pay a fair percentage of its profits" to the governor.[182]

Even more in regard to New York City, "much of this piracy was carried on under cover of privateering; and from genuine privateering [directed at Spanish shipping], the city derived a large amount of wealth."[183] Indeed, historian Douglas R. Burgess, Jr., was correct in his analysis of the contradictions and hypocrisy: "This sordid scandal of pirate patronage had been and would be played out again and again like a Renaissance comedy throughout the Atlantic world for more than three decades. Blackbeard's case was neither the last nor the worst. In the long history of piracy in the Atlantic, there were always two stories: the official and the unofficial. The first is one of heroism and valor pitted against rank treachery and treason, of brave governments with valiant navies warring against a band of seagoing miscreants that one historian has dubbed 'the lowest form of human scum.'"[184]

Thus, at the same time when Anne Bonny was sailing the Caribbean with Captain Rackham, this powerful system and its self-serving officials, such as former privateer-pirate Governor Rogers at Nassau, were determined to destroy the last remaining bands of pirates. The hypocritical authorities mustered considerable strength to eliminate them, almost as if they also wanted to wipe out the lingering memory of their own considerable crimes, collusion, and ill-gotten gains. Therefore, more pirates and their leaders would have to pay the highest price in the future, and Anne Bonny was one of those pawns caught up in a deadly game that she would be very fortunate to escape alive. In a classic case of poor timing, Anne already had been placed in a situation in which she was about to pay for the crimes of others, from government officials to other pirates.[185]

Blackbeard's demise at Ocracoke represented an era's end, even before Anne Bonny had decided to become a pirate.[186] If Blackbeard, even in his most remote North Carolina sanctuary, and other pirate captains had stood little chance for survival against the new official government vendetta to extinguish pirates, then the less experienced and much less ruthless Captain Rackham was all but doomed. It was now only a matter of time before changing times caught up with Rackham and his relatively small crew: a hard reality that Anne never realized until it was too late.

Oblivious to her own eventual fate, and how Blackbeard's severed head had been flaunted as a grisly trophy from the end of the bowsprit of the sloop *Ranger* as it sailed triumphantly into the harbor of Bath, Anne was already sailing the Caribbean's waters on borrowed time when she should have already returned to South Carolina.[187] During the Golden Age of Piracy, the pirates had clearly been too successful for their own good, and Anne Bonny and the Rackham crew were now caught in the fierce backlash from which they could never escape. Anne's life was now in peril as never before in part because pirate attacks had been so devastating that Spain's transatlantic trade and shipping were effectively halted between 1700 and 1706. Echoing the words of the Massachusetts governor in Boston, South Carolina's governor in Anne's adopted hometown of Charles Town complained of "the utter ruin of our trade" by 1718, when Rackham had embarked upon his career as a pirate captain and when Anne first became a pirate. But with the stability and lifeblood of major western European economies hanging in the balance, the inevitable backlash was more severe than any pirates, including Rackham and Anne, could possibly imagine.

By this time, all of the Great Powers of Europe—England, France, Spain, and the Netherlands—had declared war on piracy. The governors of the Bahamas and Jamaica employed Royal Navy ships to decimate the pirates and their audacious activities. One pirate leader and crew after another continued to be wiped out by a highly effective Royal Navy and specially commissioned privateers of experienced captains and seamen, bent on fulfilling their righteous missions to protect their country's commerce so that trade flowed smoothly in the Caribbean.

With a new energy, thousands of veteran seamen led by capable captains directed their efforts toward eliminating all pirates from the Caribbean's waters along with the last remaining vestiges of the "Golden Age of Piracy." But like the ill-fated Blackbeard, these sea rovers continued to conduct themselves in the same old manner as if everything still remained the same: an unbridled overconfidence, a brazen contempt for the authorities, and a philosophy of living only for the moment. This was a toxic mixture that only hastened the demise of one pirate crew after another at a rapid rate. Like the Blackbeard crew, almost all succumbed more easily than anyone expected. It was only a matter of time before Rackham and his crew were caught, swiftly tried, and executed.

By this time, the pirates had been systematically targeted for absolute destruction because they were "considered world enemy number one, to be hunted by the nations of the world and killed at almost anyone's whim. He had no home, the sea was his only residence. He was considered a stranger and an outcast from society. He had no family in the usual sense, and no children except for those outside of marriage [and]

Every day he [or she, in Anne's case] had to be prepared to die."[188]

What now reigned supreme in the Caribbean was not the rule of piracy, but an even more ruthless law that stemmed from King George I and his September 5, 1717, edict against piracy: "We strictly order our Admirals, Captains and other officers at sea, as well as Governors or Commanders of forts, castles or strongholds of our plantations and the rest of our civil and military officials to arrest those pirates who refuse to hand themselves in as according in this edict . . . ."[189] Like other European monarchs, the king of England was now waging his own personal war of no mercy on Anne Bonny and her kind, who were now nothing more than a vanishing breed. Indeed, the king's proclamation led to "the beginning of the end for piracy in the Caribbean," and especially in the center of piracy in the Caribbean, Nassau.[190]

Meanwhile, Rackham and his crew, with Anne, made plans to make their way back to New Providence Island and Nassau, after cruising the Caribbean for months. Nassau was the home port for the young couple, the unruly town where their relationship began in the heat of passion and visions of bliss. By this time, Rackham's old vessel, the *Kingston*, which he had taken command of in November 1718, had become less seaworthy. Perhaps Rackham also considered the name unlucky, because Kingston Harbor on Jamaica's southeastern coast now swarmed with British sea captains, who wanted to catch and execute pirates in order to win the king's favor. It was time to replace the recently captured ship, after she had fulfilled her primary purpose to Rackham. The port of Nassau and its harbor full of hundreds of new ships now beckoned Captain Rackham and his crew: a familiar and perceived safe haven that was no longer safe.[191]

STEALING THE WILLIAM

1720

BY THE SUMMER OF 1720, Captain Rackham and his crew were back in Nassau. Here, they frequented their old familiar haunts, especially the most popular meeting places of all, the taverns along the noisy waterfront. Before embarking upon the high seas once again, Rackham most of all now needed a new ship, and to ensure future success, he hunted for a ship that was agile, well-armed, in good shape, and most importantly, fast. He needed a vessel with a recently cleaned bottom and hull to ensure greater swiftness in order to catch large merchant ships. Rackham also needed a ship with a shallow draft to ply the inlets and bays along the coasts, such as in Cuba.

By this time, when more pirate hunters were on the prowl, a fast ship was not only a prerequisite for success but also for survival. A crew's survival depended upon the captain's judgment and navigational skills as much as a ship's swiftness, stealth, and maneuverability. Formidable opponents, especially the professional seamen of the Royal Navy, would have to be not only outwitted but also out-sailed to guarantee the Rackham crew's survival in the days ahead. Unlike the Royal Navy and merchant marine, the pirates possessed no shipyard to either repair or obtain a new vessel. Rackham's solution to this quandary was relatively simple because he had no other option: just steal a new ship.

On the night of August 22, 1720, Rackham embarked upon a new mis-

---

Opposite: A heavily armed Anne Bonny, ready for action.

sion. He led a dozen pirates to the dark shoreline at a quiet corner of Nassau Harbor, and with muffled oars, chosen members of the Rackham crew, including Anne Bonny, rowed out into the blackness of Nassau Harbor opposite the town. The rowboat headed directly toward a large ship with a single tall mast. Possessing a lofty reputation throughout Nassau, this sleek sloop in excellent condition now lay quietly at anchor in the middle of the wide channel.

Rackham's targeted vessel was a 12-ton sloop named the *William*, a light and swift vessel, and just the kind that Rackham coveted for small-scale operations. The rapier-like bowsprit, nearly as lengthy as her graceful wooden hull, provided additional canvas to generate speed. Consequently, the single-mast sloop was more maneuverable than either the much heavier two-masted brigantine or schooner, such as Royal Navy vessels. This key advantage ensured that the sloop could outdistance a pursuing warship, but not another equally swift sloop. As well, the *William*, thanks to its low draft, could be taken into the shallow waters of the bays and inlets along the lengthy coasts of Cuba, Jamaica, or the island of Hispaniola.

Anchored in Nassau's harbor on this dark, rainy night—ideal for stealing a vessel—Rackham's target was owned by Captain John Ham, who lived with his family on one of the nearby islands of the Bahamas. Most likely built in the Bahamas, the *William* was a special ship, whose swiftness and grace in movement at sea had resulted in Ham's taking of Spanish prizes, as a much-celebrated privateer. The ship was well-known in the pirate community, and Captain Rackham fairly lusted at the sight of the *William*. This ship was a dream come true, especially to an ambitious pirate captain hoping to continue his trade with renewed vigor.

Best of all for Rackham, the sloop was well-supplied, including abundant cannons and ammunition: four iron cannons situated below deck and two small swivel guns mounted on the rails. Ample reserves of gunpowder were available for flintlock muskets and pistols. Rackham had immediately sensed his opportunity when he first learned that the *William* was about to sail out of Nassau Harbor, knowing that the ship would be supplied for a long cruise. In addition, Rackham realized that the *William* had a well-maintained hull, tarred below the waterline for protection and to ensure swiftness in plying the waters: vital characteristics

Above: Anne Bonny taking aim with her flintlock pistol.

not only for the survival of his crew, but also for lengthier cruises.

Aided by a heavy rain, Captain Rackham led the 12 crew members to the high wooden side of the targeted vessel. Beside her pirate comrades on this vital mission, Anne was in the rowboat while the warm rain pelted down. Then, without having been detected, Rackham, Anne, and the other pirates climbed aboard the ship as quietly as possible. Benefitting from the element of surprise, they took possession of the *William* without difficulty. Only one or two sleepy guards were on board, but they did not want to die to save the property of Captain Ham, who was still on shore in Nassau like the rest of his crew.

Rackham gave orders to Anne and the others to raise the anchor and to set the sails. Energized to move swiftly after such a grand theft, the pirate crew flew into action, with everyone knowing their duties as prearranged by Rackham, as to escape from Nassau Harbor as soon as possible. Before long, the sleek *William*, with canvas sails flapping and full in the late-night summer breeze, moved with good speed through the harbor's waters and farther away from the twinkling lights of Nassau.

But to make a successful escape, Rackham and his crew had to first slip past the triangular Fort Nassau, which contained 28 cannons was protected by a guard ship, before they could slip out of the harbor. Fortunately, the combined effect of the rainstorm, darkness, and a light fog that reduced the visibility of the king's soldiers now worked in Rackham's favor.

The tension finally broke among Rackham's anxious crewmen, and no doubt to Anne's great relief, when the fort's rows of cannons remained silent. After passing the guns, the intense August heat and humidity no longer felt so oppressive to Anne and her comrades. With the *William* moving fast to confirm its reputation for seaworthiness, Rackham sailed out of the western entrance of Nassau Harbor at full speed. The pirates were now in the clear, and Anne and her comrades shouted themselves hoarse in wild celebration. Perhaps this bold capture of the *William*, followed by their stealthy escape in the night, were harbingers of good things to come. The newly acquired pirate ship glided through the darkness with seemingly effortless ease, with the storm's winds powering the full sails that pushed the crew out to sea and farther away from danger.

But nobody knew what the future had in store for the audacious

Rackham crew that had once again defied the odds. After stealing a well-known vessel, this cruise was far riskier than in the past, as the news of the ship's capture was sure to be spread far and wide. One reason why this crew was so small, at 12 members, was because Rackham and many of these individuals were now breaking the amnesty after having taken the king's pardon. If caught, then they would be hanged for this crime, especially when combined with acts of piracy and stealing such a well-known ship right from under the nose of authorities.[192]

Anne continued to sail dressed as a crewman dressed as a man during the day, and then also as a woman in the evenings and nights when off-duty. Evidently, she had dressed as a woman in Nassau when with Captain Rackham, and the newly gathered crew from Nassau most likely already knew that Anne was a woman by this time. It is not known, but perhaps her true identity had been discovered by accident to end the hoax that had become too difficult to maintain for such an extended period. Or perhaps Anne just decided to end it on her own on the advice of Rackham, who might have informed the crew.

The primary reason to disguise herself—to not violate the pirate code—no longer existed, because it now made no difference to Rackham's new crew of only a few men. Times had gotten so tough that Anne's sex no longer mattered after proving herself a capable and valuable crew member. She had passed all tests and had won complete acceptance among the crew members. But, of course, she wore men's clothing when performing her duties aboard ship, because of its utility and practicality—work that must have been easier for her now that there was no longer a need to hide her gender.[193]

MARY READ

If Anne's timing in deciding to take still another cruise was not bad enough, Mary Read's was even worse. She was one of the newest crew members, who had helped to set the sails and steal the *William*. Like Captain Rackham and evidently Anne as well, Mary had violated the king's pardon when she signed on for the new cruise in the Caribbean. Of Rackham's crew of a dozen, 10 were men and two were women. This rare demographic partly reflected the attrition among the pirates and how few truly bold souls continued to flout authority when it was more dangerous to do so. About 36 years old, England-born Mary Read, like Anne, was the product of an illicit love affair. Like her fellow pirates and quite unlike Anne, Mary was a member of the working class that had been long thoroughly exploited across Europe, especially England, by the wealthy and upper class.

While disguised as an ordinary seaman, perhaps as a drummer or cabin boy who attended an English officer, at age 13, Mary had "served some time" on a British man-of-war. She had then enlisted as a cadet, disguised as a man, in an English infantry regiment. As a teenager, Mary served with distinction as a common soldier in Flanders during the early part of the War of Spanish Succession from 1701 to 1714. Unable to secure an officer's rank because of her origins, despite her proven abilities, Mary then enlisted in a cavalry regiment.

But her life changed when the teenager finally found love. Mary married a Flemish comrade from her cavalry regiment, who was "a handsome young fellow." After having been discharged from military service years before the war ended, the young couple then lived together, pooled saved resources, and opened an inn. This establishment along one of the region's main roads was known as the Three Trade Horses, near Breda in the Netherlands, at the confluence of the Aa and Mark Rivers. However, their business dreams were shattered in a cruel way. Mary's husband died of an illness, apparently stemming from his years of active campaigning across Europe, and Mary's fortunes continued to plummet. When the most recent war ended in Europe, so did the thriving business that had once made the Three Trade Horses Tavern profitable.

But even more tragedy lay in store for Mary Read. She soon married a British man who was a lower-class member who worked outside the law, but while trying to provide for himself and his new wife with the limited means available, he was arrested for piracy. Mary, along with other wives and relatives—a total of 47—of the other condemned pirates, sent forth a desperate appeal to Queen Anne, begging for leniency. But the appeal was ignored by the queen, and at age 25, Mary lost her second husband in 1709, when he was hanged at the execution dock on the north bank of the Thames, where pirates had been hanged for four centuries.

Fate had once more turned against this young Englishwoman, pulling her back out of economic necessity into an old familiar role that was necessary for survival: rejoining an infantry regiment in the Netherlands, dressed as a man. But Mary's enlistment was of only short duration, perhaps because her sex was discovered. Still disguised as a man, Mary moved on, continuing her search for work to support herself. For lower-class individuals, occupations connected with the sea offered the best possibilities and opportunities. She signed on near the Atlantic coast, evidently at Amsterdam, as a crewman of a Dutch ship bound for the West Indies. From her travels across western Europe, Mary Read spoke some Dutch. However, the Dutch ship was captured by English pirates before it reached its destination, which was probably a Jamaican port. Some historians have speculated that this capture was perhaps made by Captain Rackham, after he took command from Captain Vane. As was customarily the case for pirate captains short on crewmen during a lengthy voyage, Mary, still dressed as a man, was invited to join the crew in part because she was the only English speaker among the Dutch crew. After signing the pirate articles established by crew members, Mary herself became a pirate.[194]

Adjusting easily to her new occupation, as if continuing the legacy of her second husband, Mary served as a pirate for several months before she and her crew members took the king's pardon. They then attempted to resume more conventional lives within the normal framework of colonial society, probably in Jamaica or Barbados. But as usual, funds soon ran short and jobs were few. Mary shortly learned that Woodes Rogers, as the ruthless and effective governor of Providence Island, was sending out privateers from Nassau to attack Spanish shipping.

To embark upon still another new career, she and a few male friends from her old crew traveled to Nassau. Appearing, acting, and talking like a common seaman while wearing typically baggy clothes that provided an effective disguise, she joined a privateer crew. But hardly had the ship sailed than the crew, including Mary, decided to once again turn to piracy, to ensure greater gains from "their old trade" than could be obtained by the more legitimate profession of privateering. In the pirate tradition, they simply overthrew their captain and took command of the ship in an uprising.[195]

After returning to Nassau, Mary Read joined the Rackham crew just before they embarked upon their most daring exploit: stealing the *William* right from under the governor's nose. Then, in following the traditional, male perspective-based story line of women disguised as men at sea, supposedly what developed, according to Captain Johnson, was a love relationship between the two women (Anne and Mary) behind Rackham's back and greatly at his expense. However, the imaginative Johnson was guilty of having only once again recreated a common staple of popular literature of the time. He described the familiar romance scenario with Anne, who allegedly had fallen in love with Mary, discovering her sex in an intimate encounter. Of course, this story was all part of a popular theme of the period to garner high sales: the most lurid of tales calculated to titillate a largely male audience.

As if this was not enough, the personal and sex lives of Anne and Mary have been deliberately made even more sensationalized to support the rise of a feminist or lesbian agenda that began in the 1960s, when American society finally began to change from its conservatism for the better. In the 1970s, to support this new political and social agenda, one author even suggested that the two women met at a "gay bar" in Nassau, and that they were natural products of an active gay culture in the early 1700s. Although it's an interesting thought, no evidence exists to support this speculation. Obviously, Johnson provided the initial model for even greater fictionalization and myths. Perpetuated in a successful effort to sell large numbers of books, a good many modern writers and historians have continued to faithfully portray this alleged romantic love relationship between these two young women to this day. It is not known, but the possibility exists that Anne tired of her captain or he tired of her, which might have made such an intimate relationship more likely: a case of the sisterhood of the sea proving stronger than the much-touted brotherhood of the sea.

As mentioned, however, the depiction of such a sensational romantic relationship has long served as a traditional liaison scenario to explain why women disguised themselves as men: a convenient excuse to diminish the reality that these capable women could perform with skill and as well as men and, hence, were deserving of equality. Male writers have gone to great lengths to portray what an antiquated society deemed the most deviant and immoral behavior (i.e., a lesbian relationship according

Above: Mary Read eliminates a male opponent with one thrust of her trusty sword.

to the religious-based and ultra-conservative values of the day), while overlooking the larger issue that such women were forced to dress as males in order to achieve equality in an unfair patriarchal society. As one historian correctly emphasized, the commonly depicted "scenario of an innocent female falling for a woman in soldier's disguise is so clichéd, the sources themselves cannot be trusted to give a realistic portrayal."[196]

In emphasizing the Anne-Mary liaison, Johnson might have been deliberately spinning a titillating story to virtually guarantee his book's success to a wide-eyed audience of mostly males. In keeping with upper-class values, Johnson also sought to illustrate the purported sexual "perversion" of lower-class women (a source of utter fascination to upper class males) what was little more than literary pornography: a cautionary tale for females to confirm to the wisdom of a traditional lifestyle in which women were kept securely in their lowly places allegedly for society's overall good. Such an alleged Anne-Mary sexual relationship, stemming from Johnson's penchant for poetic license to sell as many books as possible, was unlikely, but still possible.

Above: With a well-placed shot, Mary Read wins a duel with another pirate.

The portrayal of Mary Read's life—especially the old scenario that included Anne's surprise discovery of a fellow disguised woman's true sex—in Johnson's book only closely followed the traditional storyline of the stereotypical female warrior who wore men's clothing. All of these themes, including that Anne enjoyed a conventional love relationship with a pirate captain, made for very popular reading in the 18th century. Quite simply, what Johnson produced was the romance novel of his day.

Rather than a sensational discovery of her sex in a private, intimate moment that was so sensational in her day, Anne would have almost certainly recognized Mary Read, in her early 30s and at least a decade older than "Bonn," for what she actually was from the beginning: just another young woman in disguise, a role that she knew very well. Most significantly, Governor Woodes Rogers' proclamation on September 5, 1720, specifically identified not only Anne but also Mary, listing the "two women" pirates by name. If the governor knew that Mary Read was a woman, then Anne certainly would have known as well. And unlike during her first cruise from Nassau before her pregnancy, Anne was now no longer dressing as a man when not working as a member of the crew. Wearing sailor's clothing was no longer needed as a disguise for Anne, who no longer had anything to hide—no doubt a most liberating experience in itself for her.

Above: "Sisters of the Sea," Anne Bonny and Mary Read.

Because Anne had already found love with Jack Rackham, it would seem that she hardly had the time, interest, or the privacy to embark upon a new relationship on a crowded ship, which lacked seclusion. Additionally, Mary Read had already begun a romantic relationship with an officer named Thomas Bourne, whose alias was Brown. Mary became Bourne's "common-law wife" aboard ship, like Anne and Jack, and he was considered "her husband" to one and all.

Anne and Mary sailed together on the *William* only a relatively short time. Such an alleged passionate love relationship between the two women would have been extremely casual and fleeting on a small ship with little privacy, especially when Anne was sleeping at night in the captain's quarters, where she had been long assigned as a member of the captain's staff. But given human nature and the dictates of the heart, the possibility does exist that the two women had a romance affair, which might even have been a welcome respite from their male lovers who failed to fulfill certain needs..[197]

Compared to his description of Anne's life, Johnson's portrayal of Mary Read is more problematic, fitting much too easily into the well-worn stereotypical images and legends of female warriors. In his account of Read, Johnson created the enduring image of a half-crazed and blood-thirsty sociopath who was even more masculine and brave than her male counterparts both on land and sea. Johnson depicted Mary boldly defying death like some sort of superwoman, portraying her openly mocking the possibility of being hanged if caught, since it was "no great hardship, for were it not for that, every cowardly fellow would turn Pirate and so infest the seas that men of courage must starve."[198]

But most of all, and thanks to the even more remarkable occurrence of Captain Rackham now commanding the only known two female pirates to have served aboard a pirate ship during the Golden Age of Piracy, Johnson created the most sensational of all erotic stories to confirm his book's immense popularity: an alleged lesbian affair and a love triangle between Jack, Anne, and Mary. It would have been more possible for all of this extracurricular sexual activity to actually occur if heavy drinking was a factor. Or perhaps a non-monogamous relationship between the two women was a way to obtain a measure of revenge on a male lover for some unknown transgression or to demonstrate that a man was not needed. Unfortunately, the exact truth cannot be ascertained.

However, as a reformed pirate himself, and in an age in which religion was dominant, Johnson also wanted to present a moral lesson by depicting the two women in a most negative light, while providing additional religious and societal justifications for execution or death by disease (in Mary's case). In the end, Johnson provided a lesson by emphasizing that severe misery—God's punishment for sinful behavior—came at a high cost: the fate that lay in store for young women who dared to openly defy the conventional role models of a patriarchal society.[199]

But Anne's life lessons were rooted more in immediate requirements than gender stereotypes and myths. She had already learned about the need for a young woman to be assertive for her own welfare. While growing up in Ireland, perhaps Anne heard about the fabled Irish woman of unbreakable spirit and courage named Maev, who was legendary for her "rather strong physical and mental capabilities."[200] When she discovered that her husband, Conor, the provincial king of Ulster, was unworthy of her love, Maev, known for her "haughty temper," had the marriage "dissolved"—not unlike when Anne decided to end her own marriage to Jim Bonny.[201] And when one of Maev's prized cattle, a young bull, was stolen by thieves of a wealthy noble who underestimated her reaction, they soon learned that she was "not a lady who could remain quiet under such provocation."[202] Maev then took action and "proceeded to make good her claim by force of arms."[203]

Sailing the exceptionally seaworthy *William* proved to be the opening of a true Pandora's box for Anne Bonny, however. If Jack, Anne, and the other crew members believed that they would get away with stealing the ship out from under the governor's eyes without severe repercussions, then they were badly mistaken. Any pirates who thumbed their noses at this governor were in for serious trouble. On September 5, 1720, Governor Woodes Rogers issued a proclamation that not only described the *William* but also stated that the stolen vessel was manned by Captain Rackham and "two women, Ann Fulford alias Bonny and Mary Read" among the pirate crew. This revealed that Anne was now using the last name Fulford as an alias.[204]

Most ominously, this pirate-hating governor, who had been humiliated by the audacious thieves of the *William*, denounced the two women as pirates, while condemning them to an inevitable death sentence if captured. Rogers emphasized how these pirates, "the said John Rackhum [sic] and his said Company," including the mentioned "Bonny," were now "Enemies of the Crown of Great Britain, and are to be so treated and Deem'd by all his Majesty's subjects."[205]

Suffering from a bruised ego, the angry Governor Rogers had plenty of old scores to settle with this particular band of sea raiders. Captain Rackham had broken his word in dramatic fashion by resuming his old pirating career, as if Governor Rogers did not exist—a great miscalculation that revealed considerable hubris among Captain Rackham and his followers. Rogers was determined to catch and hang Rackham and his crew, including the two women. Anne was now beside her lover at the exact time when he became a marked man by the Bahamas' governor, the Royal Navy, and British forces throughout the Caribbean.

Governor Rogers was tough as nails, having waged war on the Spanish for years. He also was a famed seaman and navigator, having circumnavigated the globe at only age 29. But the old privateer, who had once profited from what was effectively piracy, was especially hard on women who violated social norms or customs. He had almost ordered a public water-ducking of one "snobbish lady" of Nassau. What was clear was that the hard-bitten Governor Rogers would not hesitate to order Anne's execution if she were caught. Without realizing it, Anne Bonny had all but signed her own death warrant when she sailed out of Nassau Harbor on the *William*.[206]

Upon first learning from Captain Ham, the *William*'s owner, that his magnificent ship had been hijacked in the night, the governor immediately ordered a swift sloop from Nassau Harbor with 45 men to set sail on September 2 in pursuit of Rackham and the *William*, three days before he issued his proclamation. This was a calculated move to get a jump on the Rackham crew before they were aware of his proclamation. To increase the odds of capturing Rackham, Rogers then ordered a second, more formidable sloop, armed with a dozen cannons and 54 veteran seamen, in pursuit of the *William*.[207]

Thanks to popular views, stereotypes, and common assumptions, modern historians and writers have fully embraced the myth of the ferocious Amazon at sea to perpetuate the traditional romantic fiction. But in truth, these widely denounced "vicious brutes," bloodthirsty psychopaths, and the "worst" criminals among the pirates were definitely not Anne Bonny or Mary Read. Contrary to these romantic myths, they were only two young women, who sought better lives and a measure of respect and equality for themselves in a harsh world.[208]

VII

ONE FINAL CRUISE AND ANNE'S LAST DAYS OF INNOCENCE
1720

AS GOVERNOR ROGERS sent forth his heavily armed sloops in pursuit of the *William*, Captain Rackham was not aware of the seriousness of the new threat, after sailing away from Nassau. Instead, eager to test the *William*'s highly touted speed and firepower, the ambitious pirate captain was once again focused on taking prizes. In his view, and quite correctly, nowhere in the Caribbean was more choice for taking fat prizes than along Jamaica's north coast. Governor Nicholas Lawes revealed as much when he wrote to London authorities in a 1718 letter, complaining of the situation that drew the opportunistic Captain Rackham like a magnet: "There is hardly any ship or vessel coming in or going out of this island that is not plundered" by pirates.[209]

Just off the coast of Jamaica, 130 miles west of what is Haiti today, Captain Rackham and his crew met with one easy success after another, as expected. During "their cruize [sic] they took a great number of ships belonging to Jamaica, and other parts of the West Indies, bound to and

---

Opposite: Saint Ann Bay, Jamaica

Above: England's jewel of the Caribbean, Jamaica.

from England."[210] The highly maneuverable sloop cut through the Caribbean's tranquil waters like a knife.

While the *William* pushed closer to Jamaica, Anne most likely sensed that only good times lay ahead for her and Captain Rackham. As back in Nassau, before she had joined in the ship's easy capture, Anne now no longer masqueraded as a man. Despite old sailor superstitions dating back centuries, the crew accepted the fact that Jack and Anne were a loving couple with nothing to hide. Nevertheless, Anne continued to be viewed as deserving of equality and respect, after having proved to be a capable sailor and pirate: an undeniable reality most recently demonstrated by her active role in the stealthy capture of the *William*. Anne alternated between wearing female attire when off duty, such as eating dinner with the crew or at night with Rackham, and when working aboard ship. Instead of wearing a nondescript hat to hide her feminine facial features as during her first voyage, she now merely wore a bandana like a head scarf—traditional women's apparel—to keep her long hair out of her face.

Unaware of Governor Rogers' proclamation and his dispatching of the two swift sloops in pursuit, Jack, Anne and Mary were now on their final cruise together, which would last less than three months. Jack Rackham and his gang of pirates spent day after day onboard the *William* in "scouring the harbours and inlets to north and west parts of Jamaica."

Here, by moving swiftly and relying on the element of surprise, Rackham "took several small craft, which proved a great booty to the rovers, but they had but few men and therefore they were obliged to run at low game, till they could increase their company."[211]

As if united by some unseen bond that only seafarers understood, the crew acted as one in ensuring that their ship continued to operate like a well-oiled machine. In part explaining the depth of this maternal-like bond, this beautiful ship was looked upon by Rackham's seafarers like an actual living being with a beating heart and immortal soul. Breaking all ties with the past, Captain Rackham, Anne, Mary, and the other crew members had entirely separated from the hypocrisies and inequalities of the land-based world that was now intent on destroying them. In this sense, this final cruise off Jamaica was the fulfillment of Anne's brightest dreams.

By the beginning of September 1720, Rackham had his way along the northeast coast of Jamaica, taking what he wanted, including "a certain Sloop of an unknown Name" on September 1st. Governor Rogers' pursuers were still nowhere to be seen, fueling a false confidence among the Rackham crew. Captain Rackham also saw no organized pursuit streaming from the ports of Jamaica. However, this situation was no accident. He had smartly avoided the busier south side of Jamaica, especially the eastern region. Here, Spanish Town, St. Catherine Province, Kingstown (now called Kingston), and Port Royal, the former great buccaneer haven, made the island's southeast side too dangerous. Located on the southeastern coast just southeast of Spanish Town, Kingstown and Port Royal in particular needed to be avoided at all costs.

Most of the Royal Navy's vessels remained absent from Jamaica's north coast, though, and Captain Rackham was gambling that it would stay that way. However, the overall pickings along the north coast, so far away from Spanish Town, Port Royal, and Kingston, were relatively slim. He captured mostly fishing vessels, but no large merchant vessels laden with booty. In search of more profitable waters that meant taking greater risks, Captain Rackham changed the *William*'s course, heading north around Cuba's eastern end and then north toward the northwestern coast of the Eleuthera Islands, northwest of New Providence Island. Stealing small-time pirate plunder instead of riches, from September 1 to

September 3, Rackham and his crew "took seven or eight fishing boats in Harbour Island [in the Bahamas], stole their nets and other tackle . . . ."[212] The confiscation of tackle—the ship's invaluable lines, ropes, and pulleys—revealed one of the basic realities of pirate life by the late summer of 1720 that sharply contradicted romantic myths—that the gains of the average pirate captain and his crew in the Caribbean at this time were much less spectacular than assumed.

Indeed, as verified in Jamaican court records that revealed Jack's and Anne's last voyage: "on the Third Day of September [and] with Force and Arms, &c. upon the High Sea, in a certain Place, distant about Two Leagues from Harbour-Island did piratically, feloniously, and in a hostile manner, attack, engage, and take, Seven certain Fishing-Boats" of "Fishermen." Here, Rackham's pirates then did "take, and carry away the Fish, and Fishing-Tackle, the value of Ten pounds, of Current Money of Jamaica, the Goods and Chattels [Slaves] of the aforesaid Fisherman . . . ."[213]

Revealing that it was too dangerous to go ashore either in Jamaica or the Bahamas (the realm of Governor Rogers) as opposed to Cuba, Rackham's crew were concerned about acquiring necessities for simple survival and to sustain the crew's daily existence (freshly caught fish), so that the cruise could continue unabated for consecutive weeks or even months if necessary. Therefore, capturing even the smallest fishing vessel and other light craft was important in sustaining the Rackham crew over a lengthy period. Most of these local Bahamian boats were large cedar canoes, which were popular with fishermen throughout the West Indies and were sufficiently large to hold 25 to 30 people. Such non-glamorous, but absolutely essential, prizes provided what was needed for everyday existence on a pirate ship: tobacco, nets, food, carpenter's tools, candles, ropes, sails, rigging, sewing kits, weapons, or a much-coveted jug of fresh water, Jamaican rum, or homemade wine.[214]

The timely capture of tackle around Harbour Island, a flat, three-and-a-half-mile-long island on Eleuthera's northeast edge, was necessary for Captain Rackham and his crew to stay out at sea on a lengthy cruise to evade capture. Anything and everything that allowed the crew to function effectively during an extended cruise was utilized by Anne and her comrades to the fullest. But Anne had other concerns than simply enjoying a relatively small measure of domesticity with Rackham

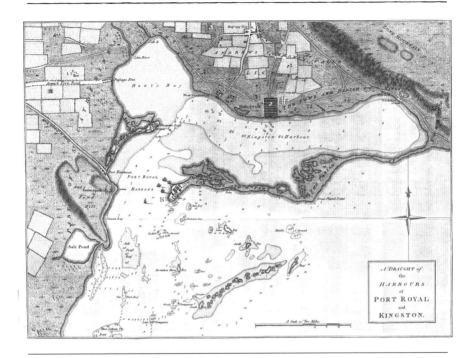

Above: Port Royal and Kingston, Jamaica, 1774.

on the pirate ship. Unlike Mary, who was already a combat veteran of fighting in Europe during imperial conflicts, Anne might well have felt the need to sharpen her skills with cutlass and pistol. If so, then Anne's preparations were timely.

Once he eventually learned the disturbing intelligence in Bahamian waters, evidently from a Harbour Island resident, that Governor Rogers had dispatched two heavily armed sloops to hunt him down, Rackham immediately departed, charting a new course to less dangerous waters. With sails raised high from tall wooden masts, the Rackham crew now headed southeast at full speed for the French side of the island of Hispaniola, Saint-Domingue, today's Haiti. Captain Rackham now ranked at the top of Governor Rogers' targets for systematic elimination, because of his multiple crimes: taking Governor Rogers' pardon in May 1719, and then breaking his word; slipping the anchor and stealing the *William* out of Nassau Harbor barely a year later and within sight of the governor's stately mansion; and now going on a wide-ranging raiding spree.

Moving swiftly with favorable winds ballooning its canvas sails, Rackham's sloop maintained a steady southeastern course. With supplies growing shorter and provisions lower with each passing day, Rackham decided to land a small party at some isolated shoreline to resupply the ship, but only for a brief period of time. And no place was better to fulfill this vital requirement than Saint-Domingue, which was rich with luminous inlets.

However, during such a lengthy cruise, and especially when targeted by pirate hunters, the most pressing problem faced by Captain Rackham was how to supply his crew with provisions and rations. But in attempting to outrun any pursuing British ships if they suddenly appeared, such a situation eliminated the possibility of any additional landings to gain supplies. Unlike Rackham's vessel, a Royal Navy ship could sail for long periods of time with a disciplined crew fed by large supplies of rations, thanks to an efficient commissary system, logistical network, and quartermaster corps to ensure a regular flow of rations.

But in contrast, an isolated pirate ship roving the Caribbean's waters was entirely on its own, without a logistical support system. The Rackham crew now paid the high price for operating so far outside the structured system of supporting life at sea when it came to crucial necessities, from rations to medical treatment. Rackham's pirates could only survive by taking provisions from captured ships or by landing to steal, or buy, trade, or hunt. Once ashore, after a beef or hog was shot down, hunting parties of pirates smoked meat for preservation or foraged for fruit, such as oranges, grapes, and mangoes. Captured vessels provided not only necessities for simple existence, but also luxuries unattainable to the lower classes. Everything taken either ashore or on land was divided fairly and equally, in contrast to the inequitable, feudal-like systems that had long existed between haves and have-nots. Anne and Mary received an equal share, because they were accepted as equals by their male cohorts.

Taking a nice prize often meant that the weak beer, watered-down wine, and stale rations on the pirate ship were replaced by robust wines from Italy and Madeira and rich foods of wealthy aristocrats. In between capturing prizes and raids onshore to obtain provisions, rations among the pirate crews were almost always not only in short supply, but also of overall poor quality as the time passed between taking prizes and going ashore. On Hispaniola, the earliest Spanish settlers had first brought hogs, goats, and cattle to the island, and now large numbers of these animals roamed wild in the island's primeval tropical forests. Here, Rackham crew members "landed, and took cattle away, with two or three French men they found near the waterside, hunting of wild hogs in the evening."[215]

With the fresh food, sides of pork and beef—both fresh for immediate consumption and smoked for the lengthy journey—and other supplies, especially good drinking water, obtained on Hispaniola, the Rackham crew very likely created a well-known pirate dish—a spicy and "hearty concoction called salmagundi." Most likely, an experienced cook accompanied the Rackham crew, and he knew how to make the popular dish enjoyed by pirates of all nationalities and races. Salmagundi was a popular dish that consisted of meat, fruit, and vegetables, such as cabbage and onions. Garlic and other flavorful spices were added for seasoning to create this spicy dish relished by hungry pirates.[216] Because unlike a well-staffed commissary department of the Royal Navy, the pirates had no way, other than the lengthy process of smoking meat, to preserve food for a lengthy voyage, Rackham probably purchased or traded for meat previously smoked by others. During wide-ranging voyages, it was almost always a case of feast or famine for pirate crews, and now the Rackham crew enjoyed one feast on the *William* off the coast of Saint-Domingue.

Shortly thereafter, on October 1, after leaving the bountiful island, good fortune suddenly smiled on the *William* and the Rackham crew about three leagues from Hispaniola. Jack struck at the opportunity suddenly presented to him when he closed in on two merchant vessels. Then, when near their victims, the pirates of the *William* fired a shot from his cannon and shouted defiance, intimidating the captains and crews. Rackham easily captured the two heavily loaded merchant sloops, which were evidently French vessels sailing either in or out of Saint-Domingue ports, such as Port-de-Paix or beautiful Cap-Français—known as "Le Cap" and the Paris of the West Indies—on the north coast. Jack Rackham's pirates then boarded the two vessels, taking what they needed from the two prizes. The booty partly consisted of "the Apparel and Tackle . . . of the Value of One Thousand Pounds of Current Money of Jamaica."

If the Rackham crew had discriminating tastes, it's possible that they invited a Frenchman of Saint-Domingue aboard the *William*, as they later would, and perhaps as a cook. If Anne was Catholic like most other people in County Cork, Ireland, she would have had a fellow Catholic aboard if a Frenchman joined the crew.[217]

JAMAICA BECKONS ONE LAST TIME

Departing Saint-Domingue, Jack Rackham headed in a new direction, turning his sights on Jamaica, where he hoped he had been forgotten—by not only Governor Rogers, who had made Rackham the most wanted man in the Caribbean at this time, but also by Jamaican authorities.[218]

But Rackham was not forgotten by his victims. The string of successes destined to be reaped by the young captain along the north coast of Jamaica for nearly a month would prove to be Rackham's (and Anne's) undoing in the end. Captain Rackham found the easy pickings as anticipated while scouring Jamaica's north coast in early and mid-October. Indeed, "they took a great number of ships belonging to Jamaica, and other parts of the West Indies, bound to and from England."[219]

Seemingly a good omen, another prize was taken by the Rackham crew on October 19th at the island's northeast edge. On "the high sea" located just outside the crescent-shaped bay of Port Maria, Rackham captured the double-masted schooner captained by Thomas Spenlow, carrying a load of goods that included 50 rolls of tobacco but no gold, jewels, or silver. Instead, they took "the Apparel and Tackle" worth "Twenty Pounds of Current Money of Jamaica." From Spenlow's crew, two Frenchmen, John Besneck and Peter Cornelian, were taken aboard the *William*. Here, just east of the larger bay and the picturesque town of Ocho Rios, Port Maria was an old buccaneer haunt. Henry Morgan had employed the heavily forested high ground of the commanding ridge on the west side of Port Maria as a lookout point, which was known as Firefly.[220]

With Anne by his side, Rackham might have been hoping to eventually emulate the life of Captain Morgan by capturing a bountiful prize that would be the haul of a lifetime. Morgan had gained riches, respect, and power on this same tropical island, Jamaica, serving as governor un-

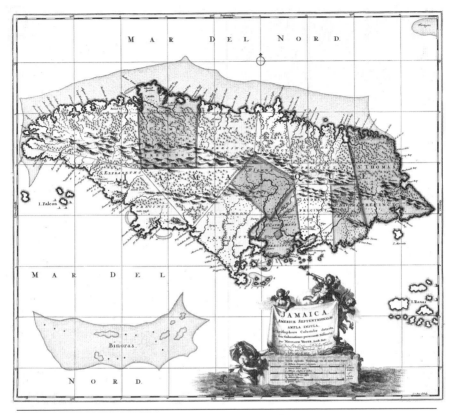

Above: The lucrative sugar island of Jamaica.

til his retirement in 1682. Then, he had lived the greatest pirate dream: the easy, pampered life of a landed, wealthy gentleman and elite member of the Jamaican plantocracy. However, what Rackham and his other pirates failed to realize at this time was that Morgan's lavish lifestyle had been as fatal as a Spanish cannonball, dooming him to an early death at age 53. After having led some of the boldest military expeditions in Western history, Morgan had continued to drink heavily in the smoky taverns and on his sugar cane plantation, as during his younger days. It took a deadly cocktail of fine liquors and rich foods to lay low the most legendary English buccaneer leader, but high living finally accomplished what no Spanish commander could. Anne, with much more modest ambitions than the legendary Morgan, now aimed for simple survival.[221]

In the tradition of the democratic brotherhood of the sea, the Rackham crew ultimately decided by vote as to where they would cruise next: a risky course along the north coast of Jamaica. It was always safer for pirates to hit and run, then change course to play it safe. However, the string of easy successes along the northern coast of Jamaica bestowed a sense of overconfidence among the captain and his crew, and instead, they kept moving west in almost a straight line, in search for new opportunities and prizes. During this cruise, the *William* benefitted from the east-west winds, which had been a factor in the crew's decision.

Even if Captain Rackham felt that this course of action was unwise, he lacked the authority to enforce his own opinion, no matter if wiser, in the democratic tradition of pirate society where decision-making was a shared experience among all crew members. If the two women, Mary and Anne, had disagreed with their fellow crew members, then they were in a minority. And if so, then the two women were overruled by the common will and consensus, often after free-spirited debate, which prevailed in the decision-making process that allowed the smooth functioning of pirate society, especially during lengthy cruises.[222]

By this time, in the early autumn of 1720, Captain Rackham and his crew were taking a great risk, although they were not aware of it. First, they had sailed too lazily and lingered too long off the north coast of Jamaica, which was England's largest and most strategic Caribbean island, and second, they were too near one of the busiest sea lanes, where merchant and slave ships often sailed.

From the south side near St. Jago de la Vega (today's Spanish Town) and with Port Royal and Kingston serving as active Royal Navy stations, British warships culled these very waters that the confident Rackham crew now sailed. What could no longer be denied was the fact that it was especially dangerous for Rackham to cruise too slowly and linger just off the coast of Jamaica for an extended period of time, as the secret to pirate survival was to never remain too long in one place or to sail in the same predictable direction day after day, and especially week after week.

This golden rule was now even more pressing when the crew was being pursued, and especially when so near the largest home port of the mighty British Navy in the Caribbean, Kingston. What the Rackham crew needed most was to find an isolated backwater that was little known by

Above: Jamaica long served as the center of English power in the Caribbean.

privateers or the Royal Navy and hide out there. The ship could then be stashed in a secluded cove on a remote island far from Jamaica and Nassau, buying precious time.[223] But Captain Rackham and his crew were not prudent or cautious during this October, when they continued to lust after additional prizes. But greed and confidence, if not hubris, rather than good judgment and reason now pushed the *William* steadily toward the setting sun.

But by this time while sailing along Jamaica's north coast, what Anne Bonny was now part of was the end of an era: the Golden Age of Piracy. Pirating in the Caribbean by October 1720 now resulted in little more than an occasional capture of small fishing boats and canoes. Booty now consisted of taking the possessions of common people, who were not unlike the pirates themselves—both socially and economically—and attempting only to survive by harvesting from the sea. Jamaica's lengthy north coast was one of Jack Rackham's favorite hunting grounds: After he had unseated Captain Vane by democratic means as the leader of the unhappy crew of the *Kingston* back in November 1718, less than two years earlier, Rackham had taken his first prizes off Jamaica's northwestern coast. At that time, he had first envisioned what was possible for him to achieve as an aggressive pirate captain. But instead, "Rackham's coasting the island [eventually] proved fatal to him" in the end.[224]

ADDITIONAL OCTOBER SUCCESSES

Located about midpoint along the island's length and situated at the east end of St. Ann's Parish, which was nestled between St. Mary Parish to the east and St. James Parish to the west, Ocho Rios was one of the most beautiful bays in Jamaica. It was here that the Captain Rackham crew suddenly struck again like a Caribbean tropical storm. Jack ordered the firing of one cannon to frighten the crew of their victim ship; the fiery blast from the gun, perhaps fired by Anne herself, sent the crew scurrying for safety and heading for the shore in rowboats. He then took the sloop without a fight or the loss of a single crewman—always the primary concern for a good pirate captain. Then the rampaging pirates captured a large fishing canoe that was lying on the beach of the wide bay of Ocho Rios. Here, on the white sands surrounded by green hills overlooking the beautiful bay, Captain Rackham and his crew went ashore. Anne, Mary and their fellow pirates were near Dunn's River Falls, which spilled down from the jungle-covered hillside to the sea and would have been a good opportunity to take on water from the mountain springs.

Then, upon setting sail after securing what was needed for the next leg of their voyage along Jamaica's north coast, the Rackham crew came across another large fishing canoe, one that contained "some Stock and Provisions," whereupon the pirates ransacked the vessel and took "most of the Things that were in her." The fact that Captain Rackham and his men spared the fishing canoe's occupants, especially one Dorothy Thomas, was a decision that would eventually prove to be a grave mistake. The havoc that the crew was wreaking on Jamaica's north side was about to become a matter of serious concern to government officials at the highest leadership level in Jamaica.

Either one of the owners of this fishing canoe or a messenger now headed across the forested hills of St. Catherine Parish on the double to Spanish Town, almost directly south of Ocho Rios, to inform the gov-

Above: Anne Bonny and Mary Read in the heat of combat.

ernor of Captain Rackham's activities on the north coast. Eager to end Rackham's plundering, an incensed Governor Nicholas Lawes immediately sent a well-manned sloop "round the island in quest of him."[225]

Captain Rackham and his crewmen had violated a basic axiom for survival, especially by the early autumn of 1720: not to become unduly careless and to always maintain prudence as past experience had long demonstrated, despite the string of successes and the thrill of the chase. After sailing out of Ocho Rios Bay, the *William* headed west past Point Fortaleza and continued along the north coast. Jamaica's lengthy shoreline seemed to draw the sloop ever westward toward the setting sun. But the plentiful rum, bright Caribbean sunshine, and picturesque scenery acted almost like a sleep-inducing tonic, reducing the crew's voyage to a crawl and dropping caution to a new low. Seemingly forgotten by the pirates, the key strategy for survival in the Caribbean was based on the availability of "so many uninhabited little islands and key, with harbours convenient . . . where, if they carry in but strong liquor, they indulge a time, and become ready for new expeditions before any intelligence can reach [the authorities] to hurt them."[226]

But Rackham and his prize-hungry crew continued to audaciously, foolishly violate the most basic and fundamental premises in the refined art of staying alive by sailing lazily under the sunny skies. No member of the *William*, especially Anne Bonny, contemplated the ugly reality that the largest hanging in American history had already taken place in late October 1718, when the gentlemanly pirate captain Stede Bonnet had met his untimely end. This pirate captain of the gentry class who loved his scholarly books more than rum and perfume-soaked prostitutes, along with 30 of his men, who represented a wide variety of nationalities, were hanged in Charles Town thanks to their lack of caution.

Captain Bonnet and his crew had committed the ultimate pirate sin of simply staying "too long" along the Carolina coast, and it meant their capture and execution before a jeering crowd. The fact that so many pirates had been hanged only two years before should have given everyone on the *William* great cause for concern. But that cautionary tale was ignored by Rackham and his crew, as they had been easily seduced by their successes.

After sailing past Runaway Bay, which had been named for slaves who had escaped the hellish sugar plantations and paddled north in desperate attempts to flee to Cuba's safety, Rackham's sloop continued to steadily sail west, passing a little place on the north coast known as Dry Bagg by the locals and pushing toward Discovery Bay, which was called Dry Harbour Bay at the time. Here, just east of the mouth of the Rio Bueno River, where it entered the sea, Rackham and the crew spied another prize.

This next target was the single-masted merchant sloop, the *Mary and Sarah*, which was anchored just inside the bay of blue about one league (three nautical miles) from shore. All hands flew to the assigned positions and battle stations, and Jack's ship descended upon its unaware victim. Jack ordered a cannon fired from the *William*, and with Thomas Dillon, who commanded the sloop, and some of the crew fleeing in row-boats to reach the shore, the captain ordered additional shots fired to reveal a more menacing threat. After being told that they were "English pirates" and no harm would come to him, a fellow Englishman, Thomas Dillon, then came aboard the *William*.

Relieved to be alive, Thomas met Jack and witnessed Anne and Mary in full pirate garb. Jack then "took the sloop and lading," another easy capture by the young captain, who only grew bolder with each new success. The pirates "did steal and carry away the sloop and her tackle." Indeed, the pirates stole "Apparel and Tackle . . . of the value of Three hundred pounds, of Current Money of Jamaica"—a nice haul.

Heady over their recent successes, the pirate crew continued to push west as the north coast continued to be just too lucrative to quit, sailing past the mouth of the Rio Bueno, which was distinguished by its "pretty harbour." Isolated and remote, Rio Bueno was an ideal "port of call," because it was small and had a friendly, ubiquitous tavern—always the pirates' delight. If the pirates went ashore to visit the small fishing community, then it was for only a short time to obtain fresh supplies. Then, after departing the vicinity of Rio Bueno, the *William* continued west.

Making good time, the *William* sailed past the small town of Falmouth, in today's Trelawny Parish, whose Anglican Parish Church steeple could be seen towering above the heart of town nestled on the coastal plain from the ship's wooden deck. Large stately mansions and sugar works dotted the landscape along the northern coastal plain that had grown prosperous from the sugar boom, along with the hurricane-resistant stone tower windmills, which crushed sugar cane stalks. Captain Rackham's sloop pushed farther west along the coast, passing a little inlet called Dunn's Hole, located in St. James Parish only a few miles east of Montego Bay. Dunn's Hole once had been known as Manatee Hole.

While heading west, the *William* flew a distinctive "white pennant"— a clever ruse of Captain Rackham's. The black flag, or the Jolly Roger, "with Death laughing," was only raised upon encountering a prize: often a successful way to intimidate a captain and civilian crew into handing over the ship without a fight in order to preserve pirate lives and precious reserves of gunpowder. When attacking a prize, Rackham also flew a flag which was distinctive and unique to his crew only: a white skull with two crossed swords underneath on a black field. The famous banner was created for the express purpose of inducing panic among the pirate's intended victims and forcing a hasty capitulation. This flag proved effective in plying the waters of the Bahamas and Jamaica, paying nice dividends. Each time a prize was targeted, the black flag was raised.

Finally, the north coast of the green island came to an abrupt end at Jamaica's extreme western tip and the pirate ship began to shift south along the coast of Hanover Parish, "rounding the island, and drawing near the westernmost point of Jamaica, called Point Negril," Jamaica.[227] This quiet place had been known as Punta Negril, as designated by the Spanish, when in September 1662 an English fleet, including a warship captained by a young Henry Morgan, had sailed out of Port Royal and anchored in another autumn at this point, before launching still another devastating buccaneer raid on the Spanish. The *William* turned south after passing Orange Bay and headed toward Negril Bay, located just north of Negril Point, which jutted out like a knife into the water.[228] The natural harbor, an ideal port for sailing ships, was bordered by a lengthy white sand beach that curved in a giant semicircle.

Unfortunately for Rackham and his followers, the beauty of this secluded place at Jamaica's western end eased what relatively little caution remained among an increasingly undisciplined crew of pirates. Negril Bay offered a quiet haven, or so it seemed. Here, about two and a half months after having departed Nassau, weary crew members could finally drop anchor and rest, relax, and thoroughly enjoy themselves.

Overconfident Jack Rackham was not demonstrating the qualities of a good captain, except in skillfully maneuvering the ship and adapting to the nuances of the north coast and its inlets. He now ignored the fact that this beautiful and seductive natural harbor was in essence a potential trap which might prove fatal. If a royal warship, or other pirate-hunting ships such as specially commissioned privateers, sailed into the harbor, then the *William* would be in serious trouble. An approaching vessel would not come from the far distant horizon to the west, where it could be seen, but would turn sharply into the harbor from either north or south. Because of visibility reduced by geography, Rackham's ship could become easily trapped inside Negril Bay. In addition, because the heavily forested hills to the east blocked the prevailing westerly winds, only a light breeze would be available, insufficient to fill canvas sails, preventing a quick escape from the bay.

But these concerns were not entertained by the Rackham crew. They had let their guard down; the captain and his sailors only wanted to celebrate their remarkable good fortune in having sailed unscathed across most of Jamaica's north coast without encountering serious trouble. In a good mood that indicated another round of heavy drinking and relaxation had begun before the anchor was dropped, the pirates had no idea that their luck had already run out. Even then, the most efficient pirate hunter in Jamaica and his privateer sloop was now rapidly descending upon Negril Bay.

Then, all of a sudden, the pirates spied a periagua (also known as a perianger in English) landing on the white sands of Negril Bay, and they watched its panicked crew spill onto the beach. They consisted of a motley, but heavily armed, group of men, some of whom had been born in England, including Thomas Quick, John Eaton, Edward Warner, and Thomas Baker. To explain their activities, these nine men later employed the lame excuse that they were out "a-turtling," which involved securing the highly coveted meat of the large marine turtle both for local consumption and for sale.

Working together, these men had recently purchased the canoe-like periagua for this specific purpose, or so they claimed. Easy to capture when stranded on the beach or when females laid their eggs in the sand, these turtles were a staple food for islanders. In fact, these eagerly sought reptiles were the "favorite dish" for both the Elizabethan buccaneers of a bygone privateering age and the relatively few remaining pirates of the Golden Age of Piracy. Most important, captured sea turtles could be kept alive aboard ship during a lengthy cruise and later slaughtered at will, creating a reserve of meat, which was always in short supply.

Meanwhile, Jack opened up discussions with the band of nine men. When asked why he was not now flying his black pirate flag, the pirate captain answered from the *William*'s railing that they were fellow Englishmen, to calm fears that they might be Spanish or French pirates, who especially enjoyed cutting non-Catholic throats. He then invited the crew of the periagua aboard to "drink a bowl of punch." As he knew, this was an offer that they could not refuse. Of course, the wily pirate captain was hoping to do more than barter for fresh food or other provisions. The captain badly needed extra crewmen.

However, Captain Rackham had not been successful in gaining additional manpower during this cruise, and new recruitment now remained a top priority. Therefore, Rackham dispatched a "canoe" to pick up the always rum-thirsty Englishmen, who were more than eager to have a drink. Shortly, the nine men boarded the sloop *William*, after having left their periagua anchored near the shore.[229]

The Rackham crew then continued to compound its already long list of mistakes and miscalculations, committing the ultimate folly of drinking for too long and letting their guard down even more. The pirates and their new friends from the old country were united in a full-fledged party aboard the *William*: the same mistake made by an equally overconfident Blackbeard in Ocracoke Inlet back in November 1718, which cost him his head.

This type of irresponsible behavior was actually nothing out of the ordinary, especially when major decisions were left in the hands of the common seamen instead of wisely made by an experienced captain with unquestioned authority, as on a British warship or merchant ship. Despite all his charisma and big talk, Jack Rackham was actually more of a small-time sea raider than a captain of legend. What Jack and his crew had failed to fully take into account were not only the repercussions stemming from their recent successes along the north coast, but also that everything had changed by this time. Now the Royal Navy and privateers, or pirate hunters, were pursuing their prey more aggressively than ever before. The people of Jamaica, whose interests and jobs were now based on commerce and the vibrancy of the plantation economy, had also changed their attitudes about piracy. They were now more eager to report the whereabouts of pirates, thanks also to the governor's liberal offers of rewards.

Completely oblivious to these new changes, what was now most important to Captain Rackham and his crew at this time at Negril Point was relaxation and consumption of large amounts of punch, the preferred intoxicant of most pirates, far more than the finest wines. Consisting of a mixture of rum, lime juice, sugar, and water, gallons of punch were poured in a large bowl, into which the thirsty pirates dipped their goblets.

Hampered by having only a small crew of around a dozen members, Jack Rackham was doing his best to recruit new pirates, and punch was the most effective recruitment tool. These Englishmen were armed "with muskets and cutlasses," which were certainly not needed against helpless turtles. Jack surmised that some of these Englishmen, if not all, almost certainly had been pirates themselves at some point. He knew that offering to share the "punch" was the best way to secure experienced members for the *William*'s depleted crew—this cocktail had long "accompanied every aspect of pirate life," and now the meeting at Negril Bay was no different. Here, the Rackham crew and their nine friends relaxed with no thought of encroaching danger, enjoying the traditional "bowl of punch," heavily spiked with a disproportionate amount of dark Jamaican rum.[230]

For the common pirates, the term "punch" evoked memories of good times beyond just mindless inebriation. For sex-starved male pirates, the busy brothels of Nassau were known as "punch houses." The popular pirate's punch was made so strong that it was completely debilitating when guzzled in large quantities. For ample good reason, this potent rum punch—stemming from the Dutch name for rum, *Kilduijvel*—was called "kill-devil" by the English and Celtic pirates. Jamaica's former governor, Sir Thomas Modyford, who had dispatched Morgan to wreak havoc among the Spanish across the Caribbean, described how "the Spaniards wondered much at the sickness of our people, until they knew the strength of their drinks, but then wondered more that they were not all dead."[231] As if the potency of the alcohol was not sufficiently lethal, the lead containers, or pipes, that carried rum and other spirits were also killers. In drinking so much alcohol, the pirates were actually "slowly poisoned" by the "rum bullion," as they christened it, stored in the lead containers.[232]

Perhaps like the unrestrained Blackbeard during his final ill-fated drinking bout back at his Ocracoke Inlet haven, Jack Rackham and his crew drank heavily of pirate's punch on this fateful evening, numbing their senses and awareness. Significantly, Anne was not part of the drunken revelry. She remained sober and watchful, just in case trouble developed, or maybe having been directed to stand watch. But the male crew members of the *William* were now doing more than simply celebrating their recent successes along Jamaica's north coast. In fact, the more realistic pirates were attempting to drown out and wash away a most unpleasant, nagging reality that could not be readily dismissed, especially when sober: the good times were dying.

Evidently, the men of the Rackham crew and the alleged turtle hunters engaged in a friendly competition as to which group could consume the most punch and show the least effects of drunkenness. As Blackbeard realized just before his head was hung from a ship's bow as a trophy, Captain Rackham and his crew were now on borrowed time.

By this time, members of the Rackham crew perhaps already knew as much, because almost everyone—except Anne and Mary—seemed to be living for the moment at Negril Bay. Disciplined crews and veteran captains had been systematically eliminated one pirate crew after another across the Caribbean. By this time, nothing could now stop these experienced seamen, England's finest, from exterminating the last remaining pirates, and it was only a matter of time before the Rackham crew was next. Blackbeard had already learned the folly of hoping to retire and live like a gentleman for his life's remainder, because this lofty ambition had been already too late for him and the ever-dwindling bands of other pirates still roaming the Caribbean.[233]

Jack Rackham and his men continued to drink excessively on this warm evening in Negril Bay, as if this celebration was their last, which was precisely the case. Anne had most likely never heard that in 1683, less than two decades before she was born, the British Admiralty had become excessively brutal, once England had turned against piracy because of the toll taken on shipping profits, indicating that efforts were already well underway to end the thriving Golden Age of Piracy. The British Admiralty had authorized the branding with a hot iron on the cheeks of captured pirates with the letter P. Therefore, if Anne was captured and such a sentence was carried out by the High Court of the Admiralty, she would be left with a disfiguring scar and a grim reminder of youthful folly.[234] As well, in March 1718, 13 of Blackbeard's crew had been hanged in Virginia's capital of Williamsburg, which would be echoed later that year with the execution of Captain Bonnet and his 30 men. But even if Anne had known about this brutal treatment dealt out to captured pirates, this would have been the least of her concerns by this time.

But this was only the beginning of the thorough decimation of the pirate crews. In late March 1722, the largest mass hanging in the history of piracy would take place at Cape Coast Castle, West Africa. At that time, Captain Bartholomew "Black Bart" Roberts, a former slaver, and 52 members of his crew would be hanged. It was well that these pirates had lived their lives to the fullest. Indeed, they had briefly lived well, dressed in fine clothing, drank the finest wine and liquor, ate like kings at a banquet, and chased whores to their hearts' delight. The pirates' creed of a short but merry life had now become a cruel Faustian bargain, which had to be paid in full to God, fate, and vengeful authorities.[235] In the end, there was no more romance or glory in the pirate's life for the more than 80 of the young men and boys of the Blackbeard and Bonnet crews, who died before a crowd of hecklers.

Here, in Negril Bay, the inevitable had finally happened, in the blink of an eye. Carelessness finally caught up to young Captain Rackham, who had long defied the odds. A swift-moving privateer—Captain Jonathan Barnet, chosen personally by Governor Lawes himself to exterminate pirates—had been methodically dogging Jack's trail for some time along the north coast of Jamaica. Unlike the unrestrained pirates, no excessive drinking now muddled the minds of either the experienced privateer captain or his disciplined crew. Day after day, this relentless hunter had sailed into each cove and inlet along Jamaica's north coast, expecting to catch Rackham and the *William* by surprise. Only when he had stopped sailing south in following the coast and then turned sharply east into Negril Bay had Captain Barnet won the game.

A startling new realization—that he was now the prey—came only too belatedly to the surprised Jack Rackham and the long-complacent *William* crew. The captain's past successes had set the stage for the crew's final downfall in Negril Bay, because having committed the folly of spending too much time in leisurely "coasting the island in this manner, proved fatal to him" and his crew.[236]

Therefore, the greatest threat suddenly appeared not on the distant horizon but in the confines of Negril Bay itself. The Rackham crew could not have been more unprepared, but in contrast, Captain Barnet was ready. Upon first glance, Jack realized that this was no ordinary threat that had suddenly emerged. Barnet was just the kind of sea captain that

Bartholomew Roberts doodgebleeven.

Above: Captain Bartholomew "Black Bart" Roberts in all his glory.

made for Rackham's worst nightmares: a well "known and experienced Stout Brisk Man," who had been hunting down pirates with a ruthless efficiency for the governor since 1715. And now, moving swiftly into the quiet waters of Negril Bay, Barnet's relentless hunt for Rackham and his small crew was over. He had now found them, thanks to the advantages of greater speed, fully loaded cannons, and "a good number of hands." In addition, Captain Barnet now had a good chance of nabbing the new English pirate recruits, only just seduced by Rackham to come aboard the *William.*

Rackham's demise was inevitable, because Barnet was the governor's point man, the tip of the spear. Governor Lawes had only recently gained significant intelligence about Captain Rackham's activities in Jamaican waters, beginning with his October capture of the sloop at Ocho Rios, and later the pirate captain's strange lack of vigilance, as if British warships and privateers were thousands of miles away. The Jamaican occupants of the canoe who escaped the pirates' clutches at Ocho Rios had then notified Governor Lawes.

And now Jack's eerily quiet sloop seemed to Captain Barnet like a ghost ship on the smooth surface of Negril Bay. Was the silent state of this ship merely a ploy orchestrated by the Captain Rackham to draw Captain Barnet nearer, before opening up with a broadside at close range? After all, the pirates in these waters had long thrived on such trickery and cunning to survive. But in fact, this was no trick. The men of the Rackham crew had been drinking liberally from their large communal "bowl of punch" and smoking fine tobacco, with their nine new friends, when they were surprised by the unexpected arrival of the heavily armed privateer sloop, which now cut through the calm waters of Negril Bay with flags flying high.[237]

Belatedly jolted into action upon catching sight of the fast-moving sloop, Jack was shocked upon ascertaining its large number of cannons. Even more, his crew discovered to their horror that "she stood directly towards her." A stunned Jack screamed orders to raise the anchor and the sails to make a desperate attempt to escape into that vast expanse of open sea that lay beyond Negril Point. However, it was almost already too late for an escape attempt by this time. Nevertheless, Captain Rackham knew that he now had no choice but to try to make a run for it to escape Negril Bay or he would be hanged.

Fortunately, the extra manpower of the recent new recruits was timely. Working frantically with every second now crucial, all hands aboard the *William* prepared to make the desperate attempt to escape, before it was too late. With the sun dropping on the western horizon, Captain Barnet's ship continued to benefit immensely from the element of surprise, having gotten the jump on the Rackham crew.

Now fearing the worst, the pirates managed to raise every sail in the frantic bid to escape with their lives, and the *William* was on its way, thanks to the late evening breeze blowing west from land. With the well-honed instincts of a natural hunter and benefitting from a seasoned crew of seamen mostly from Port Royal, Captain Barnet immediately gave chase to the surprisingly agile *William*, after turning his ship around. He now headed west toward the open sea in rapid pursuit.[238] But thanks to the excessive partaking of the large "bowl of punch," the pirate crew as well as the new English recruits were not in the best of shape for manning the ship during an escape attempt in the dark. After drawing closer to the smaller *William*, Captain Barnet saw that "some were drinking, and others walking the deck."[239]

A DEADLY RACE

The swift privateer sloop, well maintained to the highest standards in its home port, began to gain even more ground on the pirate ship. Captain Barnet yelled out for the ship to identify itself, and Captain Rackham screamed back in the darkness: "John Rackham from Cuba." In a spirited response to a demand to surrender from the Jamaica governor's top privateer, the pirates raised a chorus of defiance from the gently rocking deck of the *William*.

In keeping with pirate tactics, Captain Rackham and his crew members had replied with little more than a bluff. But the enterprising pirate captain had another trick up his sleeve, proving resourceful in a true crisis situation. Rising to the challenge, he ordered one of his two swivel guns fired at the rapidly gaining pursuers. But the shot fired into the night went badly awry—again, rum played a role—doing no damage to the Barnet ship and crew. One pirate, perhaps Anne herself, fired a musket, but even this shot whistled wide of the target. Captain Rackham was not about to surrender, although the *William* was nearly in Barnet's grasp. This weak resistance was the only defiance mustered by the groggy Rackham crew as most of them were under the punch's influence—a feeble defense that only emboldened Captain Barnet and his seamen, who realized their considerable advantage. In return, they unleashed their own close-range broadside.

The fire of cannons from the larger and more powerful sloop was accurate, inflicting direct hits to the *William*. One cannonball smashed into the boom, causing the entire sloop to shake violently. With sharp wooden splinters flying through the air and around Anne and Mary, who still stood on the sloop's deck where they struggled to maintain their balance from the impact, the entire mainsail of the *William* crashed down onto the deck, while tangles of ropes and lines rained down near the women.

The proud *William* that had once been known for its beauty and grace was now crippled, and the damage left the ship powerless. In desperation, facing his greatest dilemma as a sea captain in what was a true life-or-death situation, Jack Rackham ordered oars manned in a rowboat or canoe, in a last-ditch attempt to escape by rowing the disabled ship to safety in the blackness, but it was already much too little, too late. Captain Barnet unleashed a broadside from his heaviest cannon, and then a close, sweeping volley from muskets that raked the deck of the *William*, which was so overpowering that most of the half-drunk pirates "went down under deck" for cover. No doubt cursing his fate, Captain Jack Rackham knew that his pirate career was now over.[240]

ONE FINAL BATTLE AT SEA

But two members of the Rackham crew refused to go down into the hold. Anne and Mary stood defiantly on the deck, while all the men cowered below it. Incredibly, it was now left up to Anne Bonny and Mary Read to defend the ship on their own, and they prepared to resist!

Meanwhile, Captain Barnet maneuvered his ship close for a boarding to seize the *William*. With a drawn saber, Anne defiantly stood her ground and refused to budge, although she knew that a mob of boarders, armed with cutlasses, axes, dirks, and pistols, was ready to swarm aboard her ship and that they knew how to fight well in close quarters. Amassed at the ship's rail, Captain Barnet's men were now jumbled together like a hungry pack of wolves, preparing to storm the helpless *William*. Meanwhile, all four cannons of the *William* below deck remained perfectly silent, offering no resistance. The silence from below deck might have been deafening to Anne, who realized that the two women were now on their own as never before. Nevertheless, she and Mary prepared to defend the deck as best they could against the odds.

Even in this dire situation, the guns were still not manned by Rackham's men. They were still reeling from too much rum punch and demoralized by Captain Barnet's firepower, and they stayed completely out of the fight. Another problem that negated any hope for an organized resistance was the fact that Captain Rackham had too few able-bodied sailors to simultaneously man all of his cannons, which would have required about half a dozen sober pirates per gun to load and fire at the privateer. And no pirate now manned the two swivel guns on the railing, because they were exposed to close-range fire. At every point, the men of the *William* were doing nothing to prepare to defend the ship, after the initial resistance effort that had been pathetic in its weakness.

Meanwhile, on the *William's* deck, open and too wide to possibly defend with anything less than a full crew, only Mary Read now stood by Anne's side to face Captain Barnet's storm that was about to descend upon them. The courage of the two women had risen to the fore. Unlike their comrades, including the captain, neither woman had drunk any rum punch. Anne and Mary evidently remained abstinent deliberately to not only watch the ship, but also to defend it if necessary.

With the disabled *William* bobbing in the Caribbean's waters like a cork, Jack Rackham and his men knew that there was no escape, and perhaps reasoned, or just hoped, in their rum-soaked minds, that they might escape retribution from the High Court of the Admiralty if they were taken without weapons in their hands and offering no resistance. If so, then Anne and Mary had been abandoned to a cruel calculation. Perhaps the men below deck had simply lied about providing assistance, yelling to the two women that they were about to come atop the deck to help defend the ship, when they planned to stay put.

Anne was now on her own to defend the ship without any male assistance whatsoever, including from her own captain and lover! Only Mary remained beside her at this moment. In the end, the two young women were on their own without their captain, in the greatest crisis ever faced by the Rackham crew.[241]

Despite the odds, the two women never wavered, continuing to stand firm against the inevitable boarding of veteran seamen, preparing to meet the overpowering onslaught of Captain Barnet's entire crew. Symbolically, the two women now stood together between groups of men, feeling contempt for both. All the while with flintlock pistols and sabers, Anne and Mary prepared to fight alone on the sun-bleached deck of the *William*, wondering why their captain and comrades remained below deck in the hold. Perhaps the two women came to the unbelievable, but well-justified, conclusion that the male pirates had deliberately decided to wait out the tempest of Captain Barnet's inevitable onslaught.

Most of all, they wanted to still demonstrate that they were capable of the kind of heroics that were so well-known among male warriors who had long bragged about their courage, as if to prove that the equality and respect that they had enjoyed in pirate society was fully deserved: a case of female pirates taking the opportunity to prove that they were braver than male pirates, as part of the rivalry of genders since time immemorial. After having decided to risk their lives to the dangerous ways of piracy, Mary and Anne were not now ready to relinquish that kind of life without offering a good fight, and even one against the odds. In this sense, because of their gender, perhaps these two defiant young women had more to prove to not only themselves but also to other males (both Barnet's and Rackham's men): that they were worthy of equality both in and out of pirate society. As veteran pirates, Rackham and his male crew members might have simply realized that their numbers were too few to defend the ship, and acted accordingly. Thus, nearly a dozen male pirates hid safely in the hold, refusing to assist Anne and her sister in arms.

On the surface, this situation seems almost incomprehensible. However, a host of other reasons besides cowardice also explained why no males (not even the captain!) were on deck to defend the ship with the women. First, a rowboat was now manned by some new recruits (the Englishmen), who feared that they would be tried as pirates of the notorious Rackham crew, although they had committed no act of piracy, in a desperate effort to haul off the disabled ship. And, quite likely, a lack

Above: Anne Bonny's defiant last stand aboard the William.

of gunpowder, or the possibility that the powder supply might have been low or had become wet from a leak in the ship's hull, could mean severely limited firing capabilities. Therefore, no doubt due to a combination of factors, the four cannons below deck and the two swivel guns of the *William* remained silent, much to the consternation, if not fury, of the two women on deck. Evidently, Anne and Mary were not experienced in firing the light cannon. But most likely they had no time to attempt to load the swivel guns. In addition, the male pirates desired not to expose themselves as easy targets in the open to Captain Barnet's sharpshooters, if they attempted to load the swivel guns.

Therefore, Anne and Mary, the former private who had never surrendered in any battle on European soil and perhaps now preferred death in battle to the inevitable neck-stretching ending reserved for criminals, were determined to gamely defend the *William* on their own. With Captain Barnet's sloop now so close to the *William*, another broadside from his topside cannon would completely sweep the deck at close range with a deadly hail of grapeshot, dropping anyone and everyone on deck: Anne and Mary, in this case. In this sense, the male pirates actually demonstrated wisdom, accepting their inevitable fates and an undeniable outcome: that Rackham's helpless ship was about to be boarded, and they were all about to be captured by the governor's best pirate hunters and killers. The only way to avoid hanging was to commit suicide and at least

Above: Pirates battling hand-to-hand after boarding a ship.

deny their captors the satisfaction. Therefore, accepting their fate with typical "gallows humour," well-known pirate cynicism, and contemptuous resignation, Captain Rackham and his men now became even more fatalistic on this dark night off Negril Point.[242]

When dozens of Barnet's men, including seaman James Spatchear from Port Royal, were poised with cocked pistols and sharpened cutlasses to board the doomed *William*, "none kept the deck except Mary Read and Anne Bonny," but Anne could not have now had a better companion by her side.[243] A seasoned veteran of the War of the Spanish Succession and one who had stood firm against the French soldiers on past battlefields, Mary was a capable and trusty comrade. Like Anne Bonny when the ship was about to be boarded, she was incensed by what she rightly felt was dark infamy in the desertion by the men, including those she considered her friends. These young women were displaying an astounding amount of courage and character during the ultimate crisis.

In a towering rage, Mary suddenly dashed to the hold. As if still serving in her old British "regiment of foot" at Flanders, she "called to those under deck to come up and fight like men," but it was no use. The two women then made their final preparations for when the boarders poured onto the doomed ship's deck like a flood.[244]

Mary, who, unlike Anne, possessed military training, might have played a role in encouraging Anne to face their greatest challenge together: no longer a case of the brotherhood of the sea, but a sisterhood of the sea in defending the *William*. Like Anne, "she did not want [an ounce of] bravery" in this desperate life-or-death situation. Fueling a commitment to stand firm together to the bitter end, Mary was 14 years older than Anne, and perhaps even a surrogate mother to Anne in some ways. Very likely not only a bond of sisterhood but also a maternal bond held the two women together on deck at this crucial moment.

Anne continued to stand firm with flintlock pistol and cutlass at the ready. Standing side by side and tempting fate, Anne and Mary awaited the dreaded moment when the heavily armed members of Captain Barnet's crew swarmed aboard the all-but-defenseless sloop. Now wielding a popular pirate weapon that was excellent in close-quarter combat on deck, Anne gripped her cutlass tightly.

But Anne certainly now knew that the skill she possessed with this short, broad blade might well save her life once close combat erupted. Like Mary, she had decided that she would not surrender once the boarders poured on the deck. The two women were determined that they would have to be taken by force. Her flintlock pistol would only be good for one single shot once the boarders came over the ship's side; there would be no time to reload. Anne knew that she must count primarily upon her cutlass to defend herself during the heat of combat.

Indeed, these young women were in the prime of life, toughened by their experiences at sea, and hardened in temperament and attitude that guaranteed resistance. Both women, energetic from outdoor activities on deck as everyday seafarers, were accustomed to a vigorous life. Anne's and Mary's overall physical conditioning from the arduous daily work aboard ship had been so thorough that they were fully "able to outwrestle many men" by this time.[245]

While Captain Barnet's men prepared to board, not a single male pirate—not even Captain Rackham—came above deck to assist, although an infuriated Mary had directly challenged the men to act like men. Anne and Mary had decided to defend the ship also because they believed that they were about to be shown no mercy. By this time, they had to have been aware of Governor Rogers' burning desire and official proclamation, which had specially named them as pirates, to eliminate the Rackham crew: a guarantee that no quarter was now the fate of the crew of the *William*. However, the fact that they were women might be enough to prevent Captain Barnet's men from the no-quarter policy. If so, then Anne and Mary remained above deck in a defiant stance, in an attempt to save the male crew members below from the policy.

Mary felt even greater anger toward her male crew members than toward the threatening opponents—she had never seen such despicable behavior among the disciplined soldiers of her British regiment when she had served in the War of the Spanish Succession. She cocked both of her flintlock pistols, and prepared to unleash not only her loads but also her wrath at her fellow comrades in the ship's hold. After "finding that they did not stir, [Mary] fired her arms down the hold amongst them, killing one and wounding others": the strange case of a mini-civil war among the Rackham crew.[246]

With Captain Barnet's ship now close to the side of the *William*, grappling irons attached to long lines were thrown upon the sloop. As if pulled by ancient Rome's god of the oceans, Neptune, the giant hulls of the two ships drew together until they met with a sudden thud that shook both vessels, while Anne and Mary perhaps sought to gain their balance on the deck. With the two ships now touching, the decisive moment had come at last. Anne now faced her greatest challenge. She might have wrestled with an ancient question, wondering if she would fight or flee. The sight of Mary Read by her side may have comforted Anne, as Mary would not run or desert her, and Anne knew it.

Then, with a great shout that must have shaken the women's nerves, a howling throng of Captain Barnet's seamen poured onto the deck of Jack Rackham's sloop, after surging over the breast-high wooden gunwale in a united effort to wipe out two female pirates, who were determined to oppose them as best they could. To capture the *William*, Captain Barnet's men were armed to the teeth, anticipating tough resistance from the infamous Captain Rackham and his notorious pirate crew. However, when they swarmed upon the deck, they found no pirate crew, but only two defiant pirates defending the deck, which was now littered with debris, wood splinters, tangled rope, and rigging cut down by the broadside.

Still, Anne and Mary fought side by side with flintlock pistols and cutlasses against the encroaching boarders. Amid the noise and confusion of the close-range combat that swirled across the deck, they most likely stood back to back on the sloop's deck and away from the gunwale in order not to be cut down from behind or immediately surrounded by boarders. Even while battling against Captain Barnet's swarming men, the two women slashed with their swords and shouted defiance at their attackers, knowing that they could not possibly hold back the surging tide for long. Now that they had no time to reload pistols, Anne and Mary yelled desperately for support, attempting to rally the crew for united defense of the *William* against their common enemies. But in fact, it was already too late.

It seems that Anne and Mary had made a premeditated decision to buy as much time as possible for the male pirates to rise to the challenge. If they stood firm long enough, then surely Captain Rackham and his men would come up to the main deck and join them in the ship's defense. At this time, "no person among [the crew] were more resolute . . . as [Mary Read] and Anne Bonny; and particularly [now] at the time they were attacked [by Captain Barnet's men] and taken, when they came to close quarters, none kept the deck except Mary Read and Anne Bonny," who continued to battle against the odds.[247]

During the hand-to-hand combat on the deck of the *William*, Anne and Mary held their own much longer than anyone expected, keeping Captain Barnet's men at bay for some time. In fact, they proved themselves excellent fighters, armed with flintlock pistols and traditional seaman's hatchets, demonstrating their close-range combat skills. For some minutes, Anne and Mary gamely battled with spirit and certainly audacity, which to Captain Barnet's men was like "all the female demons a sailor's nightmares on a stormy night are made of."[248]

In a determined last stand against the odds, the women's battle skills would have made the male crew members, including Captain Rackham, proud, if they had only seen it! From the entire crew of the *William*, only two defiant members "held their places, fighting shoulder to shoulder long after their comrades had retreated, fighting unaided against the whole of Barnet's crew."[249] The astonishing sight of two female pirates holding a good many male attackers at bay might have brought a sense of admiration that could have saved the two women's lives in the end.

A possibility existed that Captain Barnet had been ordered by Governor Lawes, who wanted personally to bring the two female pirates to trial, not to kill Anne or Mary. For whatever the reason, the women were swarmed and wrestled to the ground, then disarmed of their cutlasses and empty flintlock pistols, and taken captive. All that they could do now was to curse not only the victors but also their crew who failed to come to their assistance at the time of greatest need.

All in all, to Anne's and Mary's disgust, this was one of the most disgraceful episodes in the history of pirates in the Caribbean.[250]

Thus, "even [the] two pirates such as these are no match for a whole crew, and eventually went down before the sheer weight of numbers and were captured [and] The sloop was quickly brought under control and manned, and the conflict ended with a strange suddenness as fate and the law finally caught up with Calico Jack Rackham and his notorious crew on that November day of the year 1720."[251]

Having taken the *William* without serious loss, the victorious captain rounded up the sullen prisoners, after the ship's protectors, Anne and Mary, had been roughly subdued by brute, but not lethal, force. Anne and Mary might have been spared only because Barnet's men knew about the two women pirates, including even their names, "Bonny" and "Mary Read," from Governor Rogers' September 5 proclamation.

Then, with Anne and Mary held under close guard, Barnet's sloop and the captured *William* set sail from the westernmost point of Jamaica, heading north for only a relatively short distance. After rounding the island's western edge, they then turned east and sailed along Jamaica's northwestern shore. Captain Barnet knew that the governor, now at the capital of St. Jago de la Vega (Spanish Town), would be delighted by his one-sided success in ridding Jamaican waters of the most notorious band of pirates.

On the morning after the capture of the *William*, a triumphant Captain Barnet sailed east past Orange Bay and Green Island with flags, including the Union Jack, flying. He then slipped into the small inlet known as Davis Cove, located about two-thirds of the way up the coast from Negril to the town and Bay of Lucea, where he handed the pirates over to a trusty militia officer, Major Richard James. Under heavy guard, the shackled pirates were then transported by wagon over rugged terrain, southeast across the narrow island and toward the capital. Captain Barnet and his crew reaped a reward of some 200 pounds for the capture of the Rackham crew. Made to feel less than human being during her captivity and now viewed as the worst criminal in the land, Anne probably never knew that her capture brought a great financial reward for her captors.[252]

At this time, the only solace for Anne and Mary would have been the satisfaction of putting up a very good fight on the deck of the *William*. A good many latter-day historians and writers doubted that Anne and Mary could have possibly defended themselves with such tenacity aboard the *William* because of the simple fact that they were women. These critics have emphasized that such spirited resistance by the two women was simply a case of Captain Johnson's exaggerations used to boost book sales. In describing how "none kept the deck" to fight back against Captain Barnet and his attackers except Anne and Mary, he has been accused of helping to create the myth of "the exceptional, bloodthirsty Amazons" to fit the popular stereotypes of other martial female heroes—especially of matriarchal societies—who reaped glory for their exploits in combat.[253]

But a good many first-person soldier accounts of women from many nations around the world in wartime situations, especially the most desperate ones, have long revealed a heroic side of women which was every bit as distinguished as that of men. For instance, during one of the greatest disasters in military history, one of Napoleon Bonaparte's French soldiers described how during the nightmarish retreat from Moscow and in crossing the swollen Berezina River under dark November skies to escape the encroaching Russians, especially the much-feared Cossacks, during the 1812 Campaign, women were part of this disastrous ordeal. He noticed something not only significant but also rather remarkable: "We noticed that the men seemed to suffer more, both morally and physically, than the women. The women bore their sufferings and privations with an astonished courage, enough to reflect shame on certain men, who had no courage and resignation to endure their trials [and] Very few of these women died . . . ."[254]

In much the same way and as revealed by Captain Johnson in his 1724 book, Anne and Mary were the only two members of the entire Rackham crew—and the only two female pirates to have served in the Caribbean during the history of the Golden Age of Piracy—who stood firm to defend their ship in a desperate bid to save themselves and their fellow male crew members. These two crew members were the only ones on the *William* to offer resistance to the onslaught of an entire crew of privateers: the antithesis of the pirate romance and stereotype.[255] No single incident in the Golden Age of Piracy was destined to more thoroughly shock the people and the capital of Jamaica and its aristocratic government officials, especially Governor Lawes, than the unbelievable news and "astonishing revelation . . . that the two fire-eating filibusters who had staged the sensational last stand on the deck of the pirate [ship] were not men, but women disguised as men."[256]

TRIAL FOR HER LIFE
1720

NNE WAS ABOUT TO BE put on a very public and publicized trial, presided by Jamaica's own governor, the pirate-hater Nicholas Lawes, in Jamaica. Early Jamaica had been protected by an armada of privateers, especially Captain Morgan, in the absence of the Royal Navy. Now, to protect the immense profits from the bustling slave trade, the king of England had turned against the sea raiders with a vengeance, after having declared them criminals who had to be eliminated at all costs. Among these top public enemies was now the young Irishwoman, Anne Bonny.[257]

But in truth, who were the true criminals of the Caribbean? Was it the popular definition created by a society that had first promoted piracy and then turned against it, and in both cases for its own selfish gains? In the words of historian Gabriel Kuhn, who grasped this central contradiction of the early 18th-century world to place it in much larger perspective: "Compared to the 'awful dreadfulness' of pirates, the traditional, 'relatively dreadful' attitudes—contempt for women, hatred of Aboriginal peoples, slavery—were barely to be found among them, and were often opposed directly. Women were often fully accepted, Aboriginal peoples were left mostly in peace, and some captains . . . would immediately liberate all slaves found on commandeered ships."[258] The richest city in America, New York City, had been built partly on fortunes that had been reaped from piracy and continued at this time. Indeed, "the little city with its rascally governors and its mixed population [of mostly Dutch and English], many of whom were adventurous traders ready to turn almost

---

Opposite: Church in St. Jago de la Vega (today's Spanish Town), Jamaica.

any kind of penny, was for years a favorite stamping ground of the sea rovers, and their gorgeous persons became very familiar not only to Wall Street, but throughout the whole town, where their confidential transactions with certain enterprising citizens laid the foundation of more than one existing fortune."[259]

Anne was about to go on trial for her life for having committed the same crime that the elite had long done on both sides of the Atlantic, while the high-ranking politicians, rulers, and merchants continued to violate the law to reap greater reputations and fortunes. If she were acquitted, which was all but impossible at this time, then she could walk away as a free woman. But if not so fortunate, then a hangman's noose awaited Anne and her fellow crewmen. However, escaping execution was not entirely out of the realm of possibility for them. Although Chief Justice Sir Charles Hedges declared to the jury in one pirate trial in London in 1696 that "piracy is only a term for sea robbery" and not murder, the dozen jurors at St. Jago de la Vega thought otherwise. Although all evidence indicated that the nine men on trial who had joined Rackham at Negril Bay were pirates, they were all destined to be acquitted and set free. In the near future, the sympathetic jurors would reach their decisions because the men on trial were not only Englishmen, but, more important, lower-class Londoners from the East End and fellow Jamaicans from Port Royal—just common people trying to make a living for themselves and their families, like themselves.[260] Born in Ireland and raised in South Carolina, Anne had no such advantages by the time that she was put on trial, especially because she had dared to transgress against gender stereotypes.

Indeed, Anne's trial before the High Court of Admiralty would be an entirely different matter because it would be held in Jamaica, and any pirates swarming in the waters around Jamaica posed a threat to the vast profits reaped by the British Crown itself. Such losses were a potential disaster for planters, who depended upon a steady flow of slaves to work their plantations, cutting the high stalks of sugar cane and sending the refined product back to Europe.[261]

As could be expected, Anne Bonny was about to face a host of other handicaps to any realistic possibility for a fair trial in Jamaica. Anne was not a Jamaican, nor was she even English. Her Irish/South Carolinian background was a double handicap for her in the eyes of English judges, and if Anne were Catholic, the odds were then stacked even higher against her. To the English, the Celtic Jacobite threat was very real, and it was not forgotten by the men of this generation: The crown had launched its crusade against the Bahamian pirates in part because of the fear that Nassau and the Bahamas would be transformed into a thriving Jacobite bastion.

But worst of all for Anne, the trial for pirates was always set up by the harshest and most merciless judges of the High Court of the Admiralty, which convicted and executed pirates with a routine, businesslike efficiency. It was doing the crown's dirty work, with the full support of wealthy Jamaicans, whose profits depended upon eliminating as many pirates as possible. To guarantee a quick trip to the gallows, the world of the elite and the judicial system demonized pirate defendants, even those who were more religious and less corrupt than wealthy judges who owed their fortunes to bribes. Therefore, the overall mission of the judges was to secure a quick conviction and an even quicker execution. In a very symbolic display before a kangaroo court, Anne Bonny was about to be held personally responsible for a long legacy of crimes: a perfect scapegoat.[262]

The trial of the Captain John "Calico Jack" Rackham crew began in the courthouse on November 16, 1720, at St. Jago de la Vega, today's Spanish Town. After Oliver Cromwell's conquest of the island in 1655 and the subsequent spread the Protestant faith, the English renamed the city Spanish Town, as if in tribute to their conquered religious foe. The town now served as the capital and administrative center of Jamaica since Port Royal had been largely destroyed by the earthquake in 1692.

Anne knew that the full power of the English government that rested in the stately buildings of the capital was about to come crashing down on her head. In many ways, by this time in her young life, Anne had come full circle: After defying and rebelling so many times against all manner of authority throughout her life—her father, society, tradition, and convention—she had never paid a high price for her transactions. But Anne had dramatically upped the ante when she embarked upon a free life on the high seas, and she was about to face an angry group of powerful men, who saw in Anne their greatest nightmare: a self-assertive, independent, brave, and quite formidable woman in her own right.

With its own single-minded agenda and mandate from the crown to rid the seas of pirates as quickly as possible, the High Court of the Admiralty was not at all concerned about acting on the behalf of justice and served merely to condemn and execute pirates as rapidly as possible. Anne no doubt realized as much by this time, and she also knew that merely the sight of her, sunburned in dirty sailor's clothes, before the judges who already hated Anne long before ever seeing her, would be sufficient to make their blood boil.

Any woman who disguised herself as a man and also functioned as one, in perfect equality with other men, was perhaps the most outrageous act that the court could conceive. Women in male attire were seen as "woman warriors [who] were symbols of threatening female aggression—another sign of the world gone topsy-turvy" as seen by the patriarchal order. By sending Anne Bonny to the gallows in a hurry, the men of the court were determined to make their secure patriarchal world right again.[263]

FIRST DAY OF TRIAL

Wednesday, November 16, 1720, was the day of reckoning for Captain Rackham and his crew—except Anne and Mary. The two women were to be tried at the courthouse at a later date. Headed by Sir Nicholas Lawes, who presided over the solemn proceedings, and the High Court of the Admiralty, the trial of Jack Rackham and his men was a mockery of justice, as everyone had already known the inevitable final verdict and dismal fate. Under Governor Lawes' guiding hand, these distinguished men were the personal representatives of the Lord High Admiral.

Wearing traditional black robes, these men were responsible for trying all felonies committed on the high seas. The court had been originally established to ensure that the crown and the court officials, who received no high salary as in England, received dividends from the spoils taken from captured Spanish ships by the buccaneers. With all the formal appearances of a fair court merely for ritualistic show, these officials conducted proceedings with a false taint of fairness. In truth, only one conclusion was now possible for the accused: a death by hanging. Nevertheless, maintaining the necessary façade and lofty image of dispensing righteous justice, the court laboriously went through all of the proper legal procedures as prescribed by law and proper jurisprudence. Even witnesses were gathered to formally testify against the pirates, as if they would be judged without prejudice in this showcase of hypocrisy.

The trial was swift, as preplanned by those in power. To ensure that the final verdict was all but automatic, the lack of legal representation and arguments for the defense was noticeably absent from the one-sided proceedings that were a sham formality. No legal representation was allowed for those accused of piracy. Hardly before they entered the courtroom, Jack Rackham and the male members of his crew were charged with a list of crimes "upon the high sea." These specified crimes included the taking of the two merchant ships off Hispaniola, the schooner off Port Maria Bay, Jamaica, and the merchant sloop at Dry Harbour Bay, Jamaica. Two witnesses, Thomas Spenlow, whose schooner was taken near Port Maria Bay, and James Spatchear, who was a member of Captain Barnet's crew, for the prosecution stepped forward to testify in great detail, as ordered.

It had made no difference at all that the pirates had pleaded not guilty to all four of the specific criminal charges leveled against them. Without the benefit of a legal defense and in record time, Captain Rackham and the other male crew members were condemned to be hanged by the neck until dead on the following day. "Charged with trying pirates so that the crown would be assured its share of their booty, the court was designed for efficiency," and functioned smoothly to eliminate as many pirates as swiftly as possible.[264]

It was almost as if the court wanted to hide any evidence of possible collusion with the governor, officials, or government with the pirates as soon as possible. In this way, a permanent silence was assured. Thus, Captain Rackham and his men would not long remain in their dirty jail cell at St. Jago de la Vega. Immediately after they were sentenced on November 16, preparations were made to transport the convicted pirates 13 miles southeast to Kingston.

Just they departed from St. Jago de la Vega on Thursday, November 17, Jack Rackham was granted one final request. Only recently so proud and confident, the pirate captain had only one last thing remaining to live for and to cherish, as if the enduring memories of a long-lost childhood that had vanished forever: Anne Bonny. With nothing else to lose in the last hours of his life, he asked his jailors to see Anne one last time, and his final request was granted.

Almost certainly, Jack was looking for some absolution for leading Anne to a cruel demise. But Anne, despite the fact that she was now carrying his child, or even because of it, gave no "comfort" to her captain—just as Rackham had failed to come to her aid when she attempted to defend the ship against Captain Barnet's boarders. For many reasons, Anne was extremely upset by the time that Jack, now appearing anything but gallant, was allowed into her dank cell. In this last meeting between lovers who had once shared their dreams and hopes about a bright future together: "all the comfort she gave him, was, that she was sorry to see him there, but if he had fought like a man, he need not have been hanged like a dog."[265]

In lashing out without an ounce of love or compassion for her doomed captain, Anne employed a psychological defense mechanism for her own good: the first step in the healing process to reduce the potentially shattering impact of Jack's upcoming execution. What remaining love that Anne felt toward him was now absent, because she knew that their relationship was about to be severed permanently. All Anne had was the relatively minor consolation that they had lived their lives to the fullest. By accepting their mutual tragic fates of dying young if, or when, they were caught by the authorities, and having lived like there was no tomorrow, Jack and Anne had made the most of their time together.

A TIME FOR HANGING

On fateful Friday, November 18, Captain Rackham, Ship Master George Fetherston, Quartermaster Richard Corner, John Davis, and John Howell were transported in an open cart through the dirty streets of Kingston like pigs to the slaughter. Passing by the Kingston Parish Church, Jack and his doomed men were not allowed spiritual comfort in their last hour on Earth. Under the burning sun, they proceeded slowly along the sandy road which ran along the long east-west spit of land, known as the Palisadoes, which led from Kingston to Port Royal. In keeping with the High Court of the Admiralty's process of swift trial and even swifter execution, Captain Rackham and his crewmen were unloaded and manhandled by unsympathetic guards on the way to the gallows.

A throng of excited spectators, dressed as if they were worshipping at Kingston Parish Church on a Sunday morning, had gathered to watch the execution, as the hanging of so many pirates was one of the great social events of the season. Public executions were a festive time for drinking, feasting, and a general celebration for people of all classes. Now sadly reduced from a proud pirate captain who had long terrified Englishmen across the Caribbean, Jack Rackham had for the first time in his life become a source of amusement for spectators. Onlookers eagerly wagered on how long it took their man to die at the end of a rope--and most people who believed that Captain Rackham and his pirates were fiends from hell hoped for the nightmarish agony of a lengthy strangulation, which would be God's will and just reward.[266]

Between a row of steel bayonets, the condemned men were marched to the high wooden gallows that stood like a beacon rising up from the level, sandy ground at infamous Gallows Point, east of Port Royal, where many a man had already met his maker. Mustering his last reserves of strength, Captain Rackham and his men, demonstrating a degree of courage under the circumstances, were led one by one up the ladder that leaned against one of the two uprights lining the top by a large wooden crossbeam, escorted by redcoat soldiers.

The five doomed pirates were ordered to stand still on the scaffold and were held in place just in case they refused to comply with final orders, while the executioner placed nooses of thick hemp rope around each man's neck. Because they were considered the Devil's tools, no minister administered to their spiritual needs in their last moments on Earth.[267]

With few words, Captain Rackham, no longer wearing his calico coat, and his four men, whom he had trusted and loved like brothers—especially his top officers Corner and Fetherston—stood firm while waiting for their terrible end to come. Then, the five men fell from the scaffold, halting in mid-air and dangling like apples from a tree, to the delight of the executioners, the officials, and the crowd.

The rowdy spectators shouted and cheered as the men succumbed to slow deaths. But the long, vengeful arm of the High Court of the Admiralty was still not quite finished with the earthly remains of Captain Jack Rackham. Not satisfied with the grand display he had made out of Jack, the presiding authority, Governor Lawes, and his commissioners had one last statement to make to the public at large. Because of his widespread reputation, Captain Rackham's death at the gallows would be exploited to the fullest. After he was pronounced dead, his body was taken down by the executioner, along with the bodies of his two lieutenants, and they were placed in elaborate iron harnesses for public display. These metal cages used hoops to hold the dead bodies securely in place, despite their eventual decomposition, and were then hung high from iron gibbets at prominent places: Gun Key, Plumb Point, and Bush Key, just off the Port Royal peninsula. The bodies were displayed so that they could be seen by not only the people of Port Royal and Kingston, but more importantly by the hundreds of ships and thousands of seamen who sailed into Kingston harbor in the months ahead.

At Plumb Point, Captain Rackham's body was hung up on a wind-swept mound of sand with little vegetation, farther out than Gun Key, the closest key (or cay) to Port Royal on the east-west peninsula's seaward side, also called Dead Man's Cay. For the most effective propaganda purposes, Jack's body was hung well within sight of Kingston and Port Royal and its main shipping lanes in Kingston Bay, in the key closest to the sea.

Today, Dead Man's Cay is also known as Rackham's Cay, a small beacon of sand that extended out in the bay situated just southeast and roughly parallel to Gallows Point. His body was displayed at the southern edge of Port Royal. Covered in thick coats of tar, so that these grotesque reminders of the folly of pirating were preserved for a long time, the bodies of Rackham and Corner at Gun Key and Fetherston at Bush Key stayed in their custom-built hoops of iron for years, until only their skeletons were left hanging from the chains.[268]

On Saturday, November 19, the day after Captain Rackham and his four men were hanged, another four members of his ill-fated crew were executed under the most demeaning circumstances. Noah Harwood, Patrick Carty, James Dobbin, and Thomas Earl were hanged from the same high wooden scaffold as their revered captain at Gallows Point, although because they were ordinary seamen, their bodies were not hung up for public display as horrifying examples. Instead, they were either left to rot where they lay or were buried in the pauper's cemetery of Port Royal.[269]

But the thorough decimation of the Captain Rackham crew was far from finished at the ruthless hands of the High Court of the Admiralty.

On November 20, or "on the Monday following, Thomas Brown, alias Bourne, and John Feniwick, were also executed at Gallows Point, at Port Royal," to complete the systematic destruction of the Rackham crew, which now served as a lasting example for the people of Jamaica. Brown, aforementioned, was Mary Read's common-law husband on the ship. As well, Mary, like Anne, was pregnant with her pirate husband's child.[270]

Publicly celebrating the desecration of convicted criminals was very effective in discouraging piracy. But the most powerful deterrent was the systematic decimation of the pirate leaders and their crews, and this war against piracy was reaching new heights. Between 1716 and 1726, more than 400 pirates were hanged; Captain Rackham and his male sailors were only a small fraction of this grim total.[271]

Because these much-feared High Courts of the Admiralty were so efficient in exterminating pirate crews, the cynical pirates had often psychologically coped with the prospect of capture by holding mock trials themselves. The aristocratic judges and executioners were made to look ridiculous during these trials, highlighting the fatalistic brand of pirate humor. It is not known if the Rackham crew engaged in this kind of play-acting, but it was quite likely.

For example, pirate captain Thomas Anstis held one such mock trial at a remote Cuban inlet in 1721 "to exorcise this vision of retribution" that led to the mass hanging of so many young men and boys, who were condemned without legal representation or any real chance to defend themselves. If Anne and the other Rackham crew members had hoped to keep the vengeance of the High Court of the Admiralty at bay by mock trials, then it had only backfired to hasten their downfall, by fueling a mistaken belief that the good times would last forever.[272]

ANNE FACES A GRISLY DEATH

Eleven days after Captain Rackham was hanged just outside Port Royal, the officials, judges, and commissioners turned to the matter of Anne Bonny and Mary Read. Like the other ill-fated pirates who went before them, they would not be tried under the rules of civil law but instead by the much harsher laws of the High Court of the Admiralty, in a military-like trial. This tribunal relied on the death penalty as the best means to rid the Caribbean of pirates, far more than a common court of law. Anne was now learning a bitter truth in the form of a lethal lesson: that the carefree life of a pirate was one not only without riches but also without longevity.

Since the hasty trial at St. Jago de la Vega and the hanging of Captain Rackham and his men, the prosecutors needed additional time to gather up more witnesses to testify against Anne and Mary. Evidently, the politicians were concerned about a possible backlash if they hanged two women—an act that would shock London and the English people. These young women were to be tried in the same manner as the male pirates, with no legal representation, and under identical charges that promised a swift, unceremonious death if convicted. Not content to rely upon the previous witnesses, Governor Lawes had gathered additional so-called witnesses to make sure that public sympathy for the two young women wouldn't result in the sparing of their lives, as he knew that this trial was not only the "most astonishing," but also the one "that most captured the public's imagination" on both sides of the Atlantic.

An astute politician, the governor wanted to leave no cause for complaint or protest after the two young ladies were hanged. All of these witnesses were fully prepared to emphasize that Anne and Mary were as dangerous as the male pirates. Meanwhile, the court, knowing that the two female pirates would generate even more interest in the already heavily publicized trial, had a vested interest to ensure Anne's and Mary's execution in order to showcase their own effectiveness. The women's deaths would fulfill political, social, propaganda, and professional goals of the court and crown. But first, the legal and official formalities with all of the appearances of a legitimate trial had to be acted out as part of the sham.

On Monday, November 28, 1720, the highly publicized trial of Anne Bonny and Mary Read began at the courthouse near the old Spanish plaza in St. Jago de la Vega. By this time, the news about the capture of the two female pirates had spread across Jamaica, and the novelty of female pirates drew a large crowd. Everyone wanted to get a glimpse of them.

Along with Mary, Anne Bonny was marched in chains under guard into the jam-packed courtroom to face the men who would decide their fate. She did not have to wonder for a moment what these men, in wigs and robes, were thinking. Anne knew beyond all doubt that she was about to be hanged, even before her trial began. A Machiavellian type, Lawes presided over a group of distinguished counselors, or commissioners: Samuel Moore, James Archibald, John Sadler, Thomas Bernard, and Ezekiel Gomersall, while William Nedham served as the chief justice. Royal Navy captains Thomas Davers, who commanded the HMS Adventure, and Edward Vernon sat on the court. Vernon was the commodore at Port Royal and personally commanded the HMS *Mary* as well as the British fleet in Jamaica. He had served with considerable distinction and was already on the fast track to a more promising career.[273]

At age 34, Vernon was a gifted leader destined for the rank of admiral. In the future, George Washington's older half-brother, Lawrence Washington—known as "Grog" because of the grogram cloak that he wore with regularity—would serve under Admiral Vernon during the overly ambitious 1741 British-American expedition from Jamaica to capture one of Spain's most valuable ports, Cartagena, in Colombia. When Lawrence Washington inherited his father's estate along the Potomac River, located just south of Alexandria, Virginia, he would rename the mansion Mount Vernon, in honor of his former commander. Mount Vernon was destined to become George Washington's beloved home.[274]

Already known for his bad temper, hardheadedness, and inflexible ways, Captain Vernon also hated piracy and its close cousin privateering, for not only for its criminality but also for the egalitarian system that it represented, in contrast to the autocratic Royal Navy. As he explained in his own words: "It is surprising that anyone can submit to such a wretched situation as to be a captain of a privateer, lorded over by the company's quartermaster, supported by the crew, who have chosen him for their champion [and] I fear they will generally prove a nursery of pirates."[275]

However, what Vernon and other Royal Navy officers of the court failed to realize was that the pirates operated in a true democratic manner, with common seamen holding power, a rare measure of dignity, and the right to vote on who commanded them, in a system that bound together people of different nationalities, races, and ethnic groups. Quite simply, freethinking individualists like Captain Rackham and Anne Bonny "took great pride joy in turning the rigid structure of the navy upside down," to the horror of strict martinets and ultraconservatives like Captain Vernon. This heretical sin, which mocked orthodoxy and societal norms, alone represented an outrageousness breach of the normal hierarchy and was fully deserving of death in Vernon's inflexible military mind.[276]

Likewise, the court's other distinguished members were callous, unfeeling men with strong personalities and equally strong ideas about what to do with pirates, and they were used to getting their way. Viewing Anne without pity, they were united to send as many pirates, regardless of sex, situation, or circumstance, as possible swiftly to the gallows.[277] But the greatest enemy that Anne had to face during her trial at St. Jago de la Vega was Governor Lawes himself. Some evidence has revealed that he strongly disliked self-assured women; he once denounced the manipulative "female art of getting rich in Jamaica [which is based] on two short rules—marry and bury!"[278]

Class was also a central issue at this publicized trial, with Anne and Mary facing representatives of the colonial aristocratic world in awaiting their judgment. From lowly backgrounds and troubled pasts, Anne and Mary stood together as one, as when they had defended the *William* with spirit on their own. The court register, William Norris, formally introduced the two women as "Mary Read, and Ann Bonny, alias Bonn, late of the Island of Providence [Bahamas], Spinsters," because he assumed or was told by them that neither one was married.

Standing before the court, Norris then read the charges against the two women, having allegedly committed "Piracies, Felonies, and Robberies . . . on the High Sea," in four separate cases: the exact same charges that ensured Jack Rackham and his men were quickly hanged in the bright Caribbean sunshine. Anne, of course, fully realized that her life, and that of her unborn child, was in the hands of exactly the kind of heartless aristocratic men she had hated all her life. Norris pronounced in the crowded, hot courtroom, bustling with noise and taut with tension, that Anne "did feloniously and wickedly . . . rob [and] plunder" ships at sea and took captives.[279] To the charge that warranted death in the judge's, king's, and society's eyes, but knowing that she had never murdered anyone and therefore was undeserving of execution, Anne told the court register that she was "Not Guilty."[280]

Governor Lawes and his commissioners were not moved by Anne's helplessness or her not-guilty plea. In fact, they might well have been infuriated by Anne's curt response. Mary was charged with the same offenses, and answered in the manner as Anne. Without the benefit of legal counsel or a lawyer's advice, Anne hoped to escape the death sentence by gambling that the High Court of the Admiralty simply lacked evidence that she was a pirate. Helping her case, or so it seemed, the testimony of Captain Barnet was not included in the trial, and Anne's and Mary's spirited defense of the *William* was not entirely clear-cut evidence of piracy. This desperate protection of the ship might have legally fallen under the grounds of self-defense, given the onslaught of Captain Barnet's heavily armed boarders, including perhaps non-British nationals—Frenchmen or Spaniards—under a British flag.

Whatever lingering faith that Anne might win an acquittal from the High Court of the Admiralty was abruptly shattered when Dorothy Thomas walked into the courtroom. No woman had testified against Jack Rackham and his men. But because hanging two women was hardly an everyday occurrence in the British Empire, the governor wanted a thorough prosecution without an accusation of gender bias. Thomas, who had been aboard the large canoe taken by the Rackham crew on Jamaica's north coast, was a star witness who could inflict the most harm to Anne and Mary, as she was able to provide a detailed firsthand account. If a female witness for the prosecution could be used to convict the two women, then no criticism could be raised that the court had been prejudiced or biased from a male perspective. Some sensitivity surrounded the idea of executing women by the crown, which might reflect badly on Jamaica, as Englishmen on the home isle, especially in London, looked down upon colonials almost as second-class citizens. Therefore, everything had to be done by the book. This heightened sensitivity was a result of the trial being well attended and well publicized: London would learn in detail about all of the proceedings. Most importantly, no woman had ever been hanged before for piracy in English history!

Anne and Mary were shocked when Dorothy Thomas took the stand to testify against them. Any chance of somehow escaping the death sentence now all but evaporated as soon as Thomas opened with her emotional testimony, after she had sworn her oath on the Holy Bible. Anne knew that Dorothy Thomas had witnessed her in action as a pirate in Ocho Rios Bay, Jamaica, when Jack Rackham had her come aboard the *William* after capturing the canoe. She had seen Anne fully armed and in pirate dress, carrying a machete—more fear-inspiring than a cutlass—in one hand and a flintlock pistol in the other. Thomas had watched Anne behaving just like the male members of Captain Rackham's crew of the *William*.

No doubt, Anne tensed up upon the sight of her former victim, knowing that Dorothy Thomas, who might well have felt even more outrage at the mere thought of a female pirate than an average male, would have no sympathy for her. Thomas' testimony would guarantee Anne's death sentence.

All in all, this upcoming testimony from Dorothy Thomas was about much more than just petty robbery on the water. The two women came from different worlds and classes and had entirely different outlooks on life. Dorothy Thomas had not been forced to live by her wits and resources in order to survive, resulting in risks taken by few women, like Anne Bonny had. Both Anne and Mary were illegitimate and had struggled throughout their lives, facing obstacles and difficulties that were unimaginable to Dorothy Thomas, who was a proper lady, and these realities also played their part in condemning Anne and Mary to death.

While the entire courtroom was hushed and the judges looked on intently at their chief witness for the prosecution, Dorothy Thomas presented her devastating eyewitness testimony. Anne could not refute it, given that she had not been allowed by the court to present witnesses or legal representation, and also because the court had already made up its mind long ago. Thomas testified to the court that Anne and Mary had acted and performed just like the other crew members and were indeed pirates of the first order. In her own words, they "wore Men's Jackets, and long Trousers, and Handkerchiefs tied about their Heads: and that each of them had a Machet[e] and Pistol in their Hands . . . ."[281]

The star witness also claimed that Anne and Mary were both ruthless and even more bloodthirsty than the men, including Captain Rackham. This could have been because Anne and Mary were determined to prove their worth as pirates, even more than the men of the crew, which may have been underscored by their spirited defense of their ship. Thomas also saw the two women as a direct threat to society's concepts of womanhood. She presented a scenario in which Anne and Mary "cursed and Swore at the Men, to murder [her]; and that they should kill her to prevent her coming against them."[282]

However, Thomas never explained why she was not killed by the pirates, if the situation she had described in such vivid detail had actually happened. If Anne and Mary were as bloodthirsty as claimed, then they would have killed Thomas themselves to make sure that no witness would later testify against them. The most likely explanation was that the two women behaved aggressively in order to present a façade to cow opponents and dissuade them from resisting, so that there would be no bloodshed.

Anne was now being condemned for allegedly suggesting that Dorothy Thomas should be murdered, even though Thomas had been spared from harm. Nevertheless, she was now doing everything in her power to make sure that Anne was hanged as quickly as possible. Anne was only able to sit quietly in the crowded courtroom, unable to respond. What now certainly haunted her was the ironic fact that Thomas having been spared, along with the others in the canoe at Ocho Rios Bay, had led to the timely intelligence that prompted Governor Lawes to dispatch Captain Barnet in pursuit—and ultimately led to Anne's capture.

Then, to partly verify beyond all doubt that Anne and Mary wanted to have her killed so that she would be unable to testify against them, Dorothy Thomas emphasized to the judges: "That the Reason of [her] knowing and believing them to be Women then was, by the largeness of their Breasts." As Dorothy, Anne, and the judges knew, there was now no doubt as to the identities and roles of the two women on the *William*: active and aggressive crew members that were equals among the male pirates.[283]

Nevertheless, the High Court of Admiralty was not finished in its prosecution against the two women. It seemed as if Governor Lawes and other court members were now more determined to send both Anne and Mary to the gallows than Captain Rackham himself. The active roles of Anne and Mary as pirates were reinforced by still another eyewitness, Thomas Spenlow, whose testimony had earlier helped to seal the fates of Captain Rackham and his men.

By this time, Anne's hopes for acquittal and survival had plummeted. Thomas Spenlow's own schooner had been captured by Jack Rackham on October 19 near Port Maria Bay, Jamaica, and he had seen Rackham's pirates, including Anne, after he had been brought aboard the *William*. Therefore, Spenlow's detailed first-person testimony was nearly as damaging as that of Dorothy Thomas. This young woman had seemingly become a scapegoat for every pirate robbery in the Caribbean.[284]

To make matters even worse for Anne, the two Frenchmen aboard the *William*, Peter Cornelian and John Besneck, also appeared in the courtroom to present their testimony against her. They had been captured by Rackham in a prize taken off the coast of Hispaniola and were present when Spenlow's schooner and Thomas Dillon's sloop were captured. With the aid of a translator, Simon Clarke, they told the tale of how the two pirate women were on board when the *William* struck the next day near Dry Harbour Bay. Even more damning, the Frenchmen stated under oath that Anne and Mary "were very active on Board [Rackham's ship] and willing to do any Thing; That Ann Bonny . . . handed Gun-Powder to the Men [manning the cannon], That when they saw any Vessel, gave Chase or Attacked, they wore Men's Clothes."[285]

But of all the testimony presented on this sweltering day at St. Jago de la Vega, Dorothy Thomas' was the most incriminatory—for another reason that has been largely overlooked by historians. Some possibility exists that Anne herself might have commanded the *William* at some point during the last cruise, and if so, it explains why Captain Rackham was a non-entity in the ship's defense: He had been voted out of command by the crew. It was revealed that not only Anne but also Mary possessed some measure of authority, perhaps voted upon by the crew, and that the two women had distinct leadership roles comparable to those of captain and quartermaster, especially in the final attack when they had defended the *William* off Negril Point on their own. Thomas' testimony strongly implied as much, because he stated that "the women might have commanded the others," including Jack Rackham.[286]

But as if all of this was not yet sufficient to send Anne and Mary straight to the gallows, Thomas Dillon came forth as the final witness to confirm beyond all doubt that Anne and Mary were enthusiastic and active members of Rackham's pirate crew. He was the "Master" of the "Merchant Sloop" *Mary and Sarah*, when she was taken by Captain Rackham on October 20, and he explained in detail how Rackham's *William* had descended upon his ship while anchored about one league from shore inside Dry Harbour Bay. Dillon and his men had then rowed ashore to land and "defend themselves" from the attack of this "strange sloop."

After "several Shots had been fired at them," Dillon had yelled out to request the identification of the menacing ship and its noisy crew. The *William*'s quartermaster, George Fetherston, shouted back that they were "English pirates," and asked for the master to come aboard. Identification as "English" pirates—rather than French or Spanish pirates—was a great relief, and therefore Dillon came aboard the *William*. He was then shocked to see that "Ann Bonny had a Gun in her Hand . . . ."[287]

But Dillon, still angry that his sloop had been ransacked by the Rackham crew, had much more to say to the High Court of the Admiralty—well-chosen words, if not prearranged by the corrupt and self-serving court, that continued to reduce the chances of the two women of ever reaching old age. In regard to Anne and Mary, Dillon emphasized in no uncertain terms that they "were both very profligate, cursing and swearing much, and very ready and willing to do any Thing on Board."[288]

Again, however, this behavior might well have been a case of Anne and Mary merely putting on a bold front, but of course this well-known tactic of pirate strategy was not taken into account by the High Court. Instead, one thing was perfectly clear to the courtroom and judges: When combined, the detailed personal and corroboration from multiple eyewitnesses revealed that Anne and Mary were not only key players in the functioning of the pirate crew, including in combat situations, but also undeniably held some undefined leadership roles. This only additionally incensed the judges, hastening a death sentence for the greatest infraction of all: young women performing boldly and capably as dynamic leaders over an entire crew of men. A "perfect storm" was forming to guarantee the executions of Anne and Mary.[289]

The two pirates were overwhelmed by the number of detailed testimonies from such a divergent range of witnesses. All eyewitnesses described in detail how the two women were not only pirates but played central roles in the Rackham crew's raids and robberies. Worst of all for Anne and Mary, this testimony was true and could not be denied. After they had been asked by Governor Lawes whether they had anything to say in their defense, neither Anne nor Mary said a word. Without time, resources, or connections for their legal defense, they were unable to refute the piled-on testimony, pose questions, or cross-examine the witnesses to dispute even a single word. Under these severe disadvantages,

Anne said she had no witnesses, as she had not been presented an opportunity to obtain any testimony on her behalf. All in all, there was a staggering amount of evidence and testimony piled high against the two female pirates, who realized that they had been thoroughly victimized by the system, and the two young women maintained a bitter silence.

However, this silence was not a sign of submission or lost hope. As an Englishwoman who had fought for England on European soil, Mary felt a greater sense of irony and disgust than Anne, although it took some steely nerve for both women to remain stoic and reserved under the circumstances. Jack Rackham and his men had been hanged on this same exact set of charges and with less damaging testimony, and some kind of an outburst was likely expected from the women. But they had long refused to bow to society's arbitrary dictates and were not about to start with these smug judges, who delighted in orchestrating their executions.[290]

Anne and Mary were actually in an even more disadvantageous situation than male slaves, and their lives held no comparable monetary worth. In contrast, some male slaves were even freed on rape charges involving lower-class women, because their accusations reflected badly on the lack of control by upper-class masters. A slave's execution represented a large capital loss, but Mary's and Anne's executions would cost no one anything, because no one would lose any money on their investment.[291]

On Governor Lawes' directive, Anne and Mary were removed from courtroom and sent back under guard to their dank jail cells on the premise that the court needed time to deliberate in order to come to a fair decision—another mockery of justice. This final act of so-called jurisprudence was only for show, but the court was following legal procedure to make certain that nothing appeared out of the ordinary, and to give the impression that a final decision had not been already reached. But besides the avalanche of testimony, the king had promised swift justice for all pirates in early September 1717, and that was the final word. This trial was not only a mere formality, but also nothing more than a sham.

Anne and Mary had neither killed nor harmed anyone after the capture of any prize. Meanwhile, across the Caribbean and Central America, Henry Morgan and his buccaneers had slaughtered countless Spanish men, including priests, women, and children, for tons of gold and silver. They had even tortured captives to death, in order to force them to reveal the hiding places of their riches. And of course, an untold number of Spanish women had been raped, including nuns after convents were ransacked, by Morgan's English buccaneers during raids that had laid waste to entire cities. They, however, were considered England's heroes.

Despite the fact that no woman in England or her colonies had ever been hanged as a pirate, Anne now faced the prospect of earning the dubious distinction of becoming the first to hang, along with Mary. In truth, their only crime was when Anne and Mary had defended their ship on their own against the onslaught of Captain Barnet's attackers, when they had swarmed onto Rackham's ship with cutlasses waving and pistols blazing, which was actually a case of self-defense.[292] But not only for their actions as pirates but also for what they represented, Anne and Mary had to now die. What they had accomplished was to "explode" society's "imposed limits" like very few women of their day in the Western world.[293]

CONDEMNED TO DEATH

Not surprisingly, therefore, the court "unanimously agreed" on the verdict without much contemplation. Once again, Lawes ordered that both Anne and Mary be brought forward in chains by the guards. The two young women, who wore soiled, filthy seaman's clothing and still looked like common sailors, walked forward to hear the verdict from President Sir Lawes, who proclaimed that Anne Bonny and Mary Read had been found guilty of the "Piracies, Robberies and Felonies."

Then, President Sir Lawes prepared to pass their sentences as swiftly as they had been passed upon Captain Rackham and his crew, hardly before the trial had begun. After all of the overwhelming amount of testimonies had been stacked so high against them, Anne and Mary fully realized that they were about to be hanged like their unfortunate comrades of the *William*, with their sex not only making no difference, but even garnering more widespread support for their immediate executions.[294] The decision among the court members in regard to the specific charges against the two women was unanimous on every point.

In shackles, Anne and Mary stood facing President Sir Lawes, who betrayed no emotion or sympathy toward the two unluckiest women in Jamaica. As he had inquired of Captain Rackham and his men, the chief judge and governor of Jamaica then "asked if either o[f] them had anything to say why sentence of death should not pass upon them, in like manner as had been done to all the rest."[295]

As if conducting boring, routine bureaucratic business of absolutely no importance at his work desk in the governor's mansion, Sir Lawes then pronounced his final verdict and sentence: "You, Mary Read, and Anne Bonny, alias Bonn, are to go from hence to the Place from whence you came, and from thence to the Place of Execution; where you shall be severally hang'd by the Nec, till you are severally Dead. And GOD of his infinite mercy be merciful to both your Souls."[296] But then the haughty governor, as if desiring to add insult to injury in this farce of a trial, continued his badgering of Anne and Mary by "exhorting them to bear their sufferings patiently, assuring them that if they were innocent, which he very much doubted, then their reward would be greater in the Other World."[297]

Anne's Clever Legal Maneuver

Fortunately, at this moment when their lives hung in the balance, Anne now drew from the experiences and lessons of her past. She now recalled how her own mother, Mary Brennan, had been released from a dirty Kinsale jail cell after having been incarcerated by her father's jealous first wife, because the Cormac household maid was pregnant with Anne. She had also learned a good deal from her father when he practiced law for years, not only in Ireland but also in Charles Town. Fortunately, in her greatest time of need, Anne remembered that under English law, a woman who was pregnant could not be executed, because that ended two lives, one of which was completely innocent. Perhaps to her own surprise and by employing her intellect, Anne suddenly realized that she held a legal trump card in this high-stakes game of life or death, during which the deck had been stacked so high against her.[298]

To the utter astonishment of President Sir Lawes and his aristocratic court members, Anne abruptly spoke. Shocking one and all, the attorney's daughter began to pontificate at length to the stunned judges regarding this specific point of English law. Like a gambler in a game in which the stakes could not have been higher for her, Anne now played her only high card, as an ultimate bid to save her life. At the last moment, "Anne remembers enough of her father's table-talk of unusual legal precedents that when she faces the judge, she demurely pleads-her-belly: claims the precedent that a pregnant woman is not to be hanged [and] She expounds the case law with remarkable facility," before the court.[299]

During the most dramatic moment in the history of the High Court of the Admiralty, Anne, pregnant with Jack Rackham's child, and Mary, pregnant with Thomas Bourne's child, "pleaded their bellies, being quick with child, and prayed that execution might be stayed, whereupon the court passed sentence, as in case of piracy, but ordered them back, till a proper jury should be appointed to enquire into the matter."[300] As revealed by the official court reports that recorded Anne's legal masterstroke: "After Judgment was pronounced, as aforesaid, both the Prisoners inform'd the Court, that they were both quick with Child, and prayed that Execution of the Sentence might be stayed."[301] Fortunately for them, Anne and Mary were at this point "quick with child," which pertains to at least 18 weeks of pregnancy.

If Anne's father had been present in the suddenly noisy courtroom at St. Jago de la Vega to see his daughter argue her case, as well as the looks of disbelief on the face of Governor Lawes and his court members, he certainly would have been proud. Anne's last-second legal maneuver had saved four lives (two unborn) in the blink of an eye, at a time when there seemed no hope. Her timely reliance on one of English law's finer points had been nothing short of brilliant.

President Sir Lawes' shock was sincere because no pirates had ever successfully defended themselves, as they knew nothing about the law. And even fewer had mounted an intelligent defense or sound argument. The court had been taught a legal lesson by an ill-groomed, sweaty, dirty young woman from Ireland.[302] Indeed, at this time, absolutely no one, "not even the bloodthirsty British courts [and especially the High Court of the Admiralty], could execute a pregnant woman and therefore both Bonny and Read had their sentences overturned," but only until they gave birth.[303] Governor Lawes and the court were forced to respect Anne's claim.

Because Anne or Mary did not appear pregnant at this time, they had to first be examined by a physician to determine their condition. In the words of the trial record, "the said Sentence should be respited, and then an inspection should be made." An examination by a qualified physician—a man whom Anne had saved from the rack when the prison ship, full of "thieves, the *Jewell* from Newgate" and "bound for the [sugar] plantations" was captured by Captain Rackham—revealed that both women were, in fact, pregnant. This information was then conveyed to Lawes, who was forced to realize that he had met his match in a lawyer's clever pirate daughter, Anne Bonny.[304]

At long last, God and good fortune had seemingly smiled upon Anne, when she was on the verge of death. As they had demonstrated on their last day at sea, to prove that they could excel in either a traditional male or female role in a crisis situation, "while Read and Bonny were the best warriors on Rackham's ship, they managed to escape death through the most natural of female reasons."[305]

President Sir Lawes now had no choice but to delay the executions of Anne and Mary until after they gave birth. By thwarting the hasty pace of conviction and execution, Anne had bought precious time that could result in much-needed legal assistance from outside of St. Jago de la Vega. This was the first time that the governor and the court had been outfoxed by their own laws: an embarrassing, but most historic, moment for Governor Lawes, especially considering that the defendants had had no legal representation. But the initial jubilation of the reprieve was short-lived: Anne and Mary, no doubt smiling to themselves with the successful legal maneuver, were then taken to separate jail cells and locked up.

By delaying the death sentences, Anne had bought around six more months for herself and her friend. And who knew what might happen in that time period, because of the case's high publicity that was sure to garner a response from London.[306]

During the early 18th century, the brightly painted carvings of women on the ship's bow had been prominently placed by men since times immemorial. Female imagery was calculated by the superstitious sailors to calm rough seas and to protect the crew and ship, to ensure a safe return to the home port. But even "stronger magic was embodied by pregnant women; a ship favored by a woman giving birth on the first night out of port, it was said, would never sink."[307] The old seafarer's superstition that pregnancy brought good fortune certainly proved true in the case of Anne and Mary on November 28, 1720.[308]

Autocratic Governor Lawes, certainly frustrated and probably angry, thanks to a legal technicality that had saved the two women, sat down and went to work. He wrote a letter to officials in London to describe what had happened in regard to the Rackham crew and how swift justice had eliminated these notorious pirates from the waters of Jamaica. Lawes also wrote to his superior about how, although Rackham and 10 of his crewmen had been hanged, "the women, spinsters of Providence Island, were proved to have taken an active part in piracies, wearing men's clothes and armed, etc. Being quick with child, their sentences have been suspended," until the two children were born around late April or early May 1721.[309]

REFLECTIONS FROM A JAIL CELL

The Monday night after the exhausting trial was a long one for Anne Bonny. She might well have lamented the day that she and her family had departed Kinsale and sailed across the Atlantic to Charles Town. She regretted marriage to Jim Bonny, who had been the first to seduce her into the world of piracy. Young Anne had been led astray, and the price that had to be paid for her youthful indiscretions was frightfully high. With ample time on her hands, Anne may have spent it thinking about her life back in Charles Town, which only brought more second-guessing about the risky choices she had made in life. But she likely could not forget how she could have led the easy, comfortable life of a proper lady of the gentry if she had only remained in South Carolina, married a man who met her strict father's approval, and never ventured into the world of piracy.

Anne must have realized that she had become a pirate at the worst of all times, when piracy was dying. She had learned the hard way that the authorities, the law, and the pirate hunters were catching up to those adventurous souls who had for so long defied governments, the king's laws, and free trade. An unkind fate had finally caught up to her: Anne happened to be just another unfortunate pirate who had been caught out on a limb, thanks to a reckless young captain and equally imprudent crew.

In many ways, Anne Bonny had been sentenced to death in part to pay for the crimes and sins of all those successful pirates who had come before her, for generations. Now from her dark cell at St. Jago de la Vega, awaiting the inevitable execution day after she gave birth to her second child, perhaps in Anne's dreams at night, she thought back about these things that she most loved in life. Despite her bleak situation and vivid memories of better days, she likely would not have traded any of her difficult experiences in life for the freedom that she had enjoyed as a pirate.

On the eve of meeting her maker at only 22 years old, Anne had no time for regrets. If she had been born a Catholic—as her mother almost certainly was, as she had been a poor maid of highly Catholic County Cork—and then raised a Protestant, as her father likely was, then Anne now might have found strength in both faiths. A trust in God would have steeled Anne's nerve for the upcoming ordeal of her execution. As if dropping from a scaffold was not enough, she now had to worry about the future fate of her first child in Cuba as well as the child now inside her.

Racked by bleak thoughts and a gathering sense of foreboding, Anne was now far from the young naïve girl who had departed Kinsale with high hopes. And, most of all, she was no longer the cocky, confident pirate who had terrified captives and fought against the attacking privateers aboard the *William*. At that time, Anne Bonny had proudly stood at the bridge of her ship that flew the Jolly Roger flag, when it seemed as if a carefree life of freedom would go on forever. But now, only a ghastly reality remained: the vision of a hangman.[310]

Jack Rackham and his pirates had defied the most powerful authorities on Earth and lived one day at a time because they knew that any day might well be their last. As embraced by Anne for nearly two years, the pirate philosophy to "really live, or die trying," to "live fast and die young," and of "a merry Life and a short one" had now come full circle for Anne Bonny.[311] But Anne had even more good reason for not wanting to die. She was a mother, and about to have another child of Captain Rackham's, whose body still hung high for all to see as a chilling warning to anyone who thought about becoming a pirate.[312]

Meanwhile, Anne was reminded about her future when Captain Charles Vane and one of his men were tried in St. Jago de la Vega. Anne most likely occupied a cell near his before he was hustled to the gallows. Here, the doomed Captain Vane might have said something about Jack Rackham, who had taken Vane's place when the crew voted to no longer support their captain. Vane was hanged at Gallows Point, like Captain Rackham, on March 22, 1721, and his body was "hung in chains on Gun Cay, Port Royal," near Dead Man's Cay, where Jack's body still hung.[313]

Like Captains Rackham and Vane, Anne Bonny was about to face the hangman's noose as well once her child was born, even though no evidence existed that she had harmed a single soul during her nearly two years as a pirate.[314]

A KIND INTERVENTION AT THE LAST MINUTE

Author Captain Johnson never learned the true story of what happened to Anne Bonny. While he was accurate in determining Mary's death in St. Jago de la Vega in April 1721, he could only speculate about the fate of Anne Bonny in his short biography: "She was continued in prison, to the time of her laying in, and afterwards reprieved from time to time; but what became of her since, we cannot tell; only this we know, that she was not executed."[315]

But what actually happened to Anne was more interesting than anything that Johnson could have fabricated. At some point, back in the low country of South Carolina not long after Anne's trial in Jamaica, William Cormac learned of his only child's dilemma. He had friends and business associates in Jamaica, and many merchant ships regularly passed between Charles Town, where still another efficient High Court of the Admiralty operated, and Jamaica.

William Cormac was looked upon in "favorable terms" by the governor, who had initially no idea that Anne was his daughter—she was known to the Jamaican court simply as "Ann Bonny, alias Bonn, late of the Island of [New] Providence" in the Bahamas. Anne was fortunate that her father had been a successful Charles Town merchant, who had long shipped his plantation's produce between the two places. William was also a highly respected, wealthy member of the upper class, and he was "known to a great many gentlemen, planters of Jamaica, who had dealt with him, and among whom he had a good reputation" for fair dealing.[316]

After a few weeks or months in prison, Anne revealed her maiden name of Cormac to the court, then informed them of her father's location in Charles Town. Fortunately for her, "some of [the Jamaican planters who sat in on the trial and] who had been in [South] Carolina, remembered to have seen her in his house; wherefore they were inclined to show her favour," and they assisted her by notifying her father.[317]

Back in South Carolina, William Cormac eventually received word of Anne's death sentence. This was the first time he learned that his daughter was a pirate—all that he had previously known was that she had departed with her sailor husband, Jim Bonny. Fortunately, her father had the wealth, widespread influence, and connections to Jamaica's planter class to come to his daughter's aid in her hour of greatest peril. Despite having disowned and disinherited her when she married James Bonny, he had a change of heart when his only daughter was in dire need. William Cormac used his connections to launch an attempt to rescue his daughter, either through political influence with the governor or with bribes of local officials—or both. Scant available "evidence provided by the descendants of Anne Bonny suggest that her father managed to secure her release from jail . . . ."[318] William Cormac's wealth and influence mandated a covert effort because no official record can be found of Anne's release. Captain Johnson, though, presented a convoluted scenario indicating official impropriety that hinted of bribery, writing that she was "afterwards reprieved from time to time."[319]

William Cormac essentially ransomed his daughter to win her freedom and save his unborn grandchild. A sizable bribe to Governor Lawes, one of a long line of corruptible colonial officials in America and the Caribbean, almost certainly explained how and why this female pirate disappeared so completely from the official and public record. Indeed, the governor was on "favorable terms" with William Cormac, as a fellow member of the planter class and part of the elite.

We know that Anne gave birth to her child, long after her fellow pirates had gone to the gallows, but she was never hanged. Reportedly, the cell door was left conveniently unlocked one night, after the necessary arrangements—perhaps by Governor Lawes himself through another party—had been made to smuggle Anne out of Jamaica with an alias.

Anne had been haunted by the prospect of two nightmare scenarios almost as horrific as death itself: her own impending death on Gallows Point, and the taking away of her second child after her death by hanging. According to descendants, William Cormac not only gained Anne's release but also brought "her back to Charles Town," which was almost certainly the case, because Anne could not leave Jamaica under her notorious real name. Once again, Anne gained a new lease on life and the golden opportunity for a fresh start back in America.[320] This situation explains why she was "afterwards reprieved from time to time," and eventually allowed to flee Jamaica for America with her newborn infant.[321] The fact that William Cormac owned a sugar plantation in Jamaica, with connections in high places in Jamaica and by way of a discreet payment with a bribe, helped Anne win the freedom that she thought that she would never see.

MARY READ MEETS HER MAKER, APRIL 1721

Anne's release from a steamy prison cell in the hell of the tropics saved her life, and perhaps her child, but Mary Read was not so fortunate. After surviving so many close calls with death from cannonballs, bullets, bayonets, and sabers first on Europe's battlefields and later as a pirate, she was finally stricken by something she could not even see—an invisible virus. After having been "found quick with child . . . her execution was respited, and it is possible she would have found favour, but she was seized with a violent fever soon after her trial, of which she died in prison."[322] Mary Read succumbed to the so-called "prison fever"—typhus.[323]

While Anne gave birth to her second child, Mary Read never saw the birth of her first. Worn down by too many devastating emotional reversals in life that included the hanging of two husbands for piracy—the latest being her common-law husband Thomas Bourne—she never had a chance. Mary died at age 37 in St. Jago de la Vega on April 28, 1721, and was buried with her unborn child on the same day, when her death was recorded in the register of St. Catherine Parish.[324]

A common pirate saying during the Golden Age of Piracy had nothing to do with the concept of heaven, because pirates were only too familiar with the hypocrisy of the most revered religious men. Instead, for the Caribbean pirate, the vision of a happy afterlife was centered not somewhere above in heaven but at the port of Nassau, which Mary and Anne had called home before embarking upon their ill-fated last cruise under the hard-luck Captain Rackham: "When a pirate sleeps, then he doesn't dream that he has died and gone to heaven, but that he has returned to New Providence."[325] As such, some believed that Mary Read's soul lingered afterward in Nassau rather than Jamaica.

Although her death was early, Mary had lived the way she had chosen to, taking more out life in only a few months as a pirate than she would have if had she lived to old age. To the end in her jail cell, Mary had been resigned to her tragic situation. As she explained near the end of her life: "As to hanging, the thought is no great Hardship, for were it not for that, every cowardly Fellow would turn Pyrate, and so infest the Seas, that Men of Courage must starve."[326]

Anne Bonny, though, had defied the odds not only in regard to the hangman's noose, thanks to her last-minute legal maneuvering on her own as well as her father's timely assistance, but also in regard to the ravages of disease. After all, the majority of Caribbean "pirates died at sea, and the sea became their grave."[327]

A source of great displeasure to them partly because of the undying contempt for landlubbers, Captain Jack Rackham and his crew had been denied that privilege of burial at sea. Jack had been even denied a Christian burial. After his body, hung in chains, gradually decomposed under a searing sun and pounding tropical rains month after month, his bones eventually tumbled down and into the white sands of Dead Man's Cay, where they remain at some unknown location to this day.[328]

Not only in regard to Captain Rackham's ugly demise before a jeering crowd, Anne also realized how lucky she had been upon learning the fate of the nine hapless "English men," who had boarded the *William* at Negril Point. Clearly, the timing of these young men and boys could not have been worse. They should have continued to hunt sea turtles along the beach, instead of drinking too heavily from "a bowl of punch" with the men of the Rackham crew. These Englishmen had been tried on January 24, 1721, and convicted of "going over with a piratical and felonious intent to John Rackham." Six of the men were executed on February 17 and 18 at Gallows Point, and the other three unfortunates were strung up at a later date. The judges showed no mercy to these nine men, although no witnesses testified that they had ever engaged in any pirate activity.[329] Their executions were based upon the new 1721 law known as the Expanded Piracy Act, which proclaimed that any person caught conducting business with a pirate was also guilty of the capital sin of piracy.[330]

Few details of the death of the pregnant Mary Read, isolated in a lonely jail cell far from friends and perhaps family in England, have been discovered. All that has become known was that Mary "was seized with a violent fever soon after her trial, of which she died in prison."[331] Like Anne, she was no doubt tormented by the idea that she would be hanged after childbirth and over what would happen to her child after her death. Such dark thoughts likely played a role in her rapid physical and psychological decline that made her more vulnerable to disease.

One modern novelist, James L. Nelson, in his book *The Only Life That Mattered*, perhaps said it best in regard to the early demise of Anne's friend, who was only in her 30s: "Mary looked down at her swollen belly and her child who resided there. She put her hands on her baby and she smiled, and in a whisper, she said, 'I'll take you away now, my little one. I'll take you away to a better place. I'll take you with me.'"[332]

Almost as if she willed it in the end, Mary's last act of defiance was to deny the court and her executor, not to mention a crowd of hecklers, the satisfaction of fulfilling her death sentence. It is also possible that Mary might have died in childbirth. It seems that, because she was a woman and because an innocent child had died with her, Mary was given a proper burial, unlike most who died in prison in that era. Along with other pirates who were executed by this highly efficient court, Mary Read and her child were buried behind the remains of the old stone jail, in "a common burial pit" of the prison cemetery at St. Jago de la Vega. Today, the exact location of Mary Read's final resting place is known only to God.[333]

Mary had cruised the Caribbean for only a relatively short time and had been "intending to quit it when ever a fair opportunity should offer itself" for another kind of life, but that opportunity never came for her.[334] But during that last, fatal voyage of the *William* with Captain Rackham and Anne Bonny, Mary Read had taken great pride in sailing on fair winds across the Caribbean. As Mary waxed philosophical about enjoying a free life at the risk of a grisly death, she provided the a fitting epitaph to her life as a pirate: "that if 'twas put to the choice of the pirates, they would not have the punishment less than death, the fear of which, kept some dastardly rogues honest; that many of those who are now cheating the widows and orphans, and oppressing their poor neighbours, who have no money to obtain justice, would then rob at sea, and the ocean would be crowded with rogues, like the land, and no merchant would venture out; so that the trade, in a little time, would not be worth following."[335]

COMING FULL CIRCLE, RETURN TO AMERICA
1721

ONE OF THE MISCONCEPTIONS about Anne Bonny's life was that nothing is known about her after her trial in Jamaica. As one historian recently wrote, echoing the words of many others: "Nothing more is known of Anne Bonny."[336]

While Mary ended up in a lonely grave in Jamaica, Anne returned home with her newborn child to Charles Town, after an absence of nearly three years. Like she did as a pirate, she came back to America under an alias, because a death sentence had been passed upon her and it was "never overturned." Not only her true sex but also her name had been printed in Governor Rogers' September 5, 1720, proclamation from Nassau that appeared in the *Boston Gazette*. However, she simply returned to South Carolina in conventional dress, as a young woman with an infant in her arms would have deflected any suspicions.

No one knows the exact fate of Anne's first child. Some historians and writers have speculated that the infant died in Cuba at birth, although no evidence has indicated as much. Because William Cormac had both wealth and commercial connections in nearby islands, he could have had his grandchild, almost certainly on Anne's insistence, brought back to South Carolina to rejoin its mother by a planter, lawyer, or captain friend. Because Anne had been a pirate, many male writers and historians have accepted the myth that Anne was a crazed, bloodthirsty psycho-

---

Opposite: Charles Town and its harbor, circa 1711.

path without an ounce of morality and surmised that she lacked maternal instincts and willingly abandoned her first child in Cuba. But back in South Carolina, after literally gaining a new lease on life, Anne played a more conventional and domestic role as a mother: a dramatic transition for a pirate. She had survived some of the most harrowing experiences possible for a young woman, and somehow lived to tell the tale. Perhaps she would be surprised by the joys of motherhood and find them much more rewarding and longer-lasting than the dangerous life as a pirate.

Some historians have speculated that her second child was born on April 21, 1721, in South Carolina, around five months after the trial's end in St. Jago de la Vega. But in fact, the child's birth was listed in the record of St. Catherine Parish, Jamaica. A long, rough sea voyage for a woman in the late stages of pregnancy would have been too risky for both mother and child at a time when childbirth was a leading killer among women. Anne had given birth to her child in Jamaica, and Captain Johnson indicated that she remained for some time at St. Jago de la Vega. Some evidence has indicated that the child, a son, was named either John Rackham, or John Cormac Bonny, as Anne was still legally married.[337]

But the name Bonny would have been far too dangerous to retain. And she could hardly have taken the name of one of the most infamous pirate captains in the Caribbean, Rackham. Anne had to keep her pirate past a secret once back in South Carolina, beyond the obvious fact that a death sentence still hung over her head. In the 18th-century world, a woman who was known to have dressed as a man, even to fight for one's own country in the military, was scandalous. Ida Saint-Elme learned as much when she early went to war with her husband to fight the battles of republican France. In her own words: "I put aside the garments of my sex, and assumed the press of a man [and] witnessed the Battle of Valmy." But after returning home to the Netherlands, she suffered the community's wrath and scorn: "It was known in Holland that I had gone to the war in men's clothes, and since my arrival . . . I became the object of universal curiosity and gossip," until the family was forced to move to another country.[338]

If her secret leaked out, Anne would have suffered re-arrest in a pre-revolutionary America, still under British law. Even a hint of past piracy would have brought far worse treatment from the locals than experienced by Ida Saint-Elme, because Anne had not only disguised herself as a male but also engaged in piracy rather than a patriotic struggle—a double crime sure to unleash a community's wrath.

But Anne's great secret was maintained, and once again dressed in fine clothes, Anne rejoined polite society with a quickness that indicated how she had thoroughly disinherited her pirate past out of urgent necessity. She was eager to start a new life and continued to demonstrate that she was resilient and versatile, with a distinct ability to fit into multiple environments. Here, in South Carolina's largest port, she was destined shortly to gain a new husband, Joseph Burleigh, who was visiting Charles Town from York County in the Virginia Tidewater. This was yet the latest example of class-conscious William Cormac's timely handiwork of orchestrating family affairs behind the scenes. This time, he made sure that his only daughter married into the planter-merchant class. After having been led astray in marrying the penniless sailor of ill repute, Anne evidently had no objections on this occasion: the first time that she had actually listened to and abided by her father's wishes in years.

The Cormac and Burleigh families had known each other for years, and perhaps all the way back to Ireland—although Burleigh was an English name, this might have been an Anglo-Irish family. Both were families of some means, and to keep the law off Anne's trail, William Cormac had masterminded an arranged marriage in Charles Town, so that his daughter would attain what she now most needed: a new name to hide her name, true identity, and dark past.

William also had to get Anne and her children far away from Charles Town, which contained many planters and merchants visiting from Jamaica who almost certainly were aware of Anne's trial. It was important that Anne be allowed a new start far from any major port, such as an obscure, isolated tobacco plantation in the Virginia Tidewater—around 450 miles up the coast from Charles Town, to the northeast. Situated on the north side of the Virginia Peninsula, York County extended east to the Chesapeake Bay. Anne's new husband was a member of the planter class like her father, and York County was tobacco country, unlike South Carolina, where rice dominated. However, like South Carolina, Virginia was also a land of slavery, because large numbers of slaves were needed to work the tobacco fields. Both the Virginia Tidewater and Piedmont were part of the "Tobacco Kingdom."

On December 21, 1721, Anne was married for the second time in her young life, at age 23. With his legal knowledge, William Cormac might have quietly obtained an annulment or divorce for his daughter, as upon her return to South Carolina, she was still legally married to Jim Bonny, whose whereabouts were unknown. The Virginia Peninsula, nestled between the James River to the south and the York River to the north, became Anne Burleigh's final home, where she would spend the rest of her long life in a stable marriage and in quiet contentment. Virginia contained a good many Irish immigrants during this period, which would have made her feel more at home in the Old Dominion—there was even a little town in the Virginia Tidewater called Kinsale, named by Irish immigrants.

Anne had now provided a good home and a decent life for her children. In addition to the two she had had with Captain John "Calico Jack" Rackham, she would have six more children with her new husband. According to the Burleigh family Bible, Anne became the mother of eight children in total, six of which she and Joseph raised to adulthood, after two died of illnesses. Anne's wealthy father assisted her family, leaving a large section of land to Joseph Burleigh, and the new Burleigh family became part of the established society of the Virginia Tidewater planter class of York County. In perhaps the last great irony of her life, Anne Burleigh blended in completely with the upper class of planter society, and around educated, well-dressed people who had no idea that she had sailed the Caribbean as a pirate in her youth.[339]

On July 19, 1723, and just over two years after having escaped an appointment with the hangman in Jamaica, one of Anne's countrymen met his end in Charles Town, South Carolina, a scene that Anne was lucky to not have witnessed. Along with his pirate comrades, an Irishman from County Limerick, Ireland, John Fitzgerald, was hanged at the age of 21 before a crowd on that day. But before the Irishman went to the gallows, he wrote a poem with which Anne, after her close brush with death in Jamaica, would have no doubt related and identified:

> In youthful blooming years was I, when I that practice took;
> Of perpetrating piracy, for filthy gain did look.
> To wickedness we all were bent, our lusts for to fulfill;
> To rob at sea was our intent, and perpetrate all ill.

I pray the Lord preserve you all and keep you from this end;
O let Fitz-Gerald's great downfall unto your welfare lend.
I to the Lord my soul bequeath, accept thereof I pray,
My body to the earth bequeath, dear friend, adieu for aye."[340]

During the years ahead, Anne continued to keep her past a closely guarded secret, or she might have risked an immediate annulment or divorce from Joseph Burleigh. Indeed, any revelation about Anne's pirate past or marriage to James Bonny would have brought not only disgrace to her and the family, but also to her daughters. Such scandalous information would have ruined the Burleigh girls' future prospects for marrying into respectable families in the close-knit planter society. As befitting a Tidewater upper-class family, Anne very likely went to some length to raise her daughters to be proper ladies, as if to ensure that they would never dream of running off with a handsome, smooth-talking pirate, as their mother once had.

A MOST SCANDALOUS BOOK

If any of the good people of the Virginia Tidewater region happened to pick up a copy of Captain Johnson's popular *A General History of the Robberies & Murders of the Most Notorious Pirates*, they would have had no idea that their neighbor, Mrs. Burleigh, with the fine manners of any respectable Virginia low-country wife and mother, was revealed in it, among the nefarious pirates who once raided the high seas.[341]

Captain Johnson's book was first published in 1724, and no small part of its immense popularity stemmed from a copper engraving that depicted a defiant Anne Bonny and Mary Read standing side by side, with weapons in hand. The crude illustrations were fairly accurate: Both women were shown wearing baggy pants, sailor's coats, and voluminous clothing. The publisher, Charles Riverton, who operated a small bookshop near St. Paul's Cathedral, London, understood the popular appeal of such graphic illustrations that revealed a sensational story: a titillating mix of high-seas crime, mystery, and sex. Meanwhile, back in the obscurity of Tidewater Virginia, Anne had no awareness of Captain Johnson's little book, which had devoted an entire biographical chapter to her life.

Reprints of Johnson's book soon followed, including new releases in Germany and the Netherlands, capitalizing upon the book's English-language success. Hoping to cash in, the Dutch publisher updated his 1725 translation with his own illustrations of Anne and Mary: Fierce-looking and fully armed, both women were portrayed in low-cut shirts, revealing their cleavage, with tight pants and lacings in the crotch. Perhaps Anne would have been amused to see this dramatic illustration of herself in the Dutch book, and how her highly sexualized portrait was one reason for the book's amazing success across Europe, while she was living quietly in the Virginia Tidewater and enjoying domestic life. Not only had Anne no idea of the book's publication and popularity, but she also received no compensation for the exploitation of her life story—which was a possibly libelous depiction, as she was painted as a bloodthirsty Amazon.[342]

Just one year later, in 1726, after the Dutch edition was published and not far from where Anne Burleigh now lived, a trial of captured pirates began before the Vice-Admiralty Court at Williamsburg, Virginia. This small-time crew, led by Irishman John Vidal, had prowled North Carolina waters, including Blackbeard's old hideout at Ocracoke Inlet. Unlike Anne's treatment during her Jamaica trial in 1720, the jury at the colonial capital of Virginia felt compassion for the pirate woman named Mary Harvey, who was known by the alias Martha Farlee. And unlike Mary Read, who now lay buried at St. Jago de la Vega, Martha was released on the flimsy premise that she had been coerced to join the pirate crew. Clearly, mercy had been shown to Martha because of her sex. Although Anne lived in York County not far from Williamsburg, it is almost certain that she did not attend the very public trial.[343]

Decade after decade, Anne continued to keep her secret to herself, and especially away from her children, as they might well have bragged to other kids about their mother's scandalous past. Far away from her father while living in Virginia, she could confide in no one about her pirate past. It was all the better for Anne to let it all go, because that part of Anne's life was gone forever—a romantic, distant memory that grew dimmer with the passing of each year.

But still Anne's past life as a pirate who sailed the Caribbean never completely faded away from her thoughts over the years. Even when much older, it seems unlikely that she forgot that she had been a part of an egalitarian pirate society, a close-knit community of seafarers, and a novel world that had long since disappeared from New Providence and Nassau. On cold winter days in Virginia, when temperatures dropped well below freezing, and or if she were bored with dull kitchen chores or caring for her many children, the mundane realities of the everyday traditional role as the proper wife of a respected family when she was known as Mrs. Joseph Burleigh, Anne could at least think back to those sunny days in the Caribbean and the complete sense of freedom that she had experienced to the fullest as a pirate.

Anne had served as a pirate in the first place partially in order to fight the powerful merchants, ruling class, and the aristocratic elite, to preserve what was an entirely unique way of life in the hope of retaining it as long as possible, as if knowing that it was all too good to last. She seemed to almost realize that anything so unconventional would soon slip over the horizon, never to be seen again, which proved only too true in the end. Anne undoubtedly still recalled the perfect beauty of the most elusive of all things for a young woman in her day: the exhilarating sense of freedom and equality that she enjoyed at a time when women in society had precious little agency.[344]

Indeed, one of the great myths of American history was that the founding fathers, the Declaration of Independence, and the winning of the American Revolution brought about an unprecedented degree of freedom and equality for all people. However, Thomas Jefferson's words in the Declaration of Independence were hypocritical to tens of thousands of African Americans as well as women of all races. Slavery then became permanently entrenched in the American system and way of life with the Constitution's establishment in mid-September 1787. But in pirate society, people of all races and sexes were accorded equality, and by becoming one, Anne had answered a vexing question: how and where a young woman could gain and experience greater equality.[345]

A PEACEFUL ENDING

Wearing proper clothes, eating from fine china, and surrounded by a loving family, she found the peace that she'd lacked in her youth. At some point, Joseph became a merchant instead of a plantation owner, and the Burleigh family moved farther south from York County, close to Chesapeake Bay. At some point, possibly in her 70s, she made plans to be buried in the Virginia Tidewater in a York County cemetery at a place called Sweethaven, named for its natural beauty, in a generally flat region of oaks and pines.[346]

Anne died in York County barely six months after the United States of America won its independence from Great Britain, although a peace treaty was not signed for another two years, with George Washington's and his French allies' dramatic October 1781 victory at Yorktown. Here on the York River in York County, Washington won his greatest victory, ensuring a long life for the United States of America.

Significantly, in that long struggle for America's liberty from 1775 to 1783, thousands of Irishmen played key roles—military, political, and economic—in winning the nation's independence. Irishmen even signed the Declaration of Independence in Philadelphia, such as Charles Carroll II, whose family's mansion in Maryland, Doughoregan Manor, was named for a family estate back in Ireland.

Perhaps Anne's own sons or grandsons served as patriots in battling the king's well-trained soldiers and their Hessian and Loyalist allies during the struggle for American liberty. Recognizing the fine line between hero and villain, Anne likely found some ironic amusement in the fact that, had the American rebellion against the English crown's authority been crushed, then Washington would have been hanged as she had almost been, by the same British authorities a half-century before.

Anne might have also known that hundreds of her Irish countrymen, as ship's captains and common seamen, had served on ships of the Continental Navy, in the newly formed United States Marines, and that many Irish privateers—such as Captain James Bourke, who commanded the privateer *Neptune*, and Captain Benjamin Connors, who was in charge of the *Hyder Ally*—had attacked British merchant ships, as Anne had done in her youth. Ironically, not unlike the buccaneers before Anne's day, these Irish privateer captains won acclaim as America's heroes for raiding and looting fat merchant ships like Captain Rackham and his crew had while rampaging across the Caribbean.[347]

For Anne, it was significant that the war's most decisive victory at Yorktown, when "The World Turn'd Upside Down," had successfully defied the mother country's laws, society, and even divine authority—embodied in King George III—to shock the world. The final peace treaty was signed in 1783, at a time when hundreds of American prisoners were held in Anne's native hometown of Kinsale, Ireland: the guarantee of a long life for a new nation and a people's republic, dedicated to the principle that all (white) men were created equal, although long after pirate society had proclaimed equality among pirates of all races and nationalities.[348]

While the rest of the world could hardly believe that the common people of America had successfully defied King George III to go their own way, Anne might have smiled to herself at the thought of an earlier time when common people of all races and sexes had chosen to lead their lives in a more equitable way than existed in conventional society by joining the "Brethren of the Sea." More than 50 years before the American Revolution's beginning, Anne Bonny had struck back against the king and his repressive imperialist system, rebelling against a hierarchy that had seemed to have been created for the express purpose of keeping her and other common people down.

In this sense, Anne might well have felt a sense of vindication through colonial Americans, who had created a new society that was more equal than anything ever seen under the rule of England's king, church, and society. The struggle of common Americans was not really anything new, because the colonists fought against the same enemy that had been Anne's own—and that of the Irish people for centuries. On an early spring day at an obscure place called Sweethaven in the Virginia Tidewater, perhaps Anne smiled softly to herself as she reminisced about her days as a pirate just before she died, at age 81 on April 25, 1782.[349]

Today, where the village of Sweetwater had stood, along with its cemetery, which can no longer be seen today, the remains of Anne Bonny lay unmarked. Unlike her pirate life on the Caribbean, nothing has remained of the life of Anne Bonny. Her forgotten grave is covered by a major highway, and thousands of cars speed over the bones of the most famous female pirate in history.[350]

TRANSFORMATION AND AN ENDURING LEGACY
1721-1782

THE UP-AND-DOWN COURSE and perilous existence of Anne Bonny's life was preserved forever by the publication of Captain Johnson's book in London in May 1724, only a few years after Anne returned to America to start a new life. Although Anne was at least 25 when Johnson's book was released in England, she had no idea that hundreds of London readers were busily devouring this groundbreaking work that was partially about her life.[351] Paradoxically, Anne languished in Virginia's tobacco country while she became famous across western Europe as a lawless, outrageous renegade, as the book was reprinted for years in one nation after another.

Anne's infamy was destined to live on for generations. Her life as described in Johnson's book has served as both an inspirational model and a cautionary tale for young women in pursuit of equality well into the 21st century. Quite unexpectedly, future generations of young women overlooked the admonition presented by Johnson, who had attempted to demonstrate the high price that was paid by pirates, both male and female. This lesson was ignored, though, and an entirely different lesson was taken from Anne's remarkable story: how a life of freedom, dignity,

Opposite: Cape Tiburon, Haiti.

and self-respect could be attained by a young woman in a man's world, through imagination, flexibility, and courage.

After the threat of piracy subsided by the early 1800s, the overall image of the pirate in the public's popular perception was permanently altered, evolving into romantic idols, thanks to popular writers like Walter Scott with *The Pirate* (1832) and especially Robert Louis Stevenson with *Treasure Island* (1883). These pirates were on a quest for personal freedom and independence, while struggling against an unjust system and the powerful elites, in the style of Robin Hood. But most of all, it was Charles Johnson who established a permanent place for Anne Bonny in the popular imagination and memory. His 1724 book had the most "profound and lasting influence on the European mind" in regard to pirates than any other single work. In future decades, thanks to the imagination of the bourgeoisie, Anne Bonny "became a heroine to entire flotillas of little English girls, through their surreptitious reading of Captain Johnson's" book.[352]

The telling of Anne Bonny's life story created an early foundation for the romantic female pirate, who had successfully escaped a repressive world of society's lowly expectations and a subservient role. She became an inspiring role model and symbol of women's freedom from repression to generations of women and girls on both sides of the Atlantic. In time, Anne's image evolved into that of a heroic outlaw who challenged the expectations of an unjust patriarchal society, while fulfilling her dreams and ambitions with an inordinate amount of audacity and spirit.[353]

During the French Revolution and the "Great Terror" in the early 1790s, some aristocratic French women saved themselves from the guillotine by declaring their pregnancies. It is not known, but these women might well have read Captain Johnson's 1724 book, recalling Anne Bonny's example of saving her own life and that of her unborn child at St. Jago de la Vega.[354] Anne's reputation also grew because of the Romantic era of the 19th century, which produced a flood of romantic novels and plays about the lives of pirates. First published under the title *The Female Pirate* and then republished in 1845 on the eve of America's war with Mexico, Maturin Murray Ballou of Boston authored the novel *Fanny Campbell: or the Female Pirate*, which was published by John B. Hall Publishers. He wrote his popular novel under the pseudonym Lieutenant Murray. But none of his works were more sensational than *Fanny Camp-*

bell. This was the story of the New England woman who not only went to sea as a pirate, disguised in baggy pants and a blue sailor's jacket, but also took a leadership position as a captain of a pirate ship.[355]

Like Johnson's popular book, the Ballou novel only continued to foster the mystique of the female pirate for new generations of young readers. All in all, the image of the female pirate represented "a particular working-class heroism" that was as admirable as it was impressive. In this sense and in much the same way, the romantic imagery of Anne Bonny and what she represented continued to flourish in the form of the popular story of Fanny Campbell: a female pirate who served as a working-class hero for generations of young women across America. The mythology of the female pirate of the 18th century continued to rise to new heights with the novel's popularity, cementing a central place for Anne Bonny in pirate historiography and popular memory.[356]

For example, at age 13, Emma Edmonds' life was changed forever when her mother presented her with a birthday gift: a copy of *Fanny Campbell,* the 1856 edition, which was loosely based and molded upon Anne's remarkable life. This independent young woman read the novel at a time when she felt trapped by a strict, abusive father, a patriarchal society's harsh demands, and mindless drudgery on the family farm in New Brunswick, Canada. Emma was also haunted by the "wrongs" patiently endured by her long-suffering mother, who was mired in a permanent, humiliating subservient position. Her tragic situation fueled "my love of independence and my hatred of male-tyranny," in Emma's words.[357]

Emma's most influential positive role model was the novel's female pirate, who defiantly entered into a bold, adventurous life by a "simple ingenuity of Fanny's disguise" of loose-fitting seaman's clothing. In fact, Ballou's work was the first novel that she had ever read, and it shaped her thinking and future destiny. Inspired by clever Fanny Campbell and determined not to become an abused "slave" in an inequitable environment, Emma bravely disguised herself in men's clothing, after having made the decision to never suffer "my mother's wrongs." Fanny's fictional story had stemmed from Ballou's reading of Captain Johnson's popular book, providing the model for his central character—and so, Anne Bonny's example brought an unprecedented liberation to Emma Edmonds, who wrote: "I was emancipated! and could never again be a slave."[358]

What has been forgotten about Emma's life, when she became "America's most famous female soldier" of the Civil War, was that Anne Bonny had served as the central inspirational influence of the *Fanny Campbell* novel.[359] A good many other women, besides Emma, were inspired to serve in the Civil War, in part because of Anne Bonny's legacy had inspired an entire generation of American women, hundreds of whom disguised themselves as men to serve in both Union and Confederate armies across America. Historians have overlooked this key connection between Anne Bonny and the large number of women—at least 300 and almost certainly more—who fought for their country while masquerading as men.[360]

Yet the romantic image of Anne Bonny and the female pirate would evolve in the Victorian era. What was once considered heroic and inspirational to young women like Emma Edmonds was suddenly deemed immoral and shameful, because of the artificial value system mandated by a rigid Victorian society. Women's rights, aspirations, and freedoms were crippled by a strict system of society's non-egalitarian rules that were ensured to keep women in subordinate roles in traditional society. Victorian attitudes widely denounced assertive female roles and any examples of women aspiring higher in attempts to gain equality, especially in regard to any military connection or contribution: "In our day, a certain ridicule attaches itself to the character of a woman in arms, made admirable only by such religious enthusiasms as inspired by Joan of Arc."[361]

But the Victorian period's strict rigidity likewise underwent another transformation in regard to a woman's role, but because of an emergency. Wartime crisis offered greater opportunity for women, regardless of class or social background, when everyone was needed for the war effort. The urgent requirements for women to meet the extensive demands of the First World War, from 1914 to 1918, finally restored the image of the heroic woman warrior to "a new place of honour" in society's eyes, after erasing the most repressive legacies of the Victorian era.[362]

HOLLYWOOD AND POPULAR MEMORY

Because Captain Johnson wanted to sell books, a fictionalized portrayal of Anne's life provided a means to achieve that central objective of making money. And, of course, in regard to the art of sensationalism, Hollywood picked up where Johnson left off in 1724.

Mirroring Johnson's motivations in the most sensational aspects of the story of female pirates in his 1724 book, it was only a matter of time before Hollywood got into the act, continuing to exploit this popular subject. Directed by Jacques Tourneur from a screenplay written by Philip Dunne and Arthur Caesar, the 1951 film *Anne of the Indies* presented the romantic story about a beautiful female pirate played by actress Jean Peters. Female captain Anne Providence was loosely based upon Anne Bonny, but despite the film's title, moviegoers and reviewers alike failed to realize that this captivating story was in fact based upon a real person.[363]

If not obscuring the real Anne Bonny as a historical figure, Hollywood grossly fictionalized her life. In 1954, Hollywood released *Captain William Kidd and the Slave Girl*, which presented the ridiculous scenario of the love relationship between Captain Kidd, rather than Captain Rackham, and Anne Bonny. In fact, Anne was only an infant back in Ireland when Captain Kidd was hanged. Hollywood only continued the tradition of generations of popular writers who transformed the lives of pirates into highly sexualized, romanticized, and sensationalized tales.[364]

Very likely, Anne Bonny had been inspired in part by stories of Joan of Arc, like later generations of young women influenced by portrayals of Joan in popular Hollywood films. Released in 1948, *Joan of Arc* was one such film. Starring Ingrid Bergman, this film inspired a new generation of young women of the post-World War II era. Jean Bethke Elshtain, a political scientist, described the film's impact upon her childhood aspirations, including "becoming a leader of men." She "dreamed of action, of Joan, of myself in male battle attire, fighting for morally worthy ends."[365]

Anne Bonny also shared a name with one of America's most famous female antiheroes who has become part of popular culture, Bonnie Parker. Despite living in different centuries, Parker, of Bonnie and Clyde fame, is another of America's best-known female outlaws. The popular appeal of both Anne Bonny and Bonnie Parker, American women who were among the most famed outliers in history, has extended across multiple generations. Parker and her lover, Clyde Barrow, were featured in the 1967 film *Bonnie and Clyde,* which garnered widespread acclaim and popularity as part of the growing American counterculture in the era of the Vietnam War. Basically, Jack Rackham was Anne's Clyde Barrow, as they fought the establishment together on the Caribbean.[366]

CONCLUSION

FAR MORE than a caricature of the female pirate, Anne Bonny was a real person, who persevered and ultimately succeeded in life against the odds. She defied not only nearly all of the traditional conventions of her day but also the simplistic stereotype of the psychotic female pirate of little character or morals. Contrary to the myth, she served on Captain Rackham's ship with competence and enthusiasm, faithfully performing her responsibilities as a sailor as well as in combat and in the ship's defense, just like her fellow crew members were expected to. All in all, this extraordinary Irish woman lived a multidimensional life on both sides of the Atlantic, as a mother, lover, wife, and pirate, but she served the former roles for five decades, much longer than the two years she spent in the Caribbean. Anne's life should not be simplistically defined by that very brief period. In the end, Anne Bonny proved to be far more of a real woman—human and multifaceted—than the stereotype reinforced by centuries of male writers has suggested.

Although no record exists of her having ever killed or hurt anyone as a pirate, Anne Bonny was sentenced to death by committing what was considered the ultimate social crime in the era—being a woman who behaved like a man. By choosing a life that contradicted every demeaning stereotype perpetuated about women, Anne represented a willful, deliberate rejection of the stereotypical male, the patriarchal order, and societal concepts that deemed her incapable of courage, resourcefulness, or daring.

But a price had to be paid. Anne Bonny was condemned as one of the great "enemies of the human race"—the old Roman definition of pi-

---

Opposite: Statue of Anne Bonny and Mary Read [facing] by Erik Christianson.
Photo by Silvia Guijarro Parra.

rates—and sentenced to be hanged for only doing what was necessary for her to create a better life for herself and her child. Anne found what she was looking for at sea, away from society's degradation of women, and there was nothing wrong with her reaching out and embracing her dream, according to Anne's way of thinking.

One of Anne Bonny's contemporaries, Captain Charles Bellamy, who had made his headquarters at Nassau where Jack and Anne first met, perhaps said it best when he described exactly why he and so many other independent, contrarian people, such as Anne herself, had taken to the pirate's life, unlike "all those people who will submit to be governed by Laws which rich Men have made for their own Security, for the cowardly Whelps have not the Courage otherwise to defend what they get by their Knavery . . . They villify us, the Scoundrels do, when there is only this Difference, they rob the Poor under the Cover of the Law, forsooth, and we plunder the Rich under the Protection of our own Courage."[367]

For such reasons, therefore, terrible retribution lay in store for those who openly attacked the international order, exploitative commercialism, and the very essence of mercantilism (i.e., slavery) as well as those who achieved this supreme freedom known to 18th-century women. Instead of fighting and dying as pawns for their native homeland, religion, government, and self-serving leaders, Anne and her fellow crew members served for their ultra-egalitarian society in the name of a better life. She followed her heart, natural inclinations, and instincts to fulfill her own dreams in a most unconventional way, which would not last long given the inevitable severe backlash.

Inevitably and unfortunately for Anne Bonny and the Rackham crew, it was only a matter of time before the limitless power of that privileged world of wealthy speculators, bankers, slave traders, insurance companies, and absentee sugar planters crushed them. Their fates were sealed once the highest authorities in the land decided that Anne and her comrades deserved execution for taking only a minuscule amount of their incalculable ill-gotten gains.

In truth, it always had been the aristocratic elite of Europe's great powers, reaping their vast fortunes from the slave trade, who were the real pirates in systematically destroying much of the New World's land and people in the name of God and country. The New World's riches were looted to reap fantastic profits and set the stage for the Industrial Revolution, while the elite made themselves even more wealthy by expanding slavery and the plantation system, as the most "prosperous national economies have been founded on organized piracy." And Anne was nearly executed for her opposition to this system, which she felt was morally and ethically wrong.[368] Like other members of the Rackham crew, Anne served in the Caribbean as "a means of wreaking vengeance on a society that was viewed as both oppressive and unfair."[369]

Instead of sexually charged sensationalism created by Captain Johnson, the true story of Anne Bonny's life remains timeless because of revelations about her resourcefulness, strength of will, and character. The entirety of Anne's life—not just her time as a pirate—showed that she had an irrepressible spirit, and her short career as a pirate revealed exactly what great lengths an intelligent young woman had to go in order to find a sense of personal dignity, respect, and equality in the 18th century.

Most importantly, Anne's life as a pirate was not significant because of any swashbuckling bravado or adventures in the Caribbean, but because she became an inspiring model to other women. By way of her own resourcefulness and daring, Anne Bonny enjoyed a rare high level of independence, self-esteem, and freedom unknown to the vast majority of women of her day. She was a complex person, but her decades spent in America after her trial in Jamaica has been almost completely obscured by the romanticized myth that has transcended the real person.

In a strange twist of fate, only by breaking the law and gaining notoriety as a pirate was the life of a resourceful Irish immigrant ultimately preserved in the historical record at a time when women were seldom noticed, much less recorded. The stories of such remarkable women have been long lost or deliberately erased from history, viewed as threats to society's established rules, traditions, and conventions. The real lessons of Anne's life had nothing to do with murder, theft, or buried treasure, and she proved that she was not a fake or a fraud in masquerading as a man on Captain Rackham's ship, between performing her assigned seaman's duties to almost single-handedly defending the *William*. By not employing religion as an excuse to rob and murder the innocent, as England and Spain did, she remained true to her own core belief system. In her own way, she waged her own personal war against the interests of the wealthy slave owners, the aristocracy, and the plantocracy, when England's far-flung colonies and colonial officials profited from a thriving black-market economy based upon piracy—a vast corrupt system and network of which the Rackham crew, including Anne, was not a part.

By breaking society's conventions that bound her to an inferior status because of gender bias and prejudice, Anne Bonny went her own way with a boldness, if not audacity, that has become legendary to this day. Like few women of her generation, Anne Bonny was truly ahead of her time, embracing a host of challenges that were unimaginable to almost all women of her era.[370] In novelist Thornton Wilder's *The Woman of Andros* (1930), the main character, Chrysis, told her followers the story of an ancient meeting of a large body of women who sent a male poet with an important and sage message that they wanted badly conveyed to the "world of men," including great warriors of legend: "Tell them that it is only in appearance that we are unstable. Tell them that this is because we are hard-pressed and in bitter servitude to nature, but that at heart, only asking their patience, we are as steadfast, as brave and as manly as they."[371] This message was transformed into reality and demonstrated in full in her own unique and unconventional way by Anne Bonny during a remarkable life in which she tolerated no barriers or boundaries.

When Anne died as a grandmother or perhaps even a great-grandmother in Tidewater Virginia in April 1782, 63 years after she first met Captain Rackham in the port of Nassau, she was perhaps no longer ashamed of her former life as a pirate. It would be fitting, as a pirate ship was a place where all one's past mistakes and scandals—such as Anne's illegitimate birth in Ireland—were forgiven. On a pirate ship in the Caribbean, which was the last place on Earth that almost every other woman hoped ever to be, her troubled past was gone, and she had made her fondest dreams come true—an exhilarating experience that she likely never forgot. On the high seas, she was not discriminated against, mocked or looked down upon because of her class, nationality, illegitimacy, or status as an immigrant. As such, perhaps near the end of her life in Tidewater Virginia, she still recalled the majesty of a flock of brown pelicans that glided, without flapping wings, over the breakers in search of fish, with a carefree ease that might have reminded her of her own free existence as a wide-roaming pirate under the bright Caribbean sun.

END NOTES

1. Antonia Fraser, *The Weaker Vessel*, (New York: Knopf, 1984), pp. 1-6, 9, 464-468.

2. Charles Johnson, *A General History of the Robberies and Murders of the Most Notorious Pirates*, (Guilford: The Lyons Press, 2002), p. 125.

3. Ibid., pp. 125-131; Brian Lalor, editor, *The Encyclopedia of Ireland*, (New Haven: Yale University Press, 2003), pp. 595-596; Shelley Klein, *The Most Evil Pirates in History*, (New York: Barnes and Noble, 2006), p. 131; Anne Bonny, Wikipedia, internet; Tamara J. Eastman and Constance Bond, *The Pirate Trial of Anne Bonny and Mary Read*, (Cambra: Fern Canyon Press, 2000), p. 14, 16, 18; F. O. Steele, *Women Pirates, A Brief Anthology of Thirteen Notorious Female Pirates*, (New York: Universe, Inc., 2007), p. 14; Wallace Nutting, *Ireland Beautiful*, (New York: Bonanza Books, 1975), p. 290; Anne-Bonny—An Irish diaspora story at EPIC, internet; Tamara Eastman, Petersburg, Virginia, to author, December 28, 2010, email no. 2.

4. Don N. Hagist, *British Soldiers, American War*, (Yardley: Westholme Publishing, 2012), p. 23.

5. Ibid.

6. Lalor, ed., *The Encyclopedia of Ireland*, p. 595.

7. Lalor, ed., *The Encyclopedia of Ireland*, pp. 240, 1034-1035; John P. McCormanck, Genealogy of the O'Cormacain Family of Thomond, Clare County Library, Ennis, Ireland; Mary Frances Cusack, *An Illustrated History of Ireland, From AD 400 to 1800*, (London: Bracken Books, 1995), pp. 40-41, 102-105; Don Akenson, *An Irish History of Civilization*, vol. 1, (2 vols: Montreal: McGill-Queen's University Press, 2006), pp. 65-66

8. Cusack, *An Illustrated History of Ireland, From AD 400 to 1800*, pp. 40-41.

9. Ibid., pp. 40-42.

10. Ibid., p. 42.

11. McCormack, Genealogy of the O'Cormacain Family of Thomond, CCL; Ronan Coghlan, *Irish Christian Names, An A-Z of First Names*, (London: Johnston and Bacon, 1979), p. 34.

12. Johnson, *A General History of the Robberies and Murders of the Most Notorious Pirates*, pp. 125-131; Lalor, ed., *The Encyclopedia of Ireland*, p. 104; Eastman and Bond, *The Pirate Trial of Anne Bonny and Mary Read*, pp. 14, 16, 18.

13. Johnson, *A General History of the Robberies and Murders of the Most Notorious Pirates*, pp. 125, 127; Klein, *The Most Evil Pirates in History*, p. 131.

14. Johnson, *A General History of the Robberies and Murders of the Most Notorious Pirates*, p. 125.

15. Ibid., pp. 125-127.

16. Ibid., pp. 125-128; Eastman and Bond, *The Pirate Trial of Anne Bonny and Mary Read*, p. 18; Antonia Fraser, *Cromwell, The Lord Protector*, (New York: Smithmark Publishers, 1996), pp. 326-357.

17. Johnson, *A General History of the Robberies and Murders of the Most Notorious Pirates*, pp.125-129; Brian Lalor, ed., *The Encyclopedia of Ireland*, pp. 104, 595; Klein, *The Most Evil Pirates in History*, p. 131; Nutting, *Beautiful Ireland*, pp. 9-21, 32, 39, 258.

18. Hagist, *British Soldiers*, p. 23.

19. Johnson, *A General History of the Robberies and Murders of the Most Notorious Pirates*, pp. 128-129; Klein, *The Most Evil Pirates in History*, p. 131; East and Bond, *The Pirate Trial of Anne Bonny and Mary Read*, p. 16; Eastman to author, December 28, 2010, email no. 2.

20. Nancy Roberts, *Blackbeard and Other Pirates of the Atlantic Coast*, (Winston-Salem: John F. Blair Publishers, 1993), p. 106; Johnson, *A General History of the Robberies and Murders of the Most Notorious Pirates*, p. 129.

21. Johnson, *A General History of the Robberies and Murders of the Most Notorious Pirates*, p. 125; Klein, *The Most Evil Pirates in History*, p. 131; Lalor, ed., *The Encyclopedia of Ireland*, p. 104, 595-596; Michael McNally, *Battle of the Boyne 1690, The Irish Campaign for the English Crown*, (Oxford: Osprey

Publishing Ltd., 2005), pp. 7-92.

22.   Johnson, *A General History of the Robberies and Murders of the Most Notorious Pirates*, p. 129; Lalor, ed., *The Encyclopedia of Ireland*, pp. 104, 595-596; Roberts, *Blackbeard and Other Pirates*, p. 106.

23.   Lalor, ed., *The Encyclopedia of Ireland*, pp. 104, 595-596; Johnson, *A General History of the Robberies and Murders of the Most Notorious Pirates*, p. 125, 128-129; Klein, *The Most Evil Pirates in History*, p. 131; Linda Grant DePauw, *Seafaring Women*, (Boston: Houghton Mifflin Company, 1982), p. 33.

24.   Lalor, ed., *The Encyclopedia of Ireland*, p. 875; Frederick C. Leiner, *The End of Barbary Terror, America's 1815 War Against the Pirates of North Africa*, (Oxford: Oxford University Press, 2006), pp. 1-3, 11-13, 93.

25.   Johnson, *A General History of the Robberies and Murders of the Most Notorious Pirates*, p. 129.

26.   Ibid; Ulrike Klausmann, Mari Meinzerin and Kuhn, *Women Pirates*, (Montreal: Black Rose Books, 1997), p. 196; Roberts, *Blackbeard and Other Pirates*, p. 106.

27.   Roberts, *Blackbeard and Other Pirates*, p. 106.

28.   Johnson, *A General History of the Robberies and Murders of the Most Notorious Pirates*, pp. 125-131; Klein, *The Most Evil Pirates in History*, p. 131; Roberts, *Blackbeard and Other Pirates*, p. 106.

29.   Paul Schneider, *The Adirondacks, A History of America's First Wilderness*, (New York: Henry Holt and Company, 1997), p. 91

30.   Johnson, *A General History of the Robberies and Murders of the Most Notorious Pirates*, p. 130; Nutting, *Ireland Beautiful*, p. 9.

31.   Nancy Isenberg, *Fallen Founder, The Life of Aaron Burr*, (New York: Penguin Books, 2008), p. 293.

32.   Owen B. Hunt, *The Irish and the American Revolution: Three Essays*, (Philadelphia: private printing, 1976), pp. 33-34.

33.   Ibid.

34.   Johnson, *A General History of the Robberies and Murders of the Most Notorious Pirates*, pp. 129-130.

35.   Hagist, *British Soldiers*, p. 22.

36.   Lawrence Goldstone, *Dark Bargain, Slavery, Profits, and the Struggle for the Constitution*, (New York: Walker and Company, 2005), pp. 67-69; Isabella G. Leland, *Charleston, Crossroads of History, A Story of the South Carolina Low Country*, (Woodland Hills: Windsor Publications, Inc., 1980), pp. 1-2, 5-6; Jon Latimer, *Buccaneers of the Caribbean, How Piracy Forged An Empire*, (Cambridge: Harvard University Press, 2009), pp. 77-78; Hunt, *The Irish and the American Revolution*, pp. 33-34; Ned Sublette, *The World*

That Made New Orleans, From Spanish Silver to Congo Square, (Chicago: Lawrence Hill Books, 2009), pp. 30-33; Richard R. Higgins, *The Swamp Fox, Francis Marion's Campaign in the Carolinas 1780*, (New York: Osprey Publishing, 2013), p. 10; Gregory D. Massey, *John Laurens and the American Revolution*, (Columbia: University of South Carolina Press, 2000), pp. 6, 9. Alphonso Brown, *A Gullah Guide to Charleston, Walking Through Black History*, (Charleston: The History Press, 2008), p. 41.

37.   Leland, *Charleston*, pp. 1-2; Eastman and Bond, *The Pirate Trial of Anne Bonny and Mary Read*, pp. 11, 16; Massey, *John Laurens and the American Revolution*, p. 9; Hunt, *The Irish and the American Revolution*, pp. 33-34.

38.   Leland, *Charleston*, pp. 1-11; Eastman and Bond, *The Pirate Trial of Anne Bonny and Mary Read*, p. 16.

39.   Charles Murphy, *The Irish in the American Revolution*, (Groveland: Charles Murphy Publications, 1975), p. 7; Grady McWhiney, *Cracker Culture, Celtic Ways in the Old South*, (Tuscaloosa: University of Alabama Press, 1988), pp. xxxviii-xxxix; Hunt, *The Irish and the American Revolution*, pp. 33-34.

40.   Rod Gragg, *Forged in Faith, How Faith Shaped the Birth of the Nation, 1607-1776*, (New York: Howard Books, 2010), p. 90

41.   Jay P. Dolan, *The Irish Americans*, (New York: Bloomsbury Press, 2008), pp. 8-9.

42.   Leland, *Charleston*, pp. 6, 9.

43.   Ibid., p. 14; Sublette, *The World That Made New Orleans*, pp. 30-31; Joel Williamson, *New People, Miscegenation and Mulattoes in the United States*, (New York: The Free Press, 1980), p. 34; Massey, *John Laurens and the American Revolution*, p. 9; John Bennett, *The Doctor to the Dead*, (Columbia: University of South Carolina Press, 1995), p. xvi; Douglas R. Egerton, *Year of Meteors, Stephen Douglas, Abraham Lincoln, and the Election That Brought on the Civil War*, p. 232.

44.   John Buchanan, *Jackson's Way, Andrew Jackson and the People of the Western Waters*, (New York: John Wiley and Sons, 2001), pp. 20-21.

45.   Ibid., pp. 22-23; Edward Lucie-Smith, *Outcasts of the Sea, Pirates and Piracy*, (New York: Paddington Press Ltd., 1978), pp. 178, 212.

46.   Richard Zacks, *The Pirate Hunter, The True Story of Captain Kidd*, (New York: Hyperion, 2002), pp. 8.

47.   Goldstone, *Dark Bargain*, pp. 67-72; Woodard, *The Republic of Pirates*, p. 199; Leland, *Charleston*, pp. 9, 14-16; Hunt, *The Irish and the American Revolution*, pp. 33-34; Sublette, *The World That Made New Orleans*, pp. 30-31; Bennett, *The Doctor to the Dead*, pp. xii, xxvi, 3-4; John G. Leland, *A*

History of Kiawah Island, (Charleston: Kiawah Island Company, 1977), pp. 7, 15; Brown, *A Gullah Guide to Charleston*, p. 11; Roberts, *Blackbeard and Other Pirates*, p. 107; Lalor, ed., *The Encyclopedia of Ireland*, p. 630' Buchanan, *Jackson's Way*, pp. 22-23.

48.   Johnson, *A General History of the Robberies and Murders of the Most Notorious Pirates*, pp. 129-130; Eastman and Bond, *The Pirate Trial of Anne Bonny and Mary Read*, p. 19.

49.   Kenneth M. Stampp, *The Peculiar Institution, Slavery in the Ante-Bellum South*, (New York: Vintage Books, 1956), pp. 350-361; Woodard, *The Republic of Pirates*, p. 199; Joel Williamson, *New People*, pp. xi-4, 15, 34, 41.

50.   Leland, *Charleston*, p. 13.

51.   Johnson, *A General History of the Robberies and Murders of the Most Notorious Pirates*, p. 130.

52.   Ibid; Eastman and Bond, *The Pirate Trial of Anne Bonny and Mary Read*, p. 11; Williamson, *New People*, p. 34; Leland, *A History of Kiawah*, p. 15; Roberts, *Blackbeard and Other Pirates*, p. 106; Massey, *John Laurens and the American Revolution*, pp. 9-10; Hunt, *The Irish and the American Revolution*, pp. 33-34.

53.   Johnson, *A General History of the Robberies and Murders of the Most Notorious Pirates*, p. 130; Steele, *Women Pirates*, pp. 14-15.

54.   Johnson, *A General History of the Robberies and Murders of the Most Notorious Pirates*, p. 130; Steele, *Women Pirates*, pp. 14-15; Black River, South Carolina, Wikipedia, internet; Eastman and Bond, *The Pirate Trial of Anne Bonny and Mary Read*, p. 11; Roberts, *Blackbeard and Other Pirates*, p. 106.

55.   Leland, *Charleston*, pp. 6, 10; Steele, *Women Pirates*, pp. 14-15; Botting, *The Pirates*, p. 35; Eastman and Bond, *The Pirate Trial of Anne Bonny and Mary Read*, pp. 11, 15, 19; Roberts, *Blackbeard and Other Pirates*, p. 106.

56.   Sara Hunt, editor, *Heroines, Remarkable and Inspiring Women*, (New York: Crescent Books, 1995), pp. 33-37.

57.   Lalor, ed., *The Encyclopedia of Ireland*, pp. 827-828; Ann Chambers, *Granuaile, The Life and Times of Grace O'Malley*, (Niwot: The Irish American Book Company, 1994), pp. 11-164; Linda Grant De Paw, *Seafaring Women*, (Boston: Houghton Mifflin Company, 1982), pp. 23-27; David Cordingly, *Under the Black Flag, The Romance and the Reality of Life Among the Pirates*, (New York: Harcourt Brace & Company, 1995), pp. 72-74; Johnson, *A General History of the Robberies and Murders of the Most Notorious Pirates*, pp. 121, 125, 131; Joan Druett, *She Captains, Heroines and Hellions of the Sea*, (Rockland: Wheeler Publishing, Inc., 2000), pp. 70-89; Barbara Sjoholm, *The Pirate Queen, In Search of Grace O'Malley and*

Other Legendary Women of the Sea, (Emeryville: Seal Press, 2004), pp. xxiii-35; David E. Jones, *Women Warriors, A History*, (Washington, D. C.: Brassey's, 1997), pp. 65-67; Klein, *The Most Evil Pirates in History*, pp. 17-27; Marian Broderick, *Wild Irish Women, Extraordinary Lives from History*, (Madison: University of Wisconsin Press, 2004), pp. 243-252.

58.   Sjoholm, *The Pirate Queen*, p. xvii.

59.   Broderick, *Wild Irish Women*, p. 251.

60.   Chambers, *Granuaile*, pp. 11-164, 195; Klein, *The Most Evil Pirates in History*, pp. 17-27.

61.   Chambers, *Granuaile*, pp. 11-164; Johnson, *A General History of the Robberies and Murders of the Most Notorious Pirates*, p. 131; Cordingly, *Under the Black Flag*, pp. 72-73; Klein, *The Most Evil Pirates in History*, pp. 17-27.

62.   Johnson, *A General History of the Robberies and Murders of the Most Notorious Pirates*, p. 130; Steele, *Women Pirates*, pp. 14-15; Eastman and Bond, *The Pirate Trial of Anne Bonny and Mary Read*, p. 16; Jane Landers, *Fort Mose, Gracia Real de Santa Teresa de Mose: A Free Black Town in Spanish Colonial Florida*, (St. Augustine: St. Augustine Historical Society, 1992), p. 11; John K. Mahon, *History of the Second Seminole War, 1835-1842*, (Gainesville: University of Florida Press, 1985), pp. 2-3; Roberts, *Blackbeard and Other Pirates*, p. 106.

63.   Roberts, *Blackbeard and Other Pirates*, p. 106; Broderick, *Wild Irish Women*, p. 97.

64.   Johnson, *A General History of the Robberies and Murders of the Most Notorious Pirates*, pp.125-130; Eastman and Bond, *The Pirate Trial of Anne Bonny and Mary Read*, p. 19; Eastman email to author, December 28, 2010, email no. 2; Broderick, *Wild Irish Women*, p. 97; Roberts, *Blackbeard and Other Pirates*, pp. 106-107.

65.   Steele, *Women Pirates*, pp. 14-15; Johnson, *A General History of the Robberies and Murders of the Most Notorious Pirates*, p. 130; Sublette, *The World That Made New Orleans*, p. 30; Klein, *The Most Evil Pirates in History*, pp. 131, 133; Landers, *Fort Mose*, pp. 11-12; Mahon, *History of the Second Seminole War*, p. 3; Eastman email to author, December 28, 2010, email no. 2; Roberts, *Blackbeard and Other Pirates*, p. 72.

66.   Broderick, *Wild Irish Women*, p. 97.

67.   Johnson, *A General History of the Robberies and Murders of the Most Notorious Pirates*, p. 130; Steele, *Women Pirates*, pp. 14-15; Klein, *The Most Evil Pirates in History*, pp. 131-132; Tamara Eastman, Petersburg, Virginia, to author, December 28, 2010, email no. 3; Roberts, *Blackbeard and Other Pirates*, p. 72.

68.   Leland, *Charleston*, p. 13; Johnson, *A General History of the Robberies and Murders of the*

Most Notorious Pirates, p. 125-130; Steele, *Women Pirates*, p. 15; Williamson, *New People*, p. 41; John W. Blassingame, *The Slave Community, Plantation Life in the Antebellum South*, (New York: Oxford University Press, 1972), pp. 82-83; Eastman email to author, December 28, 2010, email no. 2; Roberts, *Blackbeard and Other Pirates*, p. 72.

69.   Broderick, *Wild Irish Women*, p. 97.

70.   Johnson, *A General History of the Robberies and Murders of the Most Notorious Pirates*, pp. 125-131; Julie Wheelwright, *Amazons and Military Minds, Women Who Dressed as Men in Pursuit of Life, Liberty, and the Pursuit of Happiness*, (London: Pandora Press, 1990), p. 22; Steele, *Women Pirates*, pp. 14-15; Landers, *Fort Mose*, pp. 11-12; Mahon, *History of the Second Seminole War*, p. 3; Cordingly, *Under the Black Flag*, pp. xiii-244.

71.   Colin Woodard, *The Republic of Pirates, The True and Surprising Story of the Caribbean Pirates and the Man Who Brought Them Down*, (New York: Mariner Books, 2008), pp. 199-200; Johnson, *A General History of the Robberies and Murders of the Most Notorious Pirates*, pp. viii-x, 125-131; Goldstone, *Dark Bargain*, pp. 67-69; Leland, *Charleston*, p. 13; Stuart A. Kallen, *Life Among the Pirates*, (San Diego: Lucent Books, 1999), p. 20; Williamson, *New People*, p. 41; Steele, *Women Pirates*, pp. 14-15; Blassingame, *The Slave Community*, pp. 82-83; Broderick, *Wild Irish Women*, p. 97.

72.   Woodard, *The Republic of Pirates*, p. 139; Johnson, *A General History of the Robberies and Murders of the Most Notorious Pirates*, pp. 125-131; Cordingly, *Under the Black Flag*, p. 10; DePauw, *Seafaring Women*, p. 33; Kallen, *Life Among the Pirates*, pp. 31, 41; Steele, *Women Pirates*, pp. 14-15; Broderick, *Wild Irish Women*, p. 97; Dallas Murphy, *Round the Horn*, (New York: Perseus Books, Group, 2004), p. xi.

73.   Johnson, *A General History of the Robberies and Murders of the Most Notorious Pirates*, pp. 125-131.

74.   Woodard, *The Republic of Pirates*, p. 159.

75.   Johnson, *A General History of the Robberies and Murders of the Most Notorious Pirates*, pp. 125-131; Jo Stanley, *Bold in the Breeches, Women Pirates Across the Ages*, (New York: HarperCollins, 1995), pp. 11-12, 42; Black, *Pirates of the West Indies*, p. 109; Broderick, *Wild Irish Women*, p. 97.

76.   Johnson, *A General History of the Robberies and Murders of the Most Notorious Pirates*, pp. 103-111, 130-131; Broderick, *Wild Irish Women*, p. 98.

77.   Jon Latimer, *Buccaneers of the Caribbean, How Piracy Forged An Empire*, (Cambridge: Harvard University Press, 2009), pp. 1-6, 100-245, 247-249, 255, 257, 260, 269; Richard S. Dunn, *Sugar and Slaves, The Rise of the Planter Class in the English West Indies, 1624-1713*, (New York: W. W. Norton and Company, 1972), pp. 4-341; Michael Craton, *A History of the Bahamas*, (Waterloo: Harvard University Press, 1997), pp. 44-45; Steele, *Women Pirates*, p. 1; Sublette, *The World That Made New Orleans*, pp. 20-21; Klein, *The Most Evil Pirates in History*, pp. 38-49, 184-185; Douglas Botting, *The Pirates*, (Alexandra: Time-Life Books, 1978). p. 20; Cruz Apestegui, *Pirates of the Caribbean, Buccaneers, Privateers, Freebooters and Filibusters 1493-1720*, (Edison: Chartwell Books Inc., 2002), pp. 151-153; Clinton Black, *Tales of Old Jamaica*, (Trinidad: Longman Trinidad Ltd., 1999), pp. 1-2, 7, 53-61; Kallen, *Life Among the Pirates*, pp. 8, 63, 69; Murphy, *Round the Horn*, pp. 76-83; Lalor, ed., *The Encyclopedia of Ireland*, p. 875.

78.   Anthony Gambrill, *In Search of the Buccaneers*, (Oxford: Macmillan Caribbean, 2007), pp. 1-247; Klausmann, Meinzerin and Kuhn, *Women Pirates*, p. 25.

79.   Klausmann, Meinzerin and Kuhn, *Women Pirates*, p. 197; Klein, *The Most Evil Pirates in History*, p. 184; Robert E. Lee, *Blackbeard The Pirate, A Reappraisal of His Life and Times*, (Winston-Salem: John F. Blair Publishers, 2000), p. 9.

80.   Woodard, *The Republic of Pirates*, pp. 154, 159, 161; Johnson, *A General History of the Robberies and Murders of the Most Notorious Pirates*, p. 46; W. Jeffrey Bolster, *Black Jacks, African American Seamen in the Age of Sail*, (Cambridge: Harvard University Press, 1997), pp. 1-15; Craton, *A History of the Bahamas*, pp. 11-13, 45; Latimer, *Buccaneers of the Caribbean*, pp. 243-245, 257; Dunn, *Sugar and Slaves*, pp. 149-151; Klein, *The Most Evil Pirates in History*, p. 184; Botting, *The Pirates*, p. 28; Black, *Pirates of the West Indies*, pp. 5-6; Kallen, *Life Among the Pirates*, pp. 62-69; Lee, *Blackbeard The Pirate*, pp. 5, 9-10.

81.   Woodard, *The Republic of Pirates*, pp. 86-87, 131; Bolster, *Black Jacks*, p. 13; Klein, *The Most Evil Pirates in History*, p. 185

82.   Woodard, *The Republic of Pirates*, pp. 87-88; Akenson, *An Irish History of Civilization*, vol. 1, p. 338; Craton, *A History of the Bahamas*, pp.11-13; Klein, *The Most Evil Pirates in History*, pp. 184-185.

83.   Woodard, *The Republic of Pirates*, pp. 87-88.

84.   Klausmann, Meinzerin and Kuhn, *Women Pirates*, p. 192.

85.   Craton, *A History of the Bahamas*, pp. 11-16, 34, 45.

86.   Cordingly, *Under the Black Flag*, p. 10; Craton, *A History of the Bahamas*, pp. 45, 55, 60-61.

87.   Woodard, *The Republic of Pirates*, pp. 87-88, 131; Johnson, *A General History of the Robberies and Murders of the Most Notorious Pirates*, pp. 46, 103-116, 125-131; Craton, *A History of the Bahamas*,

pp. 11-12, 59-90; Klein, *The Most Evil Pirates in History*, p. 184; Kallen, *Life Among the Pirates*, p. 32; Lee, *Blackbeard The Pirate*, p. 12.

88.   Woodard, *The Republic of Pirates*, pp. 131-132, 139; Botting, *The Pirates*, p. 31.

89.   Woodard, *The Republic of Pirates*, pp. 131-132, 139; Johnson, *A General History of the Robberies and Murders of the Most Notorious Pirates*, pp. 125-131; Dunn, *Sugar and Slaves*, pp. 150-151; Latimer, *Buccaneers in the Caribbean*, pp. 244-245; Craton, *A History of the Bahamas*, p. 64; Botting, *The Pirates*, p. 29; Steele, *Women Pirates*, p. 4.

90.   Johnson, *A General History of the Robberies and Murders of the Most Notorious Pirates*, p. 130; Woodard, *The Republic of Pirates*, pp. 131-132, 139; Goldstone, *Dark Bargain*, pp. 69-70; Dunn, *Sugar and Slaves, The Rise of the Planter Class in the English West Indies, 1624-1713*, pp. xiii-341; Craton, *A History of the Bahamas*, pp. 11, 17, 35-40, 173, 178; Laurent Dubois, *Avengers of the New World, The Story of the Haitian Revolution*, (Cambridge: Harvard University Press, 2004), pp. 8-33; Latimer, *Buccaneers of the Caribbean*, pp. 243-255; Nutting, *Ireland Beautiful*, pp. 61-62; Roberts, *Blackbeard and Other Pirates*, p. 35; Peter Haining, *Great Irish Humor*, (New York: Barnes and Noble, 1995), pp. 14-16..

91.   Steele, *Women Pirates*, pp. 2, 14; Mc-Nally, *Battle of the Boyne 1690*, pp. 7-92; Johnson, *A General History of the Robberies and Murders of the Most Notorious Pirates*, pp. 125-131, 261, 302; Craton, *A History of the Bahamas*, pp. 83, 93; Cordingly, *Under the Black Flag*, p. 12; Botting, *The Pirates*, p. 28.

92.   Bolster, *Black Jacks*, p. 13; Johnson, *A General History of the Robberies and Murders of the Most Notorious Pirates*, pp. 125-131.

93.   Bolster, *Black Jacks*, pp. 13-14; Woodard, *The Republic of Pirates*, pp. 131-132; Craton, *A History of the Bahamas*, p. 90; Roberts, *Blackbeard and Other Pirates*, pp. 3-4, 12-16; Kallen, *Life Among the Pirates*, pp. 25, 29-30; Lee, *Blackbeard The Pirate*, pp. 5, 114, 112.

94.   Johnson, *A General History of the Robberies and Murders of the Most Notorious Pirates*, pp. 46, 103, 130; Craton, *A History of the Bahamas*, p. 90.

95.   Johnson, *A General History of the Robberies and Murders of the Most Notorious Pirates*, pp. 60-61; Klein, *The Most Evil Pirates in History*, p. 125; Lee, *Blackbeard The Pirate*, p. 112.

96.   Johnson, *A General History of the Robberies and Murders of the Most Notorious Pirates*, pp. 103, 107, 111; Kallen, *Life Among the Pirates*, p. 25; Klein, *The Most Evil Pirates in History*, p. 125; Craton, *A History of the Bahamas*, pp. 95-99.

97.   Cordingly, *Under the Black Flag*, pp. xiv, 15-17; Johnson, *A General History of the Robberies and Murders of the Most Notorious Pirates*, p. 107; Klein, *The Most Evil Pirates in History*, pp. 122, 124-125; Botting, *The Pirates*, p. 35; Roberts, *Blackbeard and Other Pirates*, p. 3.

98.   Johnson, *A General History of the Robberies & Murders of the Most Notorious Pirates*, pp. 107-108, 111-112; Klein, *The Most Evil Pirates in History*, pp. 122-124, 185; David Hancock, *Oceans of Wine, Madeira and the Emergence of American Trade and Taste*, (New Haven: Yale University Press, 2009), pp. 107-198; Cordingly, *Under the Black Flag*, p. 57; Botting, *The Pirates*, p. 57; John Esquemeling, *The Buccaneers of America*, (New York: Dover Publications, Inc., 1967), pp. ix, 59; Zacks, *The Pirate Hunter*, p. 27.

99.   Johnson, *A General History of the Robberies and Murders of the Most Notorious Pirates*, pp. 103-108, 111-113, 125-131; Klein, *The Most Evil Pirates in History*, pp. 122-125; Steele, *Women Pirates*, pp. 15-16; Cordingly, *Under the Black Flag*, pp. xiv, 11-12, 15-17, 57; Craton, *A History of the Bahamas*, pp. 98-99, 161; Roberts, *Blackbeard and Other Pirates*, pp. 72, 76.

100.   Johnson, *A General History of the Robberies and Murders of the Most Notorious Pirates*, pp. 111-112, 125-131; Klein, *The Most Evil Pirates in History*, pp. 122-125, 133; Steele, *Women Pirates*, pp. 1-2, 15-16; Klausmann, Meinzerin and Kuhn, *Women Pirates*, p. 197; Cordingly, *Under the Black Flag*, pp. xiv, 10, 15, 17-18, 57; DePauw, *Seafaring Women*, p. 33; Apestegui, *Pirates of the Caribbean*, p. 207; Kallen, *Life Among the Pirates*, pp. 24, 30; Craton, *A History of the Bahamas*, p. 99; Roberts, *Blackbeard and Other Pirates*, pp. 3, 72, 76.

101.   Lalor, ed., *The Encyclopedia of Ireland*, pp. 121-122; Broderick, *Wild Irish Women*, pp. 244, 252.

102.   Lalor, ed., *The Encyclopedia of Ireland*, pp. 121-122; Johnson, *A General History of the Robberies and Murders of the Most Notorious Pirates*, pp. 130-131; Klein, *The Most Evil Pirates in History*, pp. 122-123, 133; Stanley, ed., *Bold in Her Breeches*, p. 188; Broderick, *Wild Irish Women*, p. 244.

103.   Johnson, *A General History of the Robberies and Murders of the Most Notorious Pirates*, pp. 125-131; Stanley, ed., *Bold in Her Breeches*, p. 188.

104.   Broderick, *Wild Irish Women*, p. 97; Johnson, *A General History of the Robberies and Murders of the Most Notorious Pirates*, pp. 108, 125-131; Wheelwright, *Amazons and Military Maids*, pp. 4-13; Stanley, ed., *Bold in Her Breeches*, pp. 42-48, 52; Klein, *The Most Evil Pirates in History*, p. 133.

105.   Johnson, *A General History of the Robberies and Murders of the Most Notorious Pirates*, p. 112, 131; Klein, *The Most Evil Pirates in History*, p. 133.

106.   Zacks, *The Pirate Hunter*, pp. 4-393.

107.   *Boston News-Letter*, Boston, Massachu-

setts, February 23 to March 2, 1719; Alton Ballance, *Ocracokers*, (Chapel Hill: University of North Carolina Press, 1989), pp. 4-5, 10-13.

108. Lee, *Blackbeard the Pirate*, p. 5.

109. Johnson, *A General History of the Robberies and Murders of the Most Notorious Pirates*, pp. 125-131; Steele, *Women Pirates*, pp. 7-8; Botting, *The Pirates*, p. 24.

110. Johnson, *A General History of the Robberies and Murders of the Most Notorious Pirates*, p. 130; Wheelwright, *Amazons and Military Maids*, p. 10; Lalor, ed., *The Encyclopedia of Ireland*, pp. 121-122; Broderick, *Wild Irish Women*, pp. 244, 252.

111. Lalor, ed., *The Encyclopedia of Ireland*, pp. 121-122; Broderick, *Wild Irish Women*, p. 252.

112. Broderick, *Wild Irish Women*, pp. 239-240.

113. Edward Lucie-Smith, *Outcasts of the Sea, Pirates and Piracy*, (New York: Paddington Press, Ltd., 1978), pp. 45-46; Johnson, *A General History of the Robberies and Murders of the Most Notorious Pirates*, pp. 125-131; Lee, *Blackbeard the Pirate*, p. 120.

114. Terry Golway, *For the Cause of Liberty, A Thousand Years of Ireland's Heroes*, (New York: Simon and Schuster, 2000), pp. 33-34.

115. Johnson, *A General History of the Robberies and Murders of the Most Notorious Pirates*, p. 180; Cordingly, *Under the Black Flag*, p. 10; Eastman and Bond, *The Pirate Trial of Anne Bonny and Mary Read*, p. 21; Broderick, *Wild Irish Women*, p. 98.

116. *Washington Post*, Washington, D. C., March 26, 1899; Klausmann, Meinzerin, and Kuhn, *Women Pirates and the Politics of the Jolly Roger*, pp. 8-25, 182-183; Johnson, *A General History of the Robberies and Murders of the Most Notorious Pirates*, pp. 107-108, 125, 129, 131; Steele, *Women Pirates*, pp. 2-3, 14-15; Cordingly, *Under the Black Flag*, pp. 10-11, 14; Botting, *The Pirates*, pp. 28, 50; DePauw, *Seafaring Women*, pp. 1-4, 9-10,13; Kallen, *Life Among the Pirates*, pp. 24, 30; Dominigue Godineau, *The Women of Paris and Their French Revolution*, (Berkeley: University of California Press,1998), pp. 3, 7; The Tryals of Captain John Rackam, and Other Pirates, Public Records Office, Colonial Office Documents, Richmond, Greater London, United Kingdom.

117. Klausmann, Meinzerin, and Kuhn, *Women Pirates and the Politics of the Jolly Roger*, pp. 24-25.

118. Johnson, *A General History of the Robberies and Murders of the Most Notorious Pirates*, p. 131; The Tryals of Captain John Racham, and Other Pirates, PRO.

119. Johnson, *A General History of the Robberies and Murders of the Most Notorious Pirates*, p. 131; The Tryals of Captain John Rackam, and Other Pirates, PRO.

120. Eastman and Bond, *The Pirate Trial of Anne Bonny and Mary Read*, p. 21;Johnson, *A General History of the Robberies and Murders of the Most Notorious Pirates*, pp. 125-131, 180-181; Wheelwright, *Amazons and Military Maids*, pp. 6-19; Steele, *Women Pirates*, pp. 4, 8; Stanley, ed., *Bold in Her Breeches*, pp. 42-48; Kallen, *Life Among the Pirates*, pp. 24-25; The Tryals of Captain John Rackam, and Other Pirates, PRO; Esquemeling, *The Buccaneers of America*, pp. xxvii, 40, 59-60.

121. Johnson, *A General History of the Robberies and Murders of the Most Notorious Pirates*, p. vii; Wheelwright, *Amazons and Military Maids*, p. 11.

122. Stanley, ed., *Bold in Her Breeches*, p. 14; Johnson, *A General History of the Robberies and Murders of the Most Notorious Pirates*, pp. 125-131; Broderick, *Wild Irish Women*, pp. 98-99.

123. Druett, *She Captains*, pp. 1-152.

124. Wheelwright, *Amazons and Military Maids*, p. 11; Stanley, ed., *Bold in Her Breeches*, p. 52.

125. Klein, *The Most Evil Pirates in History*, p. 134.

126. Steele, *Woman Pirates*, p. 14; Tim McGrath, *John Barry, An American Hero*, (Yardley: Westholme: 2010), p. 10; Cordingly, *Under the Black Flag*, pp. xiv, 11; The Tryals of Captain John Rackham, and Other Pirates, PRO; *Washington Post*, March 26, 1899; Klein, *The Most Evil Pirates in History*, p. 131.

127. Kallen, *Life Among the Pirates*, p. 45.

128. Johnson, *A General History of the Robberies and Murders of the Most Notorious Pirates*, pp. 121, 131.

129. Ibid; Broderick, *Wild Irish Women*, p. 98.

130. Johnson, *A General History of the Robberies and Murders of the Most Notorious Pirates*, p. 180; Barbara Ehrenreich, *Blood Rites, Origins and History of the Passions of War*, (New York: Henry Holt and Company, 1997), pp. 125-128.

131. Stephen Crane, *The Red Badge of Courage*, (New York: Lancer Books, 1967), pp. 5-223; Stanley, ed., *Bold in Her Beeches*, p. 178; Johnson, *A General History of the Robberies and Murders of the Most Notorious Pirates*, p. 121; Ehrenreich, *Blood Rites*, pp. 125-128.

132. Stanley, ed., *Bold in Her Breeches*, p. 178; Steele, *Women Pirates*, p. 14; Cordingly, *Under the Black Flag*, pp. 10, 14-15; Botting, *The Pirates*, p. 28; David Silhanek, translator and introduction, *Homer's Illiad and Vergil's Aeneid*, (New York: Dell Publishing Company, Inc., 1969), pp. 13-160; Ehrenreich, *Blood Rites*, pp. 125-128.

133. Wheelwright, *Amazons and Military Maids*, p. 10.

134. Johnson, *A General History of the Robber-*

ies and Murders of the Most Notorious Pirates, p. 180; Klausmann, Meinzerin, and Kuhn, Women Pirates, pp. 258-259; Botting, The Pirates, pp. 46-47, 50; Kallen, Life Among the Pirates, p. 25.

135. Johnson, A General History of the Robberies and Murders of the Most Notorious Pirates, p. 181; Steele, Women Pirates, pp. xi, 3, 6-7; W. Jeffrey Bolster, Black Jacks, African American Seamen in the Age of Sail, (Cambridge: Harvard University Press, 1997), pp. 33-34; Blassingame, The Slave Community, pp. 27-32, 34-35; Klausmann, Meinzerin, and Kuhn, Women Pirates, pp. 267-268; Cordingly, Under the Black Flag, pp. 11, 15-16; Botting, The Pirates, pp. 44-45; Kallen, Life Among the Pirates, pp. 11, 21, 25, 41-43, 46-47; Lalor, ed., The Encyclopedia of Ireland, p. 754.

136. Kallen, Life Among the Pirates, pp. 25-26; Johnson, A General History of the Robberies and Murders of the Most Notorious Pirates, p. 125; Lalor, ed., The Encyclopedia of Ireland, p. 754; Kallen, Life Among the Pirates, pp. 47-48.

137. Lalor, ed., The Encyclopedia of Ireland, p. 875; Leiner, The End of Barbary Terror, pp. 13-14.

138. Johnson, A General History of the Robberies and Murders of the Most Notorious Pirates, p. 131; Kallen, Life Among the Pirates, p. 25; Eastman and Bond, The Pirate Trial of Anne Bonny and Mary Read, pp. 21-22.

139. Johnson, A General History of the Robberies and Murders of the Most Notorious Pirates, pp. 112, 131; Franklin W. Knight, Slave Society in Cuba during the Nineteenth Century, (Madison: University of Wisconsin Press, 1974), pp. 3-6, 8-9, 13-90, 106; Craton, A History of the Bahamas, p. 11; Christopher P. Baker, Cuba Handbook, (Chico: Moon Publications, Inc., 1997), p. 5; Steele, Women Pirates, pp. 3-4; Esquemeling, The Buccaneers of America, pp. 60, 75, 255-256; Murphy, Rounding the Horn, p. 79.

140. Johnson, A General History of the Robberies and Murders of the Most Notorious Pirates, p. 131; Eastman and Bond, The Pirate Trial of Anne Bonny and Mary Read, pp. 21-22.

141. Johnson, A General History of the Robberies and Murders of the Most Notorious Pirates, pp. 112, 125-131; Wheelwright, Amazons and Military Maids, p. 17; Klausmann, Meinzerin, and Kuhn, Women Pirates, p. 230; Eastman and Bond, The Pirate Trial of Anne Bonny and Mary Read, pp. 22, 24; Druett, She Captains, p. 136; Cordingly, Under the Black Flag, pp. xiv, xx; Klein, The Most Evil Pirates in History, p. 133.

142. Druett, She Captains, p. 136; Eastman and Bond, The Pirate Trail of Anne Bonny and Mary Read, p. 24; Cordingly, Under the Black Flag, p. 57; The Tryals of Captain John Rackam, and other Pirates, PRO.

143. Klein, The Most Evil Pirates in History, p. 124.

144. Ibid., p. 122.

145. Johnson, A General History of the Robberies and Murders of the Most Notorious Pirates, pp. 104, 131.

146. Johnson, A General History of the Robberies and Murders of the Most Notorious Pirates, pp. 111-115, 131; Knight, Slave Society in Cuba during the Nineteenth Century, pp. 8-9, 89; Lucie-Smith, Outcasts of the Sea, pp. 177-178.

147. Johnson, A General History of the Robberies and Murders of the Most Notorious Pirates, p. 112; DePauw, Seafaring Women, p. 30.

148. Johnson, A General History of the Robberies and Murders of the Most Notorious Pirates, p. 131; Black, Pirates of the West Indies, p. 113; Eastman and Bond, The Trial of Anne Bonny and Mary Read, pp. 21-22.

149. Johnson, A General History of the Robberies and Murders of the Most Notorious Pirates, pp. 19-21, 112, 131; Klein, The Most Evil Pirates in History, p. 124; Steele, Women Pirates, pp. 16-17.

150. Calendar of State Papers, vol. xxxii, p. 463iii, December 28, 1720, Public Records Office, Kew, England.

151. Johnson, A General History of the Robberies and Murders of the Most Notorious Pirates, pp. 19-21.

152. Ibid., pp. 20, 112, 131; The Tryals of Captain John Rackam, and Other Pirates, PRO.

153. Calendar of State Papers, vol. xxxii, p. 463iii, December 28, 1720; PRO; Johnson, A General History of the Robberies and Murders of the Most Notorious Pirates, pp. 112, 131; Trinidad, Cuba, Wikipedia; Knight, Slave Society in Cuba, pp. 3-9; Esquemeling, The Buccaneers of America, pp. 130-132.

154. Johnson, A General History of the Robberies and Murders of the Most Notorious Pirates, pp.112, 131; Knight, Slave Society in Cuba during the Nineteenth Century, pp. 8-9, 43, 89; Eastman and Bond, The Pirate Trial of Anne Bonny and Mary Read, pp. 21-22.

155. Johnson, A General History of the Robberies and Murders of the Most Notorious Pirates, p. 112; Klein, The Most Evil Pirates in History, p. 124; Knight, Slave Society in Cuba during the Nineteenth Century, pp. 8-9.

156. Baker, Cuba Handbook, pp. 2-5; Craton, A History of the Bahamas, pp. 11-12; Calendar of State Papers, vol. xxxii, p. 463iii, December 28, 1720, PRO; Johnson, A General History of the Robberies and Murders of the Most Notorious Pirates, pp. 112, 131

157. Johnson, A General History of the Robberies and Murders of the Most Notorious Pirates, pp.

110, 112, 115-116, 125, 131; Baker, *Cuba Handbook*, p. 11; Craton, *A History of the Bahamas*, pp. 11-12; Baker, *Cuba Handbook*, pp. 144-145; Botting, *The Pirates*, p. 45; Eastman and Bond, *The Pirate Trial of Anne Bonny and Mary Read*, p. 22.

158.   Johnson, *A General History of the Robberies and Murders of the Most Notorious Pirates*, pp. 112, 131.

159.   Ibid., pp. 19-21, 112-113, 131; Black, *Pirates of the West Indies*, pp. 113-114; Calendar of State Papers, vol. xxxii, p. 463iii, December 28, 1720, PRO

160.   Johnson, *A General History of the Robberies and Murders of the Most Notorious Pirates*, pp. 112-113, 131; Eastman and Bond, *The Pirate Trial of Anne Bonny and Mary Read*, pp. 21-22.

161.   Johnson, *A General History of the Robberies and Murders of the Most Notorious Pirates*, pp. 112-113, 131; Calendar of States Papers, vol. xxxii, p. 463iii, December 28, 1720, PRO; Eastman and Bond, *The Pirate Trial of Anne Bonny and Mary Read*, pp. 21-22

162.   Johnson, *A General History of the Robberies and Murders of the Most Notorious Pirates*, pp. 112-113, 125-131.

163.   Ibid., pp. 125-131; Klausmann, Meinzerin, and Kuhn, *Women Pirates*, p. 235; Lucie-Smith, *Outcasts of the Sea*, pp. 24, 158, 162.

164.   Klein, *The Most Evil Pirates in History*, p. 125.

165.   Akenson, *An Irish History of Civilization*, vol. 1, p. 335; Cordingly, *Under the Black Flag*, p. 231; Lucie-Smith, *Outcasts of the Sea*, p. 113; Apestegui, *Pirates of the Caribbean*, pp. 20, 164-166; Kallen, *Life Among the Pirates*, pp. 15-16, 62; Gambrill, *In Search of the Buccaneers*, pp. 59-60.

166.   Atkenson, *An Irish History of Civilization*, vol. 1, pp. 335, 342-343; Dunn, *Sugar and Slaves*, pp. 164-165; Latimer, *Buccaneers of the Caribbean*, pp. 4-5; Botting, *The Pirates*, p. 15; Eastman and Bond, *The Pirate Trial of Bonny and Read*, p. 16; Eastman email to author, December 28, 2010, no. 2.

167.   Woodard, *The Republic of Pirates*, pp. 131, 153-154, 155, 158-159, 162-163, 176, 213-214; Bolster, *Black Jacks*, p. 13; Blassingame, *The Slave Community*, pp. 119-121; Latimer, *Buccaneers of the Caribbean*, pp. 135-136, 165, 169, 183, 244-245, 266; Steele, *Women Pirates*, p. 4; Johnson, *A General History of the Robberies and Murders of the Most Notorious Pirates*, pp. 179-181; Klausmann, Meinzerin, and Kuhn, *Women Pirates*, pp. 180, 230; Sublette, *The World That Made New Orleans*, p. 43; Cordingly, *Under the Black Flag*, p. 231; Apestegui, *Pirates of the Caribbean*, pp. 51, 54-55, 185-186; Kallen, *Life Among the Pirates*, pp. 29-30.

168.   Klausmann, Meinzerin, and Kuhn, *Women Pirates*, p. 237; Druett, *She Captains*, p. 148; Myron

and Bunch, eds., *Women Remembered*, p. 89.

169.   Woodard, *The Republic of Pirates*, pp. 159, 165, 167.

170.   Ibid., pp. 131-132, 154, 158-159, 163; William H. McNeill, *The Pursuit of Power*, (Chicago: The University of Chicago Press, 1982), p. 156.

171.   Johnson, *A General History of the Robberies and Murders of the Most Notorious Pirates*, p. 1; Sublette, *The World That Made New Orleans*, p. 43; Botting, *The Pirates*, p. 20.

172.   Johnson, *A General History of the Robberies and Murders of the Most Notorious Pirates*, pp. 1, 73, 111, 125-126; 260-261, 302, 309; Bolster, *Black Jacks*, p. 15; Richard Sanders, *If a Pirate I Must Be . . . The True Story of "Black Bart," King of the Pirates*, (New York: Skyhorse Publishing, 2009),p. 95; Dunn, *Sugar and Slaves*, pp. 150-151; Latimer, *Buccaneers of the Caribbean*, pp. 244-245; Sublette, *The World That Made New Orleans*, pp. 30-31; Craton, *A History of the Bahamas*, pp. 83, 93-99; Botting, *The Pirates*, pp. 20, 28, 50; Cordingly, *Under the Black Flag*, pp. 87-88; Kallen, *Life Among the Pirates*, pp. 74-75

173.   Bolster, *Black Jacks*, pp. 13, 15; Dunn, *Sugar and Slaves*, pp. 150-151; Latimer, *Buccaneers of the Caribbean*, pp. 244-245.

174.   Johnson, *A General History of the Robberies and Murders of the Most Notorious Pirates*, pp. 63-79; Woodard, *The Republic of Pirates*, pp. 277, 300-301; Leland, *Charleston*, pp. 5, 11; Dunn, *Sugar and Slaves*, pp. 64-165; Latimer, *Buccaneers in the Caribbean*, pp. 243-246.

175.   B. W. Higman, *Proslavery Priest, The Atlantic World of John Lindsay, 1729-1788*, (Kingston: University of West Indies Press, 2011), p. 209.

176.   Ibid.

177.   Klein, *The Most Evil Pirates in History*, pp. 82-86; Douglas R. Burgess, Jr., *The Pirates' Pact, The Secret Alliances Between History's Most Notorious Buccaneers and Colonial America*, (Camden: International Marine/Ragged Mountain Press, 2008), p. xiv-xv; Steele, *Women Pirates*, pp. 14-15.

178.   David Shears, *Ocracoke, Its History and People*, (Washington, D. C.: Starfish Press, 1989), pp. 1, 16, 27, 30-31; Steele, *Women Pirates*, p. 14; Klein, *The Most Evil Pirates in History*, pp. 83-84.

179.   Shears, *Ocracoke*, pp. 27, 29-33; Klein, *The Most Evil Pirates in History*, pp. 83-85; Burgess, *The Pirates' Pact*, p. 3; Cordingly, *Under the Black Flag*, p. 71; Druett, *She Captains*, pp. 144-145; Klein, *The Most Evil Pirates in History*, pp. 83-84.

180.   Shears, *Ocracoke*, pp. 33-34; Burgess, *The Pirates' Pact*, pp. 2-7; Johnson, *A General History of the Robberies and Murders of the Most Notorious Pirates*, pp. 54-59, 61-62; Kallen, *Life Among the Pirates*, p. 78

181. Burgess, *The Pirates' Pact*, pp. xi-265; Latimer, *Buccaneers of the Caribbean*, pp. 100-281; Steele, *Women Pirates*, pp. 3-4, 7-8; Kallen, *Life Among the Pirates*, pp. 13-14, 39, 80; Klein, *The Most Evil Pirates in History*, pp. 7, 83-84; Esquemeling, *The Buccaneers of America*, pp. 130-131.

182. *New York, A Collection from Harper's Magazine*, (New York: Gallery Books, 1991), p.118.

183. Ibid.

184. Burgess, *The Pirates' Pact*, p. 11.

185. *Boston Gazette*, Boston, Massachusetts, October 10 to 17, 1720; Johnson, *A General History of the Robberies and Murders of the Most Notorious Pirates*, pp. 125-131; Burgess, *The Pirates' Pact*, pp. xi-265; Stanley, ed., *Bold in Her Breeches*, p. 185

186. Johnson, *A General History of the Robberies and Murders of the Most Notorious Pirates*, pp. 111, 125-131.

187. Ibid., pp. 111, 58-59; Burgess, *The Pirates' Pact*, p. 9; Stanley, ed., *Bold in Her Breeches*, p. 185; Botting, *The Pirates*, p. 20

188. Klausmann, Meinzerin and Kuhn, *Women Pirates*, p. 230; Stanley, ed., *Bold in Her Breeches*, p. 185; Botting, *The Pirates*, pp. 20, 24; Apestegui, *The Pirates of the Caribbean*, pp. 194, 203; Kallen, *Life Among the Pirates*, pp. 8, 19, 29; Johnson, *A General History of the Robberies and Murders of the Most Notorious Pirates*, pp. 111-112, 130-131.

189. Apestegui, *The Pirates of the Caribbean*, p. 208; Kallen, *Life Among the Pirates*, p. 70.

190. Apestegui, *The Pirates of the Caribbean*, p. 208; Kallen, *Life Among the Pirates*, p. 70; Johnson, *A General History of the Robberies and Murders of the Most Notorious Pirates*, pp. 125-131.

191. Johnson, *A General History of the Robberies and Murders of the Most Notorious Pirates*, pp. 111-113, 131; Klein, *The Most Evil Pirates in History*, pp. 125-126.

192. *Boston Gazette*, October 10 and 17, 1720; Cordingly, *Under the Black Flag*, pp. 56-57; Botting, *The Pirates*, pp. 31-34, 57; Craton, *A History of the Bahamas*, pp. 79, 111, 129; Kallen, *Life Among the Pirates*, pp. 11, 35; Johnson, *A General History of the Robberies and Murders of the Most Notorious Pirates*, pp. 113, 120-121; Klein, *The Most Evil Pirates in History*, p. 126; The Tryals of Captain John Racham, and Other Pirates, PRO.

193. The Tryals of Captain John Rackam, and Other Pirates, PRO; Johnson, *A General History of the Robberies and Murders of the Most Notorious Pirates*, pp. 120-121.

194. *Boston Gazette*, October 10 and 17, 1720; Cordingly, *Under the Black Flag*, pp. 56, 223-224, 226, 249; Johnson, *A General History of the Robberies and Murders of the Most Notorious Pirates*, pp. 119-120; Stanley, ed., *Bold in Her Breeches*, pp. 185-186; Eastman email to author, December 28, 2010, email no. 3; Tamara Eastman, Petersburg, Virginia, email to author, December 30, 2010; Female Pirates, World History Site, internet; Johnson, *A General History of the Robberies and Murders of the Most Notorious Pirates*, pp. 25, 28-29, 120-121

195. Johnson, *A General History of the Robberies and Murders of the Most Notorious Pirates*, pp. 119-121; Eastman email to author, December 28, 2010, no. 3, and 30, 2010; Female Pirates, World History Site, internet.

196. *Boston Gazette*, October 10 and 17, 1720; Wheelwright, *Amazons and Military Maids*, p. 12; Klausmann, Meinzerin, and Kuhn, *Women Pirates*, p. 180; Nancy Myron and Charlotte Bunch, eds., *Women Remembered, A Collection of Biographies From The Furies*, (Baltimore: Diana Press, 1974), pp. 77-89; Johnson, *A General History of the Robberies and Murders of the Most Notorious Pirates*, pp. vii-viii, 120-122; Stanley, ed., *Bold in Her Breeches*, pp. 32, 187; Druett, *She Captains*, pp. 149-150.

197. Johnson, *A General History of the Robberies and Murders of the Most Notorious Pirates*, pp. 115-131; Stanley, ed., *Bold in Her Breeches*, pp. 181-182; Cordingly, *Under the Black Flag*, p. 58; Myron and Bunch, eds., *Women Remembered*, pp. 84-86; The Tryals of Captain John Rackam, and Other Pirates, PRO; Eastman email to author, December 28, 2010, no. 3, and December 30, 2010; Female Pirates, World History Site, internet.

198. Johnson, *A General History of the Robberies and Murders of the Most Notorious Pirates*, pp. 117-124; Stanley, ed., *Bold in Her Breeches*, pp. 182-188.

199. Stanley, ed., *Bold in Her Breeches*, pp. 182-188; Johnson, *A General History of the Robberies and Murders of the Most Notorious Pirates*, pp. 117-131; Cordingly, *Under the Black Flag*, p. 59.

200. Cusack, *An Illustrated History of Ireland, From AD 400 to 1800*, p. 92.

201. Ibid.

202. Ibid., pp. 92-93.

203. Ibid., p. 93.

204. *Boston Gazette*, October 10 and 17, 1720; Cordingly, *Under the Black Flag*, p. 58.

205. *Boston Gazette*, October 10 and 17, 1720; Cordingly, *Under the Black Flag*, p. 58

206. *Boston Gazette*, October 10 and 17, 1720; Craton, *A History of the Bahamas*, pp. 93-101; Edward Leslie, *Desperate Journeys, Abandoned Souls*, (London: Papermac, 1991), pp. 1-2.

207. *Boston Gazette*, October 10 and 17, 1720; Cordingly, *Under the Black Flag*, pp. 57-58.

208. Klein, *The Most Evil Pirates in History*, p. 8.

209. *Boston Gazette*, October 10 and 17, 1720; Lucie-Smith, *Outcasts of the Sea*, p. 194.

210. Johnson, *A General History of the Robberies and Murders of the Most Notorious Pirates*, p. 122.

211. *Boston Gazette*, October 10 and 17, 1720; Johnson, *A General History of the Robberies and Murders of the Most Notorious Pirates*, p. 113; Cordingly, *Under the Black Flag*, pp. 11, 56-59; *Washington Post*, March 26, 1899; The Tryals of Captain John Rackam, and Other Pirates, PRO.

212. *Boston Gazette*, October 10 and 17, 1720; Johnson, *A General History of the Robberies and Murders of the Most Notorious Pirates*, p. 113; David Buckley, *The Right to be Proud, A Brief Guide to Jamaican Heritage Sits*, (Kingston: MAPCO Business Partners, 2005), pp. 37, 51-53; Cordingly, *Under the Black Flag*, pp. xiv, 58; DePauw, *Seafaring Women*, pp. 5-6, 13; Lucie-Smith, *Outcasts of the Sea*, p. 9; The Tryals of Captain John Rackam, and Other Pirates, PRO.

213. The Tryals of Captain John Rackam, and Other Pirates, PRO.

214. Ibid; Johnson, *A General History of the Robberies and Murders of the Most Notorious Pirates*, p. 113; Kallen, *Life Among the Pirates*, pp. 11, 25, 36, 48, 56; Esquemeling, *The Buccaneers of America*, pp. 26, 89.

215. *Boston Gazette*, October 10 and 17, 1720; The Tryals of Captain John Rackam, and Other Pirates, PRO; Johnson, *A General History of the Robberies and Murders of the Most Notorious Pirates*, pp. 113, 117-131; Botting, *The Pirates*, p. 45; DePauw, *Seafaring Women*, p. 28; Druett, *She Captains*, p. 136; Lucie-Smith, *Outcasts of the Sea*, p. 6; Kallen, *Life Among the Pirates*, pp. 11, 45, 48, 56; Klein, *The Most Evil Pirates in History*, p. 138; Esquemeling, *The Buccaneers of America*, pp. xxiv-xxxvi, 9, 38, 40.

216. *Boston Gazette*, October 10 and 17, 1720; Johnson, *A General History of the Robberies and Murders of the Most Notorious Pirates*, p. 113; Botting, *The Pirates*, p. 45; Apestegui, *Pirates of the Caribbean*, p. 169; Kallen, *Life Among the Pirates*, p. 56.

217. *Boston Gazette*, October 10 and 17, 1720; Johnson, *A General History of the Robberies and Murders of the Most Notorious Pirates*, pp. 113, 115; Klausmann, Meinzerin, and Kuhn, *Women Pirates*, p. 250; Cordingly, *Under the Black Flag*, p. 58; The Tryals of Captain John Rackam, and Other Pirates, PRO.

218. Johnson, *A General History of the Robberies and Murders of the Most Notorious Pirates*, p. 113; Cordingly, *Under the Black Flag*, p. 58; Klein, *The Most Evil Pirates in History*, p. 124.

219. *Boston Gazette*, October 10 and 17, 1720; Johnson, *A General History of the Robberies and Murders of the Most Notorious Pirates*, pp. 113, 122; Latimer, *Buccaneers of the Caribbean*, pp. 278-281; Cord-

ingly, *Under the Black Flag*, pp. 56-59.

220. *Boston Gazette*, October 10 and 17, 1720; Johnson, *A General History of the Robberies and Murders of the Most Notorious Pirates*, p. 113; Buckley, *The Right to be Proud*, pp. 30-31; Cordingly, *Under the Black Flag*, pp. 58-59; The Tryals of Captain John Rackam and Other Pirates, PRO.

221. Cordingly, *Under the Black Flag*, p. 50; Klein, *The Most Evil Pirates in History*, pp. 38-49; Johnson, *A General History of the Robberies and Murders of the Most Notorious Pirates*, p. 125; Lucie-Smith, *Outcasts of the Sea*, p. 166; Edward Long, *The History of Jamaica*, vol. 1, (2 vols., New York: Arno Press, 1972), p. 376; Apestegui, *Pirates of the Caribbean*, p. 179; Klein, *The Most Evil Pirates in History*, pp. 38-50.

222. *Boston Gazette*, October 10 and 17, 1720; Johnson, *A General History of the Robberies and Murders of the Most Notorious Pirates*, pp. 113, 122,131; Klausmann, Meinzerin, and Kuhn, *Women Pirates*, pp. 258-259; Philip Sherlock, *The Story of the Jamaican People*, (Kingston: Ian Randle Publishers, 1998), p. 155; Kallen, *Life Among the Pirates*, p. 25.

223. Sanders, *If a Pirate I must be . . .*," pp. 94-95, 104; Dunn, *Sugar and Slaves*, p. 148; Klausmann, Meinzerin, and Kuhn, *Women Pirates*, p. 180; Johnson, *A General History of the Robberies and Murders of the Most Notorious Pirates*, p. 122; Buckley, *The Right to be Proud*, pp. 37, 51-53; Cordingly, *Under the Black Flag*, p. 59.

224. *Boston Gazette*, October 10 and 17, 1720; Johnson, *A General History of the Robberies & Murders of the Most Notorious Pirates*, pp. 111-113, 122; Peter Earle, *Sack of Panama, Sir Henry Morgan's Adventures on the Spanish Main*, (New York: The Viking Press, 1981), pp. 9-249; Klein, *The Most Evil Pirates in History*, pp. 38-50, 108, 124; Sherlock and Bennett, *The Story of the Jamaican People*, p. 155; Cordingly, *Under the Black Flag*, p. 59.

225. *Boston Gazette*, October 10 and 17, 1720; Johnson, *A General History of the Robberies and Murders of the Most Notorious Pirates*, pp. 113-114; Buckley, *The Right to be Proud*, pp. 30-31; The Tryals of Captain John Rackham, and Other Pirates, PRO.

226. *Boston Gazette*, October 10 and 17, 1720; Johnson, *A General History of the Robberies and Murders of the Most Notorious Pirates*, pp. 6-7, 113, 122; Sanders, *If a Pirate I must be . . .*," pp. 94-95, 104; Cordingly, *Under the Black Flag*, p. 59; Long, *The History of Jamaica*, vol. 1, pp. 376-377 map.

227. *Boston Gazette*, October 10 and 17, 1720; Long, *The History of Jamaica*, vol. 1, pp. 376-377 map; Johnson, *A General History of the Robberies and Murders of the Most Notorious Pirates*, pp. 68-79, 113-114, 122; Latimer, *Buccaneers of the Caribbean*, pp. 265-

266; Klausmann, Meinzerin, and Kuhn, *Women Pirates*, pp. 251-252; Buckly, *The Right to be Proud*, pp. 8-9, 14,18-19, 25-26; Sherlock and Bennett, *The Story of the Jamaican People*, pp. 151-153; Black, *Pirates of the West Indies*, pp. 101, 118; Cordingly, *Under the Black Flag*, pp. 11, 14, 16, 59, 245, 249; Botting, *The Pirates*, pp. 48-49; Kallen, *Life Among the Pirates*, p. 22; The Tryals of Captain John Rackam, and Other Pirates, PRO; Higman, *Proslavery Priest*, pp. 217, 223.

228. Long, *The History of Jamaica*, vol. 1, pp. 376-377 map; Latimer, *Buccaneers of the Caribbean*, pp. 136-137; Johnson, *A General History of the Robberies and Murders of the Most Notorious Pirates*, pp. 114-115; Black, *Pirates of the West Indies*, p. 101; Cordingly, *Under the Black Flag*, p. 56; Kallen, *Life Among the Pirates*, pp. 21, 40-41; Gambrill, *In Search of the Buccaneers*, pp. 75-79; Long, *The History of Jamaica*, vol. 1, pp. 376-377 map; The Tryals of Captain John Rackam, and Other Pirates, PRO

229. *Boston Gazette*, October 10 and 17, 1720; The Tryals of Captain John Rackam, and Other Pirates, PRO; Johnson, *A General History of the Robberies and Murders of the Most Notorious Pirates*, pp. 113-116, 121; Sherlock and Bennett, *The Story of the Jamaican People*, p. 114; Botting, *The Pirates*, pp. 26, 44; Lucie-Smith, *Outcasts of the Sea*, pp. 134-138, 148, 174; Black, *Pirates of the West Indies*, p. 102; Kallen, *Life Among the Pirates*, p. 36; Esquemeling, *The Buccaneers of America*, pp. 26, 89.

230. *Boston Gazette*, October 10 and 17, 1720; Johnson, *A General History of the Robberies and Murders of the Most Notorious Pirates*, pp. 12-14, 109-116, 122; Sanders, *If a Pirate I must be . . . ,*" pp. 120; Klein, *The Most Evil Pirates in History*, pp. 85-86, 121-125; Sherlock and Bennett, *The Story of the Jamaican People*, pp. 113-114; Cordingly, *Under the Black Flag*, pp. 58-59, 249.

231. Klein, *The Most Evil Pirates in History*, p. 185; Cordingly, *Under the Black Flag*, 50; Apestegui, *Pirates of the Caribbean*, p. 169.

232. Gambrill, *In Search of the Buccaneers*, p. 247.

233. *Boston Gazette*, October 10 and 17, 1720; Johnson, *A General History of the Robberies and Murders of the Most Notorious Pirates*, pp. 113, 115-116, 131; Klein, *The Most Evil Pirates in History*, pp. 83-86; Klausmann, Meinzerin, and Kuhn, *Women Pirates*, p. 180; Stanley, ed., *Bold in Her Breeches*, p. 32; Cordingly, *Under the Black Flag*, p. 58; Botting, *The Pirates*, p. 24; Black, *History of the West Indies*, p. 102.

234. Steele, *Women Pirates*, p. 5; Botting, *The Pirates*, p. 20; Johnson, *A General History of the Robberies and Murders of the Most Notorious Pirates*, p. 125.

235. *Boston Gazette*, October 10 and 17, 1720; Johnson, *A General History of the Robberies and Murders of the Most Notorious Pirates*, pp. 161, 253-259; Steele, *Women Pirates*, pp. 5, 7-8; Cordingly, *Under the Black Flag*, p. 246.

236. *Boston Gazette*, October 10 and 17, 1720; Johnson, *A General History of the Robberies and Murders of the Most Notorious Pirates*, pp. 113, 115; Cordingly, *Under the Black Flag*, pp. 57-59, 245; Black, *Pirates of the West Indies*, pp. 102, 113-114.

237. *Boston Gazette*, October 10 and 17, 1720; Johnson, *A General History of the Robberies and Murders of the Most Notorious Pirates*, pp. 111, 113-116; Sherlock and Bennett, *The Story of the Jamaican People*, pp. 113-114; Cordingly, *Under the Black Flag*, pp. 58-59, 260, note 7; Kallen, *Life Among the Pirates*, p. 35.

238. *Boston Gazette*, October 10 and 17, 1720; Johnson, *A General History of the Robberies and Murders of the Most Notorious Pirates*, pp. 114-116; Cordingly, *Under the Black Flag*, p. 59; Botting, *The Pirates*, pp. 32-34; Black, *Pirates of the West Indies*, p. 102; The Tryals of Captain John Rackam, and Other Pirates, PRO.

239. *Boston Gazette*, October 10 and 17, 1720; Johnson, *A General History of the Robberies and Murders of the Most Notorious Pirates*, pp. 115-116.

240. *Boston Gazette*, October 10 and 17, 1720; Johnson, *A General History of the Robberies and Murders of the Most Notorious Pirates*, pp. 115, 131; Steele, *Women Pirates*, p. 18; Cordingly, *Under the Black Flag*, pp. 56, 59; Black, *Pirates of the West Indies*, pp. 102-103; Klein, *The Most Evil Pirates in History*, pp. 126-127.

241. *Boston Gazette*, October 10 and 17, 1720; Johnson, *A General History of the Robberies and Murders of the Most Notorious Pirates*, pp. 115, 121, 131; Klausmann, Meinzerin, and Kuhn, *Women Pirates*, pp. 256-257; Steele, *Women Pirates*, p. 18; Cordingly, *Under the Black Flag*, p. 56; Kallen, *Life Among the Pirates*, p. 51; Black, *Pirates of the West Indies*, p. 103; The Tryals of Captain John Rackam, and Other Pirates, PRO.

242. *Boston Gazette*, October 10 and 17, 1720; The Tryals of Captain John Rackham, and Other Pirates, PRO; Johnson, *A General History of the Robberies and Murders of the Most Notorious Pirates*, pp. 114-116, 118-121, 131; Klausmann, Meinzerin, and Kuhn, *Women Pirates*, pp. 243-245; Black, *Pirates of the West Indies*, pp. 101, 103; Stanley, ed., *Bold in the Breeches*, pp. 41-48; Cordingly, *Under the Black Flag*, p. 56.

243. *Boston Gazette*, October 10 and 17, 1720; Johnson, *A General History of the Robberies and Murders of the Most Notorious Pirates*, p. 121; Black, *Pirates of the West Indies*, p. 103; The Tryals of Captain John Rackam, and other Pirates, PRO.

244. Johnson, *A General History of the Robberies and Murders of the Most Notorious Pirates*, pp. 118-119, 121; Black, *Pirates of the West Indies*, p. 103.

245. *Boston Gazette*, October 10 and 17, 1720; Johnson, *A General History of the Robberies and Murders of the Most Notorious Pirates*, pp. 118-131; Steele, *Women Pirates*, p. 19; Marcus Tanner, *Ireland's Holy Wars, The Struggle for a Nation's Soul*, (New Haven: Yale University Press, 2001), pp. 1-175; Cordingly, *Under the Black Flag*, pp. 11, 14, Terry Golway, *For the Cause of Liberty, A Thousands Years of Ireland's Heroes*, (New York: Simon and Schuster, 2000), pp. 9-41; Myron and Bunch, *Women Remember*, p. 86; Kallen, *Life Among the Pirates*, pp. 50-51; Female Pirates, World History Site, internet; Eastman email to author, December 30, 2010; Cusack, *An Illustrated History of Ireland from AD 400 to 1800*, pp. 500-503.

246. *Boston Gazette*, October 10 and 17, 1720; Johnson, *A General History of the Robberies and Murders of the Most Notorious Pirates*, pp. 118-121, 131; Cordingly, *Under the Black Flags*, p. 58; Black, *Pirates of the West Indies*, p. 103.

247. *Boston Gazette*, October 10 and 17, 1720; Johnson, *A General History of the Robberies and Murders of the Most Notorious Pirates*, pp. 118-121, 131; Black, *Pirates of the West Indies*, p. 101; Steele, *Women Pirates*, p. 19; Cordingly, *Under the Black Flag*, p. 59; Black, *Pirates of the West Indies*, p. 103; Klein, *The Most Evil Pirates in History*, p. 138.

248. *Boston Gazette*, October 10 and 17, 1720; Myron and Bunch, eds., *Women Remembered*, p. 88; Black, *Pirates of the West Indies*, p. 103; Cordingly, *Under the Black Flag*, p. 14; Johnson, *A General History of the Robberies and Murders of the Most Notorious Pirates*, pp. 118-121, 131.

249. *Boston Gazette*, October 10 and 17, 1720; Black, *Pirates of the West Indies*, p. 103.

250. *Boston Gazette*, October 10 and 17, 1720; Johnson, *A General History of the Robberies and Murders of the Most Notorious Pirates*, pp. 115-116, 121, 131; Steele, *Women Pirates*, p. 19; Cordingly, *Under the Black Flag*, p. 59.

251. Black, *Pirates of the West Indies*, p. 103.

252. *Boston Gazette*, October 10 and 17, 1720; Buckley, *The Right to be Proud*, pp. 8-9; Corindingly, *Under the Black Flag*, p. 59; Black, *Pirates of the West Indies*, p. 103.

253. *Boston Gazette*, October 10 and 17, 1720; Stanley, ed., *Bold in Her Breeches*, pp. 178, 181-182; Johnson, *A General History of the Robberies and Murders of the Most Notorious Pirates*, pp. 121-122; The Tryals of Captain John Rackham, and Other Pirates, PRO.

254. Alexander Mikaberidze, *The Battle of the Berezina, Napoleon's Great Escape*, (Bransley: Pen &

Sword Books, Ltd., 2010), p. 2000; Johnson, *A General History of the Robberies and Murders of the Most Notorious Pirates*, pp. 121-122.

255. *Boston Gazette*, October 10 and 17, 1720; Johnson, *A General History of the Robberies and Murders of the Most Notorious Pirates*, pp. 121-122; Cordingly, *Under the Black Flag*, p. 59; Black, *Pirates of the West Indies*, p. 103.

256. Black, *Pirates of the West Indies*, p. 103.

257. *Boston Gazette*, October 10 and 17, 1720; Latimer, *Buccaneers of the Caribbean*, pp. 135-281; Dunn, *Sugar and Slaves*, pp. 149-223; Steele, *Women Pirates*, p. 7; Klausmann, Meinzerin, and Kuhn, *Women Pirates*, pp. 180, 184; Johnson, *A General History of the Robberies and Murders of the Most Notorious Pirates*, pp. 12-14; Esquemeling, *The Buccaneers of America*, pp. xxxvii, 138-139; The Tryals of Captain John Rackham, and Other Pirates, PRO.

258. Klausmann, Meinzerin, and Kuhn, *Women Pirates*, p. 237; Stanley, ed., *Bold in Her Breeches*, p. 32.

259. *New York*, pp. 118, 140.

260. Burgess, *The Pirates' Pact*, pp. 12-14; Klausmann, Meinzerin, and Kuhn, *Women Pirates*, pp. 236-237; Stanley, *Bold in Her Breeches*, pp. 178-179.

261. The Tryals of Captain John Rackam, and Other Pirates, PRO; Dunn, *Sugar and Slaves*, pp. 150-151; Latimer, *Buccaneers of the Caribbean*, pp. 244-245; Klausmann, Meinzerin, and Kuhn, *Women Pirates*, p. 180; Stanley, *Bold in Her Breeches*, pp. 178-179.

262. The Tryals of Captain John Rackam, and Other Pirates, PRO; Johnson, *A General History of the Robberies and Murders of the Most Notorious Pirates*, pp. 73, 125-131, 261, 302; Burgess, *The Pirates' Pact*, pp. 13-14; Dunn, *Sugar and Slaves*, pp. 150-151; Latimer, *Buccaneers of the Caribbean*, pp. 244-245; Stanley, ed., *Bold in Her Breeches*, pp. 178-179; Craton, *A History of the Bahamas*, p. 93.

263. The Tryals of Captain John Rackham, and Other Pirates, PRO; Wheelwright, *Amazons and Military Maids*, pp. 6-8; Buckley, *The Right to be Proud*, p. 37; Johnson, *A General History of the Robberies and Murders of the Most Notorious Pirates*, pp. 125-131; Stanley, ed., *Bold in Her Breeches*, pp. 178-179; Spanish Town, Jamaica, Wikipedia, internet; Cordingly, *Under the Black Flag*, pp. 11, 14, 62; Apestegui, *Pirates of the Caribbean*, p. 207; Travelin' to Pirate Country, A Visit to Jamaica, Part III, Spanish Town and Kingston, internet; Higman, *Proslavery Priest*, pp. 124-125, 130.

264. Stanley, ed., *Bold in Her Breeches*, pp. 178-179; Klein, *The Most Evil Pirates in History*, p. 128; Cordingly, *Under the Black Flag*, pp. 62, 228; Long,

The History of Jamaica, vol. 1, pp. 77-79; The Tryals of Captain John Rackam, and Other Pirates, PRO.

265. The Tryals of Captain John Rackam, and Other Pirates, PRO; Johnson, *A General History of the Robberies and Murders of the Most Notorious Pirates*, pp. 111-116, 121-122, 125-131; Cordingly, *Under the Black Flag*, p. 228; Kallen, *Life Among the Pirates*, p. 25.

266. The Tryals of Captain John Rackam, and Other Pirates, PRO; Johnson, *A General History of the Robberies and Murders of the Most Notorious Pirates*, p. 131; Buckley, *The Right to be Proud*, p. 54; Stanley, ed., *Bold in Her Breeches*, pp. 178-179; Steele, *Women Pirates*, p. 5; Kallen, *Life Among the Pirates*, p. 72; Travelin' to Pirate Country, A Visit to Jamaica, Part II, The Port Royal Development Project, internet.

267. The Tryals of Captain John Rackam, and Other Pirates, PRO; Johnson, *A General History of the Robberies and Murders of the Most Notorious Pirates*, p. 114; Cordingly, *Under the Black Flag*, p. 63.

268. The Tryals of Captain John Rackham, and other Pirates, PRO; Johnson, *A General History of the Robberies and Murders of the Most Notorious Pirates*, pp. 5, 114; Steele, *Women Pirates*, pp. 5, 20; Cordingly, *Under the Black Flag*, pp. 63, 224-226; Black, *Pirates of the West Indies*, p. 116; Kallen, *Life Among the Pirates*, p. 74; Klein, *The Most Evil Pirates in History*, p. 128; Eastman and Bond, *The Pirate Trial of Anne Bonny and Mary Read*, p. 37; Travelin' to Pirate Country, A Visit to Jamaica, Part II, The Port Royal Development Project, internet.

269. Johnson, *A General History of the Robberies and Murders of the Most Notorious Pirates*, p. 5; The Tryals of Captain John Rackam and other Pirates, PRO.

270. The Tryals of Captain John Rackam, and Other Pirates, PRO; Eastman to author, December 30, 2010.

271. Cordingly, *Under the Black Flag*, pp. 227-230; The Tryals of Captain John Rackam, and Other Pirates, PRO.

272. The Tryals of Captain John Rackam, and Other Pirates, PRO; Notting, *The Pirates*, pp. 46-47; Johnson, *A General History of the Robberies and Murders of the Most Notorious Pirates*, pp. 264-266; Kallen, *Life Among the Pirates*, p. 72.

273. The Tryals of Captain John Rackham and Other Pirates, PRO; Edward Vernon, Wikipedia, internet; Steele, *Women Pirates*, pp. 5, 20; Stanley, ed., *Bold in Her Breeches*, pp. 178-179; Cordingly, *Under the Black Flag*, pp. 62, 203, 228-229; Gambrill, *In Search of the Buccaneers*, p. 80; Klein, *The Most Evil Pirates in History*, pp. 130-131, 136; Johnson, *A General Histories of the Robberies and Murders of the Most*

Notorious Pirates, pp. 117-131; Eastman email to author, December 30, 2010.

274. Edward G. Lengel, *General George Washington, A Military Life*, (New York: Random House, 2005), pp. 3-13; Edward Vernon, Wikipedia, internet.

275. The Tryals of Captain John Rackam, and Other Pirates, PRO; Lucie-Smith, *Outcasts of the Sea*, p. 175.

276. The Tryals of Captain John Rackam, and Other Pirates, PRO; Kallen, *Life Among the Pirates*, pp. 24-25.

277. The Tryals of Captain John Rackam, and Other Pirates, PRO; Lengel, *General George Washington*, p. 5; Edward Vernon, Wikipedia, internet; Cordingly, *Under the Black Flag*, p. 228.

278. The Tryals of Captain John Rackam, and Other Pirates, PRO; Black, *Tales of Old Jamaica*, p. 89.

279. Stanley, ed., *Bold in Her Breeches*, p. 179; Klein, *The Most Evil Pirates in History*, p. 128; Johnson, *A General History of the Robberies and Murders of the Most Notorious Pirates*, pp. 117-124, 125-131; The Tryals of Captain John Rackam, and Other Pirates, PRO.

280. Stanley, ed., *Bold in Her Breeches*, p. 179; The Tryals of Captain John Rackam, and Other Pirates, PRO.

281. Stanley, ed., *Bold in Her Breeches*, pp. 178-179; Steele, *Women Pirates*, pp. 20-21; The Tryals of Captain John Rackam and Other Pirates, PRO; Cordingly, *Under the Black Flag*, p. 228; Johnson, *A General History of the Robberies and Murders of the Most Notorious Pirates*, pp. 112-113, 117-131

282. Stanley, ed., *Bold in Her Breeches*, pp. 178-179; Klein, *The Most Evil of Pirates*, pp. 122-128; The Tryals of Captain John Rackam, and Other Pirates, PRO.

283. Stanley, ed., *Bold in Her Breeches*, p. 179; The Tryals of Captain John Rackham, and Other Pirates, PRO; Steele, *Women Pirates*, pp. 14-15; Stanley, *Bold in Her Britches*, pp. 181-182; Eastman and Bond, *The Pirate Trial of Anne Bonny and Mary Read*, p. 25; Johnson, *A General History of the Robberies and Murders of the Most Notorious Pirates*, p. 113.

284. Stanley, ed., *Bold in Her Breeches*, pp. 179-180; Cordingly, *Under the Black Flag*, p. 228; The Tryals of Captain John Rackham, and Other Pirates, PRO

285. The Tryals of Captain John Rackam. and Other Pirates, PRO; Stanley, ed., *Bold in Her Breeches*, p. 180; Johnson, *A General History of the Robberies and Murders of the Most Notorious Pirates*, p. 115.

286. The Tryals of Captain John Rackam, and Other Pirates, PRO; Stanley, ed., *Bold in Her Breeches*, p. 180.

287. Stanley, ed., *Bold in Her Breeches*, p. 180; The Tryals of Captain John Rackam, and Other Pirates, PRO; Johnson, *A General History of the Robberies and Murders of the Most Notorious Pirates*, p. 113.

288. The Tryals of Captain John Rackam, and Other Pirates, PRO; Stanley, ed., *Bold in Her Breeches*, p. 180

289. Stanley, ed., *Bold in Her Breeches*, pp. 180-182; The Tryals of Captain John Rackam, and Other Pirates, PRO.

290. Stanley, ed., *Bold in Her Breeches*, pp. 179-180; Steele, *Women Pirates*, p. 21; Cordingly, *Under the Black Flag*, pp. 228-229; The Tryals of Captain John Rackam, and Other Pirates, PRO.

291. Diane Miller Sommerville, *Rape and Race in the Nineteenth-Century South*, (Chapel Hill: The University of North Carolina Press, 2004), pp. 4-5.

292. The Tryals of Captain John Rackam, and Other Pirates, PRO; Klausmann, Meinzerin and Kuhn, *Women Pirates*, p. 193; Johnson, *A General History of the Robberies and Murders of the Most Notorious Pirates*, p. 121; Stanley, ed., *Bold in Her Beeches*, pp. 33, 178-179; Cordingly, *Under the Black Flag*, pp. 64, 228-229; Kallen, *Life Among the Pirates*, p. 72; Esquemeling, *The Buccaneers of America*, pp. 220-222, 228-229; Apestegui, *Pirates of the Caribbean*, p. 208; Eastman email to author, December 30, 2010.

293. Klausmann, Meinzerin and Kuhn, *Women Pirates*, p. 193; Stanley, ed., *Bold in Her Beeches*, pp. 33, 178-179; Cordingly, *Under the Black Flag*, pp. 228-229; Black, *Tales of Old Jamaica*, p. 89.

294. The Tryals of Captain John Rackam, and Other Pirates, PRO; Stanley, ed., *Bold in Her Beeches*, pp. 180-181; Klein, *The Most Evil Pirates in History*, p. 128; Cordingly, *Under the Black Flag*, pp. 64, 228-229; Black, *Tales of Old Jamaica*, p. 89.

295. Johnson, *A General History of the Robberies and Murders of the Most Notorious Pirates*, p. 116; Cordingly, *Under the Black Flag*, p. 228.

296. Steele, *Women Pirates*, p. 21; Cordingly, *Under the Black Flag*, pp. 64-65; The Tryals of Captain John Rackam, and Other Pirates, PRO.

297. The Tryals of Captain John Rackam, and Other Pirates, PRO; Black, *Pirates of the West Indies*, p. 116.

298. The Tryals of Captain John Rackam, and Other Pirates, PRO; Johnson, *A General History of the Robberies and Murders of the Most Notorious Pirates*, pp. 114, 116, 125-131; Akenson, *An Irish History of Civilization*, vol. 1, pp. 345-346; Cordingly, *Under the Black Flag*, p. 65.

299. Akenson, *An Irish History of Civilization*, vol. 1, p. 346; Cordingly, *Under the Black Flag*, pp. 65, 228; Kallen, *Life Among the Pirates*, p. 9; The Tryals of Captain John Rackham, and Other Pirates, PRO.

300. The Tryals of Captain John Rackam, and Other Pirates, PRO; Johnson, *A General History of the Robberies and Murders of the Most Notorious Pirates*, p. 116; Eastman email to author, December 30, 2010.

301. The Tryals of Captain John Rackam, and Other Pirates, PRO.

302. The Tryals of Captain John Rackam, and Other Pirates, PRO; Johnson, *A General History of the Robberies and Murders of the Most Notorious Pirates*, pp. 125-130; Akenson, *An Irish History of Civilization*, vol. 1, p. 346; Cordingly, *Under the Black Flag*, p. 228; Steele, *Women Pirates*, p. 21.

303. The Tryals of Captain John Rackam, and Other Pirates, PRO; Klein, *The Most Evil Pirates in History*, p. 140.

304. The Tryals of Captain John Rackam, and Other Pirates, PRO; Stanley, ed., *Bold in Her Breeches*, p. 182; Steele, *Women Pirates*, p. 21; Cordingly, *Under the Black Flag*, p. 65; Myron and Bunch, eds., *Women Remembered*, p. 88; Johnson, *A General History of the Robberies and Murders of the Most Notorious Pirates*, pp. 111-112.

305. The Tryals of Captain John Rackam, and Other Pirates, PRO; Stanley, ed., *Bold in Her Breeches*, p. 185; Johnson, *A General History of the Robberies and Murders of the Most Notorious Pirates*, pp. 114, 121.

306. The Tryals of Captain John Rackam, and Other Pirates, PRO; Steele, *Women Pirates*, p. 21; Akenson, *An Irish History of Civilization*, vol. 1, p. 346; Cordingly, *Under the Black Flag*, pp. 65, 228.

307. DePauw, *Seafaring Women*, p. 14.

308. Ibid.

309. The Tryals of Captain John Rackam, and Other Pirates, PRO; Eastman and Bond, *The Pirate Trial of Anne Bonny and Mary Read*, p. 40.

310. Johnson, *A General History of the Robberies and Murders of the Most Notorious Pirates*, pp. 125-131; Lalor, ed., *The Encyclopedia of Ireland*, p. 104; The Tryals of Captain John Rackam, and Other Pirates, PRO; Eastman and Bond, *The Pirate Trial of Anne Bonny and Mary Read*, pp. 14-45; Steele, *Woman Pirates*, pp. 14-15; Cordingly, *Under the Black Flag*, pp. xiii-247.

311. Klausmann, Meinzerin, and Kuhn, *Women Pirates*, pp. 243-245; Johnson, *A General History of the Robberies and Murders of the Most Notorious Pirates*, pp. 114, 131.

312. Johnson, *A General History of the Robberies & Murders of the Most Notorious Pirates*, pp. 112, 131; Eastman and Bond, *The Pirate Trial of Anne Bonny and Mary Read*, p. 24

313. The Tryals of Captain John Rackam, and Other Pirates, PRO; Cordingly, *Under the Black Flag*, pp. 63, 225, 246; Johnson, *A General History of the*

Robberies and Murders of the Most Notorious Pirates, pp. 103-110.

314.   The Tryals of Captain John Rackam, and Other Pirates, PRO.

315.   Johnson, *A General History of the Robberies and Murders of the Most Notorious Pirates*, pp. 124, 131.

316.   Johnson, *A General History of the Robberies and Murders of the Most Notorious Pirates*, pp. 130-131; Eastman and Bond, The Pirate Trial of Anne Bonny and Mary Read, p. 9; Steele, *Women Pirates*, pp. 14-15; Eastman email to author, December 28, 2010, email no. 3; The Tryals of Captain John Rackam, and Other Pirates, PRO.

317.   Johnson, *A General History of the Robberies and Murders of the Most Notorious Pirates*, p. 131; Black, *Pirates of the West Indies*, p. 117; Eastman and Bond, *The Pirate Trial of Anne Bonny and Mary Read*, pp. 42-44; The Tryals of Captain John Rackam, and Other Pirates, PRO; Eastman email to author, December 28, 2010, email no. 3

318.   Oxford Dictionary of National Biography, Anne Bonny, internet; Black, *Pirates of the West Indies*, p. 117; Johnson, *A General History of the Robberies and Murders of the Most Notorious Pirates*, pp. 130-131; Eastman email to author, December 28, 2010, email no. 3; Eastman and Bond, *The Pirate Trial of Anne Bonny and Mary Read*, pp. 42-43.

319.   Johnson, *A General History of the Robberies and Murders of the Most Notorious Pirates*, p. 131; Eastman email to author, December 28, 2010, email no. 3.

320.   Oxford Dictionary of National Biography, Anne Bonny, internet; Anne Bonny, Wikipedia, internet; Black, *Pirates of the West Indies*, p. 117; Eastman email to author, December 28, 2010, email no. 3; Eastman and Bond, *The Pirate Trial of Anne Bonny and Mary Read*, pp. 43-44.

321.   Johnson, *A General History of the Robberies and Murders of the Most Notorious Pirates*, pp. 13-131; Eastman email to author, December 28, 2010, email no. 3; Oxford Dictionary of National Biography, Anne Bonny, internet; Steele, *Women Pirates*, pp. 14-15.

322.   Johnson, *A General History of the Robberies and Murders of the Most Notorious Pirates*, pp.117, 124; Cordingly, *Under the Black Flag*, p. 65.

323.   Broderick, *Wild Irish Women*, p. 100.

324.   Cordingly, *Under the Black Flag*, p. 65; Eastman email to author, December 28, no. 3; Eastman email to author, December 30, 2010; Female Pirates, World History Site, internet; Johnson, *A General History of the Robberies and Murders of the Most Notorious Pirates*, p. 124.

325.   Johnson, *A General History of the Robberies and Murders of the Most Notorious Pirates*, pp. 117-124; Klausmann, Meinzerin, and Kuhn, *Women Pirates*, p. 246.

326.   Johnson, *A General History of the Robberies and Murders of the Most Notorious Pirates*, p. 124.

327.   Klausmann, Meinzerin, and Kuhn, *Women Pirates*, p. 263; Cordingly, *Under the Black Flag*, p. 65; Atkenson, *An Irish History of Civilization*, vol., p. 346; Johnson, *A General History of the Robberies and Murders of the Most Notorious Pirates*, p. 131; Oxford Dictionary of National Biography, Anne Bonny.

328.   Johnson, *A General History of the Robberies and Murders of the Most Notorious Pirates*, p. 114; Cordingly, *Under the Black Flag*, p. 63

329.   The Tryals of Captain John Rackam, and Other Pirates, PRO; Johnson, *A General History of the Robberies and Murders of the Most Notorious Pirates*, pp. 115-116; Stanley, ed., *Bold in Her Breeches*, pp. 178-179; Cordingly, *Under the Black Flag*, p. 65.

330.   Steele, *Women Pirates*, p. 6; Johnson, *A General History of the Robberies and Murders of the Most Notorious Pirates*, pp. 115-116.

331.   The Tryals of Captain John Rackam, and Other Pirates, PRO; Johnson, *A General of the Robberies and Murders of the Most Notorious Pirates*, p. 124.

332.   James L. Nelson, *The Only Life That Mattered, The Short and Merry Lives of Anne Bonny, Mary Read, and Calico Jack Rackham*, (Ithaca: McBooks Press, Inc., 2004), p. 408

333.   Kallen, *Life Among the Pirates*, pp. 34, 74; Eastman email to author, December 30, 2010; Eastman and Bond, *The Pirate Trial of Anne Bonny and Mary Read*, pp. 40-41.

334.   Johnson, *A General History of the Robberies and Murders of the Most Notorious Pirates*, p. 121.

335.   Ibid.

336.   Broderick, *Wild Irish Women*, p. 100.

337.   *Boston Gazette*, October 7 and 10, 1720; Oxford Dictionary of National Biography, Anne Bonny; internet; Johnson, *A General History of the Robberies & Murders of the Most Notorious Pirates*, pp. 130-131; Druett, She Captains, p. 140; Klausmann, Meinzerin, and Kuhn, *Women Pirates*, p. 193; Eastman and Bond, *The Pirate Trial of Anne Bonny and Mary Read*, p. 22; Cordingly, *Under the Black Flag*, p. 63; Eastman email to author, December 28, 2010, email no. 3; Female Pirates, World History Site, internet.

338.   Ida Saint-Elme, *Memoirs of a Contemporary*, (New York: Doubleday, Page and Company, 1902), pp. 10-12; Eastman email to author, December 28, 2010, email no. 3.

339.   Oxford Dictionary of National Biography Anne Bonny, internet; David Stapleton, "Pirate Roster," internet; "Anne Bonny," Answers.com, in-

ternet; Johnson, *A General History of the Robberies and Murders of the Most Notorious Pirates*, pp. 125-131; Charles Murphy, *The Irish in the American Revolution*, pp. 1-14; Sherman Crawford, *Forgotten Tales of South Carolina*, (Charleston: The History Press, 2011), p. 72; Stampp, *The Peculiar Institution*, pp. 7-8, 47-48, 53; Eastman email to author, December 28, 2010, email no. 2 and 3; McWhiney, *Cracker Culture*, pp. xxi-50; Female Pirates, World History Site, internet; Eastman and Bond, *The Pirate Trial of Anne Bonny and Mary Read*, pp. 44-45.

340. Cordingly, *Under the Black Flag*, p. 240.

341. Oxford Dictionary of National Biography, Anne Bonny, internet; David Stapleton, "Pirate Roster," internet; "Anne Bonny," Answers.com, internet; Johnson, *A General History of the Robberies and Murders of the Most Notorious Pirates*, pp. 125-131.

342. Johnson, *A General History of the Robberies and Murders of the Most Notorious Pirates*, p. vii-viii; Druett, *She Captains*, pp. 158-159; Oxford Dictionary of National Biography, Anne Bonny, internet.

343. Oxford Dictionary of National Biography, Anne Bonny, internet; Druitt, *She Captains*, pp. 154-155; The Tryal of Captain John Rackam, and Other Pirates, PRO; Johnson, *A General History of the Robberies and Murders of the Most Notorious Pirates*, p. 124.

344. Johnson, *A General History of the Robberies and Murders of the Most Notorious Pirates*, pp. 125-131; Oxford Dictionary of National Biography, Anne Bonny, internet; Margaret Hodges, *Blue Mountain Guide*, (Kingston: The Natural History Society of Jamaica, 1993), pp. 1-39; Carmichael, *Forgotten Tales of South Carolina*, pp. 67-72.

345. David S. Reynolds, *John Brown Abolitionist, The Man Who Killed Slavery, Sparked the Civil War, and Seeded Civil Rights*, (New York: Alfred A. Knopf, 2005), p. 263; Cordingly, *Under the Black Flag*, pp. 11-16; The Tryal of Captain John Rackam, and Other Pirates, PRO; Klausmann, Meinzerin and Kuhn, *Women Pirates*, pp. 235-275; Lawrence Goldstone, *Dark Bargain, Slavery, Profits, and the Struggle for the Constitution*, (New York: Walker and Company, 2005), pp. 1-195.

346. Oxford Dictionary of National Biography, Anne Bonny, internet; "Anne Bonny," Answers.com, internet; Kallen, *Life Among the Pirates*, p. 34; Tamara Eastman, Petersburg, Virginia, email to author, December 28, 2010, no. 1; Michael Arditti, "Women Pirates of the West Indies," (2006), internet; Carmichael, *Forgotten Tales of South Carolina*, p. 72.

347. Robert G. Ferris, *Signers of the Declaration, Historic Places Commemorating the Signing of the Declaration of Independence*, (Washington, D. C.: United States Department of the Interior National Park Service, 1975), pp. 43-45; Phillip Thomas Tucker, *How the Irish Won the American Revolution, A New Look at the Forgotten Heroes of America's War of Independence*, (New York: Skyhorse Publishing, 2015), pp. 1-339; Thomas Fleming, *Washington's Secret War, The Hidden History of Valley Forge*, (New York: HarperCollins, 2005), pp. 141-142; Murphy, *The Irish in the American Revolution*, pp. 1-103; Patrick J. Haltigan, *The Irish in the American Revolution and their Early Influence in the Colonies*, (Washington, D. C.: Patrick J. Haltigan Publisher, 1908), pp. 9-619; Michael J. O'Brien, *A Hidden Phase of American History, Ireland's Part in America's Struggle for Liberty*, (New York: Dodd, Mead and Company, 1920), pp. 1-441; Thomas Fleming, *Liberty!, The American Revolution*, (New York: Viking, 1997), pp. 326-336; Lengel, *General George Washington*, pp. 3-13; Burke Davis, *The Campaign That Won America, The Story of Yorktown*, (New York: The Dial Press, 1970), pp. 3-289; The Tryals of Captain John Rackam and Other Pirates, PRO; Arditti, "Women Pirates of the West Indies," (2006), internet; Eastman email to author, December 28, 2010, no. 1.

348. Fleming, *Liberty!*, pp. 326-336; Murphy, *The Irish in the American Revolution*, p. 34; Davis, *The Campaign That Won America*, pp. 3-289; Cordingly, *Under the Black Flag*, pp. 10-17.

349. Oxford Dictionary of National Biography, internet, Anne Bonny; Johnson, *A General History of the Robberies and Murders of the Most Notorious Pirates*, pp. 111-116,131; The Tryals of Captain John Rackam, and Other Pirates, PRO; Klein, *The Most Evil Pirates in History*, pp. 122-140; Cordingly, *Under the Black Flag*, pp. 10-17; Hodges, ed., *Blue Mountain Guide*, p. 31; Arditti, "Women Pirates of the West Indies," (2006), internet; Eastman email to author, December 28, 2010, no. 1.

350. Eastman email to author, December 28, 2010, no. 1; Arditti, "Women Pirates of the West Indies," (2006), internet.

351. Johnson, *A General History of the Robberies and Murders of the Most Notorious Pirates*, pp. vii, 125-131; 34; Druett, *She Captains*, pp. 158-159; Eastman and Bond, *The Pirate Trial of Anne Bonny and Mary Read*, p. 16; Oxford Dictionary of National Biography, internet, Anne Bonny; Arditti, "Women Pirates of the West Indies," (2006), internet; Eastman email to author, December 28, 2010, no. 2.

352. Akenson, *An Irish History of Civilization*, vol. 1, p. 346; Druett, *She Captains*, pp. 158-159; Johnson, *A General History of the Robberies and Murders of the Most Notorious Pirates*, pp. 125-131; Lucie-Smith, *Outcasts of the Sea*, pp. 8-16, 21, 23; Kallen, *Life*

Among the Pirates, p. 10; Cordingly, *Under the Black Flag*, pp. 3-9, 170-171; Arditti, "Women of the West Indies," (2006), internet; Eastman email to author, December 28, 2010.

353.   Stanley, *Bold in Her Breeches*, p. 176-177; Johnson, *A General History of the Robberies and Murders of the Most Notorious Pirates*, pp. 125-131.

354.   The Tryals of Captain John Rackham, and Other Pirates, PRO; Johnson, *A General History of the Robberies and Murders of the Most Notorious Pirates*, p. 131; Druett, *She Captains*, pp. 151, 158-159; J. Christopher Herold, *A Life of Madame de Stael, Mistress to an Age*, (New York: Times-Life Books, 1958), p. 201.

355.   Wheelwright, *Amazons and Military Maids*, p. 22; Maturin Murray Ballou, Wikipedia, internet; Stanley, ed., *Bold in Her Breeches*, pp. 194-197; Lucie-Smith, *Outcasts of the Sea*, pp. 11-12; Cordingly, *Under the Black Flag*, p. 171.

356.   Stanley, ed., *Bold in Her Breeches*, pp. 194-197.

357.   Wheelwright, *Amazons and Military Maids*, pp. 21-22; Stanley, ed., *Bold in Her Breeches*, p. 196.

358.   Wheelwright, *Amazons and Military Maids*, pp. 21-22; Stanley, ed., *Bold in Her Breeches*, p. 196.

359.   Wheelwright, *Amazons and Military Maids*, pp. 21-24.

360.   Ibid; Webb Garrison, *Amazing Women of the Civil War*, (Nashville: Rutledge Hill Press, 1999), pp. 7-55.

361.   Ibid., p. 19.

362.   Ibid.

363.   *New York Times*, October 25, 1951; Anne of the Indies, Wikipedia, internet.

364.   Cordingly, *Under the Black Flag*, pp. 176-177; Klein, *The Most Evil Pirates in History*, pp. 51-63.

365.   Wheelwright, *Amazons and Military Maids*, p. 13.

366.   *The Chronicle of the Movies*, (New York: Crescent Books, 1991), p. 274.

367.   The Tryal of Captain John Rackam, and Other Pirates, PRO; Cordingly, *Under the Black Flag*, pp. 150-151; Fraser, *The Weaker Vessel*, pp. 1-6, 9; Burgess, *The Pirates' Pact*, p. xi; Johnson, *A General History of the Robberies and Murders of the Most Notorious Pirates*, pp. 125-131; Klausmann, Meinzerin and Kuhn, *Women Pirates*, pp. 229-246; Stanley, ed., *Bold in Her Breeches*, pp. iv-xvi14-15, 20-21; Steele, *Women Pirates*, p. 8; Botting, *The Pirates*, pp. 29-31; Lucie-Smith, *Outcasts of the Sea*, p. 26; Oxford Dictionary of National Biography, Anne Bonny, internet; Eastman and Bond, *The Pirate Trial of Anne Bonny and Mary Read*, pp. 44-45; Eastman email to author, De-cember 28, 2010, no. 1.

368.   The Tryal of Captain John Rackam, and Other Pirates, PRO; Johnson, *A General History of the Robberies and Murders of the Most Notorious Pirates*, pp. 13-14, 125-131; Klausmann, Meinzerin and Kuhn, *Women Pirates*, pp. 229-246; Sherlock and Bennett, *The Story of the Jamaican People*, pp. 161-162; Stanley, *Bold in Her Breeches*, pp. 20-21; Dunn, *Sugar and Slaves*, pp. 3-341; Myron and Bunch, eds., *Women Remembered*, p. 89; Latimer, *Buccaneers of the Caribbean*, pp. 165, 169, 266, 279, 242-281; Botting, *The Pirates*, pp. 29-31; Druett, *Women Pirates*, p. 148; Dunn, *Sugar and Slaves*, pp. 3-341; Cordingly, *Under the Black Flag*, p. 12; Lucie-Smith, *Outcasts of the Sea*, pp. 9, 212; Fraser, *The Weaker Vessel*, pp. 1-6, 9, 467.

369.   Druett, *She Captains*, p. 148; Johnson, *A General History of the Robberies and Murders of the Most Notorious Pirates*, pp. 123-131.

370.   Johnson, *A General History of the Robberies and Murders of the Most Notorious Pirates*, pp. 111-131; Oxford Dictionary of National Biography, Anne Bonny, interest: The Tryal of Captain John Rackham, and Other Pirates, PRO; Cordingly, *Under the Black Flag*, pp. xiii-240; Steele, *Women Pirates*, pp. 1-23; Fraser, *The Weaker Vessel*, pp. 1-6, 9, 464-468; The Tryal of Captain John Rackam, and Other Pirates, POC; R. F. Foster, editor, *The Oxford History of Ireland*, (New York: Oxford University Press, 1992), pp. 99-143; Eastman and Bond, *The Pirate Trial of Anne Bonny and Mary Read*, pp. 44-45; Eastman email to author, December 28, 2010, email no. 1 and no. 2.

371.   Thornton Wilder, *The Woman of Andros*, (New York: Penguin Books, 1969), p. 26.

www.FeralHouse.com

www.processmediainc.com